HIGH PLAY IS "AN EXCITING BOOK BECAUSE IT DEALS WITH WHAT IS PERHAPS THE LAST FRONTIER—THE NATURE OF MAN."
                    —*ARE JOURNAL*

Its author, Harmon Hartzell Bro, Ph.D., is a psychotherapist who has specialized in the study of dreams and other altered states of consciousness, as these have been used to heighten creativity in traditions of both East and West.

He has taught at Harvard University and Syracuse University, and is a contributor to the *Encyclopedia Britannica,* as well as the author of *Paradoxes of Rebirth,* a study of the thought of Martin Buber. His books on dreams include *Dreams in the Life of Prayer* and *Edgar Cayce on Dreams,* and his books on heightened creativity include *Begin a New Life* and *Edgar Cayce on Religion and Psychic Experience.*

For information on ordering any of the above books, please turn to page 288.

HIGH PLAY

Turning On Without Drugs

by Harmon Hartzell Bro

Introduction by Hugh Lynn Cayce

A KINNEY SERVICE COMPANY
NEW YORK

To EARL AND JOYCE KRUSE—
  sponsors of this book
  and companions in exploring high play
  since I first assigned *Moby Dick*
  to a sophomore class

Library of Congress Catalog Card Number: 77-131569

This Paperback Library Edition is published by arrangement with Coward-McCann & Geoghegan Inc.

Paperback Library is a division of Coronet Communications, Inc. Its trademark, consisting of the words "Paperback Library" accompanied by an open book, is registered in the United States Patent Office. *Coronet Communications, Inc., 315 Park Avenue South, New York, N.Y. 10010.*

INTRODUCTION

The author of this book, Harmon Hartzell Bro, is one of the few men alive today who heard Edgar Cayce give five hundred or more psychic readings. First as a young Protestant minister, and later as a psychologist of religion, he has become as much at home in psychotherapy as he is in university teaching, and in research on dreams and other phenomena of the human mind and spirit.

As I read the first half of this book, I realized that Harmon had skillfully drawn upon the research experience of a mutual friend, Walter Pahnke, psychiatrist, who is a recognized authority on hallucinogenic drugs. Dr. Pahnke has been involved in some of the most unusual, the most exciting and at times most rewarding experimentation with these mind-expanding drugs. Thus, Dr. Bro has been able to present a balanced evaluation pointing out the major insights which have resulted from drug use, and at the same time he has highlighted the major dangers in the drug approach to expanded consciousness.

In the last half of the book, Harmon leads the reader into some particularly challenging and safer explorations of the mind and spirit. This book should get, as quickly as possible, into the hands of thousands of young people who are now beginning to seek a more rewarding and more controllable "trip" into the world of heightened and creative consciousness.

But you don't have to take my word for this. Read the book. It will truly "turn you on."

HUGH LYNN CAYCE

CONTENTS

Part I

TURNING ON AS HIGH PLAY

CHAPTER ONE

THE CHALLENGE OF THE
PSYCHEDELIC ADVENTURE

The woman had been given LSD several hours before. Now she was sobbing. "I've been so phony, so phony." She wept hard, her whole body shaking as she leaned toward the psychologist on the couch beside her and seized his hand.

The psychologist responded as he had trained himself: he responded as a human being to someone weeping. He slipped his arm around her and pulled her over until her head was in his lap. "Cry it out," he said. "You've been wanting to do this for a long time." He held her firmly while she sobbed and shook.

The nurse across the room waited. Soon she would be needed, she knew, to straighten the pillows on the comfortable big couch, and then to ease the woman back to recline for a period of music heard through oversize head-

11

phones. She understood that as a nurse she was important in the room. Her starched but gentle professionalism complemented the informal manner of the therapist, who sat there across the room in his shirt sleeves, his tie loosened, holding his patient and calling her by her first name. Further, she as a nurse was woman, as the therapist was man; the patient would need to relate to both while her spinning mind took her back to girlhood and then on into her marriage, during the long hours of the LSD session in the experimental building of the state mental hospital.

The nurse and the psychologist both knew that the weeping of the drugged woman was no chemically induced jag, which long experience had taught them to distinguish from honest human tears. They knew it was the product of dynamics which they had seen in several weeks of intensive therapy sessions to prepare their neurotic patient for LSD —weeks which had made them not only her therapy team but her friends. They understood how their patient had turned toward her husband an unaccountable hate, a hate which she actually felt toward her mother and, ultimately, toward herself. They remembered how she had supported and fed that hate with such delusions that she had once turned her husband over to the FBI, accusing him of being a bank robber instead of a conscientious businessman. They knew how she had slept outside her home in the family car for weeks of lonely nights, convinced that her husband wanted to kill her. And they recalled that when she had been brought to the hospital in a police patrol car, she had kept insisting that it was her husband who needed treatment, despite her doctor's explanations to her.

They could see that now, in her time of weeping in the LSD session, she had come to that honest facing of one's self where all deep therapy succeeds or fails. And they were doing what the human race has always known to do at such moments of truth: being there, and caring. Later in the session, they would help her to strengthen the insights won in her tearful confession and catharsis by getting her to talk, while still under the influence of the drug, about her children and husband and parents, whose photographs were on the coffee table in front of the couch.

But they would not stop the session when they had walked her through the maze of her childhood and family dynamics, helping her to convince herself that there was a center to her labyrinth, a place of sunlight in the blind corridors of her life. For they were proceeding on the assumption, generated in hundreds of similar LSD sessions, that therapy would go deepest and last longest when it continued past repair work, taking the subject into entirely new rooms and wings of the psyche. They were going to try to help their patient reach her best human potentials, and remember them, while the LSD had her moving and exploring.

They would lead her to speak of the beauty of a rose in a vase which they would put before her. And they would ask her about the same enchanting colors and proportions in the art prints which were on the coffee table beside the family photographs. They would set her to responding aloud to the wonder she felt in hearing stately and soaring music. They would get her to laugh at her own remembered defensiveness and posing; yet they would help her to see that it had taken strength and imagination for her to stay so stubbornly sick—the same kind of strength and imagination which she now could use for adventures in a new life. They would help her to find within her hate the superior stance which she had taken when she condemned herself and others; but they would look with her for some vision of authentic excellence which could be rescued from the hate-producing superiority.

They would ask about her dearest and deepest religious intuitions, if she brought them up. They would be midwives to her best self, if they could, while provoking her to tease them and to enjoy them, and to joke when she had to go to the bathroom. They knew that if they were in luck, their little treatment room, so snug and tastefully appointed in its corner of the huge hospital grounds, could become for their patient a captain's cabin, a place where she could find adventure and direction, and a hope of control over the voyage of her years.

13

As the hours go by and the drug begins to wear off, they bring in the woman's husband. He sits down gingerly on the couch beside her, his face showing both hope that his wife has changed and guardedness lest she rebuff him still. She smiles at him and hugs him as she has not done for many months. Holding him close for a moment, she leans back and looks him frankly in the face. "I've made it, honey," she says. "It's all going to be okay." He holds her arm and stares at her, then slumps a bit in relief. All the signs of her face and voice and manner suggest that he has his wife back, whole and entire, ready to take up the daily round with him and with their children.

She leans toward him again and adds one small sentence, in their shy moment of closeness before the doctor and nurse. Her face in a grave smile, she says, "I found God."

In the months and years that follow, this housewife does not return to her neurosis. Instead, she joins that surprisingly high percentage of neurotics, especially severe alcoholics, who have been successfully treated in the U.S. and Canada by a combination of the best of psychotherapy with LSD, followed by group therapy to carry forward the healing effects. She has no desire for further LSD sessions, but finds herself engrossed in her family and in her work as a schoolteacher—while not forgetting to retrace her steps inwardly, from time to time, to that point of ultimate hope which she found in her LSD session. She is not without problems, for she has to change the encrusted style of years of her life. She has low times, as everyone does; and also some lonely and fearful times as she works through the deep, sullen resentfulness which her therapy exposed in her. She finds that she has to choose, in little decisions made scores of times daily, to build up rather than destroy those around her. But she trusts the strength and the imagination which she saw so clearly in herself, and she trusts the helping One who seemed so real that day in the hospital.

Her own prognosis proves correct; she has made it. Before long she finds her recovery confirmed by her own panel of experts, the group which none can mislead: her family.

What had happened to her in that experimental hospital room where LSD was being studied under a government grant? Had her gains come from crowning the preparatory therapy sessions with that marathon session, in which the music and the flowers, doctor and nurse, art and memories, sense and nonsense had become for her a microcosm of the best in the human venture? Perhaps. But similar marathon therapy for others, conducted without LSD by the same doctor and nurse, had not produced such deep and permanent results in so short a time. The speed of the therapy seemed to be a gift of the drug. Or had she experienced the hope of aid from LSD, added to her own saved-up feelings which had been banked and made white-hot by her illness, so that her forces of torment became her purgation and elevation? Perhaps. But similar therapy efforts with others, told they were getting a psychedelic drug but receiving only a stimulant, had not been so productive in marathon sessions. The mounting hope through the session seemed to be reinforced by real changes induced hour after hour by the LSD.

Somehow, through her drug experience she had seemed to come undrugged. The tight smirk that had so long touched her smile was gone. The stagy posing of her body was gone. Her mind and heart and body had become pliable, responsive, alert, loving. She was spontaneous. She was funny. She was fun. The sickening, mind-bending poisons of mental illness seemed drained from her, leaving her not spent and indifferent, but awake. She was not simply non-drugged afterward, not simply returned to passable normalcy. She appeared thoroughly undrugged from chronic emotions and uptightness. She seemed to have snapped out of her nightmare with a spin that had sent her somewhere important, inside. And as the months went by after her therapy, she seemed to stretch to a stature not previously hers, developing new talents as a writer, building new friendships, reasoning out new convictions. She went beyond functional adequacy toward

15

her own optimums, becoming a refreshing, unique person —"self-actualizing," in the low-key phrase of the psychological theorist Maslow.

Her adventure had truly been "psychedelic"—meaning "mind-manifesting," as Osmond had suggested when he coined the term. Like similar adventures of hundreds upon hundreds of experimental subjects given LSD and related drugs under expert medical care, her experience was significant for three kinds of psychology.

It was significant for academic psychology, that careful comparative study which exposes how man behaves as a biological organism. This is the psychology which has built upon findings from Pavlov's dogs, from Kohler's apes, from babies who back away from visually simulated cliffs, from students learning nonsense syllables on rotating drums, to produce ever-better methods for society's daily work: running its machines, rearing its children, recalling its social security numbers, and plotting graphs of its own death rates. For such biological psychology, experiments with LSD point to a chemical basis for states of mind and trains of thought, advancing the claims of those who emphasize endocrine-gland effects rather than brain and nerve action alone. Indeed, LSD experiments call attention to every content of the bloodstream which might affect thought: residues from emotional discharges in vigorous dreaming, toxins from illness, sugar levels at different times of day and night, effects of particular diets and vitamins (now freshly studied as a cause for schizophrenia), poisons from poor eliminations, and traces of supposedly harmless medicines. The research also points to the body's capacity to generate its own mind-bending chemicals, in those cases where experiences like that of the housewife are spontaneously reinstated for minutes or hours, long after the drug has left the bloodstream (as shown by radioactive tracing).

The housewife's psychedelic adventure was also significant for medical psychology, that psychology which exposes how the mind distorts in mental illness and can be aided to recover. This psychology has built upon findings

16

from infantile sexuality, from responses to Rorschach inkblots, from hypnotic states, from cases of shock treatments and of shocking traumas, to disclose patterns within the wildness of neurotic and psychotic symptoms. It has developed treatments by chemical cures and talking cures alike, as well as by the bittersweet bonds of transference and group therapy. For medical psychology, LSD therapy offers the hope of methods through which the mind "locked in" upon compulsions and thought trains (as a missile is "locked in" on its target by its radar) might be "unlocked," so that new connections of meaning might emerge out of a drug-fluidized state of mind. And in those cases where LSD works best, as it does not in all therapy, it offers the hope of unbelievable speed when combined with traditional healing methods. By itself, the drug works no magic healing. But as a catalyst its aid to therapy is sometimes beyond price.

However, the major challenge of the housewife's psychedelic transformation was for a kind of psychology still barely represented in college textbooks: optimum psychology. This psychology, so young as not to have a generally accepted name, studies how men reach their optimums in dealing not only with machines, but with truth, with beauty, with goodness, and even with holiness. It has built upon findings from notable biographies, from cases of those performing heroically under battle stress, from much-contested ESP experiments, from breakthrough insights of those recovering from mental illness, from records of mystical experiences in East and West, from studies of the best problem solving by brainstorming and incubation, and from drug states and other types of "peak experiences"—as Maslow has labeled those states which seem to free an individual to reach his highest stature. The products of research in optimum psychology have so far not been definitive, and its research tools—such as brain-wave recorders and polygraphs (lie detectors)—are still so few that the entire venture of this psychology has often been pushed aside in classroom, clinic, and laboratory. Yet optimum psychology, still barely touched in conven-

17

tional psychology courses, is being quietly advanced onto the social agenda as "the psychology of altered states of consciousness" by the content of such drug experiences as that of the neurotic housewife.

For she was not alone. Amid the thousands on thousands, both sick and well, who have taken various mind-bending drugs (with or without medical supervision), there has been a continuing minority of those who have reached such psychedelic optimums as to find their lives changed—sometimes permanently. While most others have drug trips which are merely colorful, changing them but little, and while another minority has drug experiences which are tragic, there remains this puzzling segment of drug takers which reports moving into optimum states and talents. The few in this minority keep telling of transformative insights into themselves and their universe; they speak of the "joyous cosmology," as Alan Watts describes the vistas which they think they see as reality. They report extraordinary inward lifts, which enable some of them to change permanently toward nobler lives. Such lifts were recounted by participants in Walter Pahnke's carefully prepared and now famous Good Friday experiment in Boston University's Marsh Chapel, made the subject of Pahnke's doctoral dissertation in religion at Harvard.

The major challenge of the psychedelic adventure may well be to optimum psychology. Three of the six models upon which drug taking has suddenly grown to staggering dimensions in modern America are models directly concerned with reaching optimums in the lives of those who use the mind-altering drugs.

The medical model for taking mind-affecting drugs is not a model for reaching optimums, though it is an important model in the culture. Like the rest of medicine, this model embodies a search for recovery from disability. It presents itself to the would-be drug user with the credentials of having accomplished a phenomenal gain in the treatment of mental illness through tranquilizers and related drugs, which have cut down the number of beds occupied in mental institutions for the first time in recent

18

centuries. Responding to this medical model, the drug user tells himself that there must be specific chemicals to relieve his troubled mind and emotions, just as there are specific drugs to alleviate headaches, ulcers, muscle aches, tired eyes, menopause upsets, and constipation. Perhaps, he reasons, the psychedelic and other mind-affecting drugs are such specific chemicals, still in their early stages of development, and safe if he is cautious. So he experiments with his moods, metabolism, and fantasy, assuring himself that he will be more careful than he has been with alcohol. He finds himself bolstered in his venture by advertising which shows him that there is a drug for his cough center, a drug which will seem to cure his bad manners, a drug which will go far toward turning his noxious breath into sexy aroma, a harmless drugstore compound to put him gently to sleep, and a tonic to make him feel peppy if his blood is tired. Behind his medical model for drug use are strong cultural patterns which magnify instant result through technology—in foods, in fabrics, in automation, in communication, and even in atomic warfare; his times feature miracle cures, miracle devices, miracle success stories. He is soaked in the ethos of that part of modern science which emphasizes detached magic—results without personal involvement through action on Nature as man's plaything to be exploited. Insofar as he accepts such a magical mind-set, he may find it easy to tinker with his body for instant benefits while ignoring long-range consequences, just as research scientists may be tempted to ignore the consequences of developing nuclear fission or germ warfare, and just as business may be tempted to ignore the consequences of industrial pollution.

The second model for contemporary use of drugs to affect the mind is also less concerned with optimums than with recovery from disability. This model focuses on social disability. It is the ghetto model, drawn from black segments of disadvantaged city life in which the use of the harder addictive drugs has a long history. The appeal of drugs in the ghetto setting has complex sources, but a major stimulus to such drug use may well be the bitter predicament of living in a society which touts its shiny wares on every hand, yet leaves a minority unable to buy them. The same cultural forces which promote looting in the aftermath of rioting appear to foster the pursuit of drug-induced fantasies; drug taking in the ghetto both defies the social system and sets up a substitute circuit to its popular sensate values. The lonely drug user may feel himself powerless to change his society, but he knows he can at least temporarily change his state of mind and desires, while in the process finding brief solidarity with others who defy the established order of things.

As the ghetto model for drug use has moved out from its original confines (in the company of other ghetto models for clothing, hair styles, music, and language), many in the surrounding youth subculture, and some in adult suburban culture, have found drug taking a symbolic way of entering the pain of the black man's experience in American society. Such drug use touches on authentic concerns of optimum psychology, including sacrificial covenanting with others. But the primary thrust of the ghetto model is still toward recovery from disability, toward independence and freedom from restraint—upon which a search for optimums may later be mounted. Taking drugs on this model, then, may represent anyone's struggle for proud identity as a precondition for reaching his tallest stature.

A third model, and perhaps the major model for contemporary drug taking, comes out of comfortable suburban white homes, where again the concern is for adequate function, rather than for optimums. In this suburban model, drugs are taken socially to free the play of human feelings. Alcohol makes parties go better and conversations seem more intimate. Pills to take off weight, and dietetically sweetened foods, offer human shapes thought to be socially more marketable and worthy of self-regard. Sleeping pills allow rest without worry, so that the user may look more debonair the next day, while pep pills may make him seem as busy and alert as any competitor in his status market. Tobacco offers that graceful sharing in momentary silence which is often hard to find in rushed lives. Sedation can cover grief at death loss of a loved one, relieving friends and relatives from having to venture beneath surface condolences but also postponing needed grief-work until a time when it is more difficult to do alone. And the Pill takes some of the risk out of encounters not so freely attempted before the advent of such hormone-affecting drugs, although the social consequences have not yet been worked out for the easy transfer from "Shall we?" to "What's next?" As the ghetto drugs are dramatic in signifying tragic pain and its overcoming by human spirit, the suburban drugs are alluring in their promise of risk-free and pain-free social pleasure. Yet the sense of having chemically polluted his body lingers in the mind of many a social drug user, and he is startled to find how strongly he feels that man should not poison the streams around him, even while he continues to dump his social chemicals into his private bloodstream.

Alongside these models from medicine, the ghetto, and the suburbs is a fourth model for modern drug taking which is directly concerned with the achievement of optimums. This model is offered by a smaller number of drug users, though the number has high visibility in contemporary culture. It is presented by intellectuals and artists who use chemicals to enhance their creativity, to put them into an "on" state of skill and awareness, to give them peace of mind, and to clarify their vision of ultimates. From the learned and eloquent Huxley—whose book *The Doors of Perception* was one of the first to set forth the mysteries of psychedelic adventure (followed by his Utopian novel, *Island*)—to the saucy and stringent Beatles, there have been not a few to testify to the optimums glimpsed or incarnated with the aid of chemicals. Some have spoken of social optimums, suggested by tranquil drug states which mock war and racial violence. Others have spoken of individual optimums, known both in drug-quickened visions and in drug-heightened feelings of compassion and patience. Behind this model shines the dim but exciting light of the way of mysticism in both East and West, offering

21

states in which man may be consciously aware of the presence of God, or aware of the divine spark in his soul which moves him towards his optimums. Not every thinker or artist proves able to deliver on the promise which he finds in his drug-altered states of mind, for some appear to retreat from the discipline of fashioning forms into the lush Eden of primal visions. Yet the concern for new forms of civilization and individuality which this model embodies gives it much of its force.

A fifth model for today's drug taking comes with a long history in rural and nomadic cultures of the past, given heraldic dignity by medieval pomp. It is the practice of celebrating definitive changes in the lives of individuals and of groups, through feasts and drinking and holidays which blow the mind out of its usual routines. In this model the concern is again with optimums; for the hope which it embodies, however poorly verbalized or realized, is to free the mind to reach the fullest meanings in a time of transition. Whenever a moment of truth is sought and found, ancient traditions may prescribe adding a chemical stimulus to allow the mind to continue its spontaneous psychedelic work of self-transformation. Sometimes the stimulus is by intake which affects the blood chemistry (as in the drinking at a wake), and sometimes the stimulus is by output which also affects the blood chemistry (as in enduring the hardships of an initiation).

The life of each individual offers a number of spontaneously psychedelic or "mind-manifesting" turning points, when the mind must stretch into new ways of being human. Some of these times, which Van Gennep tagged as requiring *rites de passage,* are the transition from adolescence to adulthood, marriage, entry into a totem (or college), childbirth, recovery from grave illness or peril, loss of parents or spouse, and preparing for death. Such critical periods have their festivities, their solemn ceremonies, their initiations, varying from culture to culture; some of the vehicles are as formal as weddings and some as informal as prenuptial bachelor parties. How each effort seeks to alter the blood chemistry of participants may be

22

seen in the frequent use of alcohol or the rarer use of fasting, as it may also be seen in the use of exhilarating or ennobling ritual, risk, or play. But in the life-span of an individual it is not only the crossing of bridges between segments of the life journey which calls for chemical action on the bloodstream. There are also the times when an individual makes a stride towards his personal optimums. He may develop the kind of courage and wisdom which Jonah needed in order to challenge the makers of Nineveh's ghettos; if he does not have companions and rites in which to celebrate, at last, his release from an engulfing, whale-like depression, he may find his psychedelic transformation difficult to sustain. Or the individual may achieve at last the kind of humbling found by righteous Job, when he glimpsed upon his ash heap the wonders of subhuman creation and required more celebration than a few talkative friends could provide. At such times of individual optimums, layers of the mind well outside of consciousness seem to move in mindquakes, giving up their hidden treasures and requiring some kind of ritual chemical action.

In much the same way, but for whole peoples rather than for individuals, the parade of the seasons brings a round of national holidays, and a deeper round of religious holy days, which stir up tentative psychedelic changes. The gentling effects of even commercialized Christmas are a notable example. To forward the action of such mild psychedelic effects there are rites, places, myths and covenants—some of which may also be called into play for such times of crisis-growth of a people as the death of their leader, their release from oppression, or their gain or loss of harvest. Where social rites to affect the bloodstream in this fashion are missing, then groups and movements may be observed trying to invent them afresh by designating certain dates for annual remembrance, or by holding a moratorium on accustomed activities, or by making a pilgrimage to a national capital or retreating to a place of renewal of spirit. Even modern man's hurried shopping rituals, from January white sales to December toy-sale binges, may be viewed as his half-conscious attempts to play upon the spontaneous psychedelic currents of his mind as it gropes towards collective optimums. Accordingly, part of the modern taking of drugs must be seen as proceeding upon a very old model—often beneath the surface of conscious reflection in urban life, but not gone from what Jung called the collective unconscious, or Hindus call karmic memory, and most Westerners merely call tradition. This model of ceremonial eating, drinking, and turning on in times of personal and social transition finds exact expression in the general taking of LSD at a hippie wedding. While much of the concern in such psychedelic drugging is for heightened social pleasure, modeled upon suburban alcohol patterns and containing legitimate sexual elements, there is also present a deeper model of seeking an altered state of mind which can plumb the full and true meanings in the transition at hand. Not everyone can be sufficiently psychedelic by weeping at weddings or at funerals—perhaps in part because the meanings which are glimpsed transcend the vistas given by emotions alone.

Finally, there is a model for modern drug taking which is also built on concern for optimums but does not wait for times of transition in the lives of individuals or in the affairs of groups and peoples. This model is well represented by the Christian act of taking communion; it is the model of renewing both vision and covenantal bonds under the stimulus of chemistry. Modern Christian celebrants of communion who view the sacrament as a colorful symbolic memorial forget that at its origin (when communion competed in Rome with such charged rites as the *taurobolium,* a bloodbath under a platform holding a slaughtered bull), the action of alcohol and bread was heightened by elements which today's research on LSD has shown to be immensely effective in directing the force and action of even mildly psychoactive chemicals. These elements include confession (as practiced by the neurotic housewife before and during her taking of LSD); fasting and periods of silence; risking and sharing with a small loved group (as done with her therapy team by the housewife under LSD); and reinforcement by symbolic signs and sounds and tales (accomplished for the housewife by music and photos, art and talk). Under such conditions, heightened in their effects by earnest prayer and high hope, those who took communion in its early history may well have had just what they claimed: psychedelic experiences of immeasurable importance to them, including direct awareness of the helping action of the divine (as the neurotic housewife also claimed, in her time of healing).

Further examples of the sacramental model for regular drug taking may be found in the Jewish blessing and sharing of wine in the home at the start of the Sabbath; in the dramatic eating of peyote buttons by Indians worshiping in the Southwest; and perhaps even in the quiet elegance of the Zen tea ceremony. Parallels may be found in many old cultures—including the Hindu use of the now lost drug *soma,* the Persian use of its variant *haoma,* and the ritual use of mushrooms in Egypt and elsewhere. More important than any one chemical used in such ceremonies may have been the recognition that some sort of quieting and cleansing and quickening is essential for the human body, quite apart from times of crisis and moments of truth, in order for the mind and spirit of man to keep in touch with their optimums. Today's drug users who gather regularly in small friendship groups, in communes, in encounter groups, or at wooded or seaside retreats, to embark together on a socio-chemical adventure of changed consciousness—all such are in the company of a long procession who have thought such shared renewal appropriate. Whatever the drug and the rite, the sacramental effort tends to have a double character: it is a mutual plumbing of potentials for greatness, and it is a testing of group and individual progress towards these potentials. Whether drug use, and drug abuse, will yield in the next century to other methods will surely depend in part on what optimum psychology develops as less dangerous routes to the same prized discoveries. Without alternative means for sensing how rich might be his love, how honest his truth, how lovely his works, many a modern drug user will laugh

25

at attempts to curb his chemical habits and rites. And without equally far-reaching procedures for helping him to test himself, to measure his changes and his failures, to assess his progress along a meaningful ladder of growth, he will ignore admonitions to temper his chemical ways —ways which in the long march of history are more hallowed than he may realize.

The task of this book is to explore some alternatives to drug taking which may offer less erratic rewards and less dangerous side effects than does the use of mind-bending chemicals.

For the drug method of altering consciousness towards optimums is at times immensely dangerous, whether the drugs used be deleriants (found in glue sniffing); hallucinogens (such as LSD and its mild consort, marijuana); stimulants (such as amphetamines); depressants (barbiturates, tranquilizers, heroin and related drugs); or that historic semiaddictive drug which both Islam and Buddhism outlawed centuries ago, alcohol. The success of the psychologist using LSD with the neurotic housewife has not always been repeated by the same psychologist, a man whom his colleagues recognize as a genius at psychotherapy, as well as vastly experienced in the use of LSD. Beside his limited though dramatic successes, and the successes of other researchers, must be placed the bitterly sad cases of those few who have taken the same drug under far different circumstances and reached far different results: driving a car over a friend, stepping out a window to death, or beginning a heady journey into use of the harder, addictive drugs whose name is slow death to the user.

Today more and more people know at first hand someone who has so assaulted his mind with even nonaddictive drugs that he experiences mild or acute hallucinosis—inability to stop hallucinating, even when he is not taking drugs. Today more and more people know someone personally whose physical health has collapsed under "speed" drugs taken to heighten his performance at tasks of word or study; they know someone else who wears the "spaced out" vacant stare of one who has lost touch with others in his own private escape world. And others—as many as half the students in the author's psychology classes—have seen a friend in the dehumanizing agonies of craving or withdrawal from heroin or morphine or cocaine.

Why do both youth and adults risk such danger in mind-bending drugs? Part of the answer lies in sanctions and catalysts which reinforce the action of the models described above. For those who farm, manufacture, and peddle illegal drugs, there are economic gains so great as to generate a sizable international traffic assuring that nearly half of all the mind-altering drugs from pharmaceutical houses may find their way to consumers without medical supervision. There are social forces which carry along drug use as symbolic of the conflict of the generations or of reformers in conflict with established authority. There are educational trends, some of which bore the young into seeking diversion with drugs, and some of which properly train the young to be as curious about the inner space of the mind as about the outer space of the planets. There are mass media, which call attention to the novelties of drug experiences in the very act of exposing their excesses or making them central to television melodrama. Behind all of these modifying forces are deeper currents of malaise and boredom in an increasingly other-directed society which drifts toward surface living at the expense of emotional depth and vitality, to what Fromm has called a "marketing orientation" that appears as readily in lovemaking as in moneymaking. But the most persistent force in drug taking, despite its medical, psychological, and legal risks, may be the human hunger for optimums.

The psychedelic adventure poses for optimum psychology such questions as these: How big are human beings? How far can they reach toward love and goodness and truth? How much of their best can they learn to share with others? How can altered states help them to keep the adventuresomeness, the goodwill, the playfulness, which mankind loves in its children? What mind-altering force might be substituted for pain as a catalyst of human greatness?

Finding the answers to such questions requires positing a model of optimum behavior—a model with which various states and activities may be compared in the effort to single out critical processes for careful study and experimentation.

Freud introduced a sexual model. He distinguished between maturely "genital" and immaturely "pregenital" behavior. The former he saw as the fully adult capacity to give and receive in intercourse, taking the risks and responsibilities of close ties with another person, and freeing each participant to go with the drive and pleasure of powerful sexual emotions. He found it not too difficult to generalize his picture of genital optimums until he could fit it as a tracing over many activities of work, play, and loving; he could speak of genital behavior wherever an individual truly and spontaneously gave of himself to another, and received in return what was truly and spontaneously given to him. For contrast, Freud outlined several pregenital types. There were the oral types, distinguished by their gaping gullibility and by their dependence on others to suckle and stimulate them, even with words and ideas, so that they might feel alive and might function in both sexual and nonsexual ways. There were the anal types, distinguished by their chronic withholding of feelings, ideas, and belongings, which they meticulously arranged and saved until such time as they could manipulate responses from others by presenting their feces-like accumulations of thoughts and deeds and things. And there were the phallic types, inclined towards showing off in things sexual and nonsexual, substituting competitively won attention for productivity with others. Building on these constructs of pregenital types, Karen Horney and others following Freud suggested that each individual in his relations with others shows trends "towards," "away," and "against" which might keep him from full mutuality and self-expression; these types and trends in a sexual

28

metaphor have become classic modern versions of less-than-optimum behavior.

But the sexual metaphor, although a potent one in Freud's Victorian culture, may lack some impact in a more sensate contemporary culture where the consumption economy puts a premium on the pursuit of thrills, and where the advertising of intimate bras and deodorants occupies almost as much space in the prime-time evening newscasts as reports of disasters and heroism. In such a climate, the Freudian sexual model may seem to emphasize sheer gratification and sensuality to the exclusion of mutuality between partners which Freud saw as part of full genitality. The metaphor of aggression, which Freud also used, might be more serviceable. A language of types of anger, violence, and power striving, some dirty and some clean with respect to manipulating others and deluding oneself, has much promise in a time of riots and protests, and racial conflicts. But like the sexual metaphor, the aggression metaphor may easily be used in the modern scene to stress colors and piquancies of emotions at the expense of the interpersonal action which demands attention in any construction of optimums.

An alternative model, though certainly not without its own limitations, comes from the reports of those who use drugs to affect the mind. It is the model of play.

The sense of play runs like a golden thread through the most prized of psychedelic drug experiences. There is first the play of perceptions and images which beggars speech when the mind-altering drug takes full effect. Forms on forms stream at the beholder, and music turns into light, light into people, and people into worlds which again become music, as the mind tosses forth treasures as though it could never run out. But the note of play is also struck when the psychedelic experience is invaded by panics, demons, and darkness. The subject who is well-prepared, and who has a good and loving coach, is encouraged to take on the darkness—not by fighting it but by walking gravely and openly into it, to see what it has to give him. The tension in the drug-altered mind at such moments may be immense. Sometimes courage fails and the subject wants out—whereupon his demons may grow worse and insanity may threaten him for a time. But in those experiences where the psychedelically drugged subject can confront his demons and his darkness without forcing himself, yet without holding anything back—then something like the fine, free, cool game of the confident athlete begins. The individual plays for each play, not for points; he takes one step at a time in his drug-induced journey, and without protecting himself. Then his darkness characteristically splits, revealing to him light and pattern and deep helpful meaning. Looking back, the one who has placed himself under the spell of a psychedelic drug may say, "That's when I saw the very worst in myself— my meanness and phoniness and manipulation and greed; I saw these exposed, and yet saw them as capable of something good." His imagery of fire at this point turns to sparkling sunlight of reason; his dark cave becomes a life-carrying womb; his dragon turns into a horse to be ridden; his threatening murderer only strips off the artificial masks of others in his vision. He sees his evil, with the aid of the drug, as containing its own seeds of goodness, ready to blossom if only he can stand before the evil in the full and ungrasping effort to meet what is there—in fearless play.

Something of play also lights journeys in therapy conducted without drugs. The play may be seen when the endlessly protective person finally strips himself for risky action with and for others. Play may be seen when the narcissistic person looks at last to see who is on the rest of the team, or when the snob kneels to play jacks with the rest of the human race. Further, there is play found in the optimums where workmen sling boxes off a truck, or a secretary types off letters in spirits as bouncy as her flirtations in the office. There is solemn, unpretentious play in the earnest worship processional and in the good stories which relatives tell of a man after his funeral. There is play in the dance of the mind among the anecdotes of a biographer and among the branching paths of a new theory. For while play is often constrasted with work or study or worship, as if it were something trivial or momentary in comparison with these, play may in fact be central to all of them, and no stranger to pain. The real opposite of such play as appears in the psychedelic adventure is not effort, or gravity, but the lack of these.

When there is indifference, there is no play. That indifference may show itself in the catatonic schizophrenic, or in the prosperous administrator who has so fused with his job as to become a set of specifications rather than an original and originating person; in both, play is missing. Where there is only compulsion, there is no play. The compulsion may show itself in the hand-washing ritual of the rage-filled person, or in the nagging of a wife who stays married to a husband to whom she has been unfaithful, in order to hate him and hurt herself; in both processes, play is missing. Where there is no seriousness, there is no play. The lack of seriousness may show itself in the windy flights of speech by the paranoiac, or in the cute sophistication of the one who thinks himself above his peers; in neither behavior is there play.

What, then, counts in play?

People under the influence of LSD sometimes say, "The universe is playing back at me," or "The chair seemed to answer me, to breathe right after I did." Clouds, floods, floors, strangers—all seem to be streaming centers of being, ready to respond if taken on. Allowing for their extravagance of expression, these reports suggest several features of play as a model for optimum turning on in any activity.

To begin with, play has a kind of doubleness. There is the player and something beyond his surface consciousness which responds to him. In lighter moments of fantasy or wishful thinking, this doubleness is reduced almost to vanishing, because so little is allowed to surprise the beholder. But in real play, something is at hand which may overtake or outflank or astonish the player as if he can trust it not to destroy him. His delight may be in the free bouncing of a ball, in the unexpected retorts of a waitress,

31

in the sudden resonance of lower notes on a clarinet, in the unfolding of architectural variations on a building at which he stares, in the stream of autonomous visions from a deeply introspective state, or in the small shocks which bring laughter from an almost-frightened child tossed into the air. This primal doubleness, from which surprise and fitting challenge stream forth to meet but not to inundate the player, constitutes the base of play and is what so easily makes it an emblem of the art and game of living. Sometimes the double or opponent or partner in play is an object, which the player chases and tracks and dodges. Sometimes it is a form, an idea, a scheme, which he struggles to tug into shape or to comprehend. Sometimes it is a person. But whether it is matter, meter, or man—or all three—he finds that play begins with something beyond his surface self which acts on him unpredictably.

Second, the individual at play lowers his defenses toward whatever confronts or puzzles him. For the time being he acts in trust or in hope, without everlastingly checking to see whether he is bleeding or beheaded. In any kind of play, men are a bit more ready than usual to be fools in order to have a rollicking fast game, here or hereafter.

Third, the person at play may now and then act as a total being, while he is open, untangled from his weapons and harness and shield. His conscious skill and unconscious hunch meet in a flash of judgment, and he throws the ball to George—who baskets it, even though George has been off his stride for a couple of weeks. The same kind of optimum total engagement occurs in making love (as Freud said), in discussing a proposition, in building a barn, or wherever else the action is full of play. Memory and mood, strategy and stampede, picture and passion, the positive and the possible—all meet in one act called forth by play, when there is no time to sort, but only to be there and produce. The psychologist of optimums says that conscious and unconscious regions of the mind appear to interact more freely and richly in play than in most other kinds of behavior.

Fourth, spontaneity marks play as truly as does total engagement. Taoist tradition celebrates such spontaneity in Chinese scrolls, where a spacious and cloud-flecked vista offers an emptied background against which the artist attempts to flash his sketch of gnarled tree and winging bird, created in one swift set of spontaneous strokes. Similarly, Zen Buddhism has taught archery as one quick spontaneous movement of pulling and release, as it has taught wrestling through being prepared by not being prepared—for the spontaneous spring of an opponent who may leap from any direction at any time of day. Zen philosophy has offered parallel versions of living and loving and knowing, by means of totally engaged spontaneous acts of creative response to each situation. But the West has its own versions of play in the unified and spontaneous act. Socrates is endeared to men of later centuries for lifting his voice in grave-playful exchanges, reaching for the prizes of truth and integrity which seem to be grasped only by helping other players to touch them as well. Francis of Assisi steps into men's hearts when he walks naked from his father and his own playboy finery, in one bold move where playboy now plays man, the fool for God. And Jesus acts the total spontaneous response when he suddenly scrawls in the dust beside a captured adulteress, turning back on her accusers the heat of the private guilts they had thought to project on her, and asking the man without sin to throw the first stone. Such sudden and fitting responses, in all their seriousness, have the character of play at its best.

Fifth, play makes possible some moments of objectivity, free of compulsions. The lowering of defenses and following of spontaneous promptings also works to free that which confronts the player. Rock is allowed to have its grain and bulk for the sculptor, and characters unfold their mystery for actors. The wilderness is treasured, not patronized, by vacationing city dwellers. Opponents and teammates are freed to be themselves. In the best of drug states, many a person who discovers undefensive, total, and spontaneous play promptly and physically embraces his friend or psychiatrist—and then encourages the other to make his own move. Similarly, when crisis or joy or elevation of spirit turns people free without drugs, they stumble into alert and undriven objectivity. As one ball club plays great ball, so does the other, on the court or field or diamond. Freedom and integrity build freedom and integrity. Skill whets skill. Imagination sparks imagination. Play evokes play.

In summary, then, when play is present in turned-on work, love, study, recreation, or worship, it has the features of doubleness, openness, total engagement, spontaneity, and objectivity. Players are not so much doing it as caught up in it, relishing whatever can surprise them, exchanging customary suits of mail for movable shields which are also toboggans, and responding with total acts of skill and spontaneity which waken and welcome the same from others.

Just such a model of optimum behavior was suggested by an uneducated American photographer, a tall Southerner named Edgar Cayce whose puzzling skills and mature philosophy, exhibited in a trance state of altered consciousness, made him a showcase of optimums. When he looked from his own psychedelic but drugless state at the highest human behavior in any activity, he saw much the same model as did the housewife who took LSD in her therapy. He saw optimum behavior as "co-creating with God."

CHAPTER TWO

HIGH PLAY AND LOW PLAY

Early in his young manhood in Kentucky, Edgar Cayce discovered that he could extend the time and spirit of his prayers into twice-daily periods of deep quiet where he lost consciousness, yet could speak complete, helpful discourses on the needs of individuals who sought his aid. For the same reasons which made him a Sunday school teacher all of his life, he sought first to use his abilities chiefly for children and youth, especially for those who needed medical diagnosis and prescription of treatments. Soon he was producing similar medical counsel for adults; he found that in trance he could report detailed and accurate medical observations, organ system by organ system, on people whom he had never seen and might never see. Further, his own quiet voice, while he was in trance, was specifying remarkably thorough and balanced treatment regimes, ranging from surgery to diet, from drugs to physiotherapy, and sometimes emphasizing prayer. Most of the Kentucky doctors who heard of him ignored him, but a few were fascinated, conducted preliminary experiments on him, and verified his strange capacities when they were reported to a national medical society meeting in Boston in 1910. What Cayce did seemed manifestly impossible, yet he kept on doing it in thousands of striking medical cases until his death in 1945.

What bewildered such observers as the present writer (who studied Cayce in action for eight months shortly before his death and later wrote a doctoral dissertation about him at the University of Chicago) was not only Cayce's obvious medical accuracy on verifiable details about people whom he had not seen, but his incredible trance directory service. Somehow he could instantly name needed medical specialists in any part of the country and locate out-of-the-way drugs, as well as report on tiny changes in drug compounds manufactured in distant cities as soon as these changes were made. Because of his impressive medical vocabulary and his grasp of physiology and chemistry, he was a one-man museum of medical history, a one-man clinic encompassing the major specialties, and a one-man research laboratory—as when, for example, he described in detail vitamins and viruses which in some cases were not discovered by experts until after his death (and in other cases still await full confirmation). Yet Cayce had not been educated beyond grade school and could render little medical service outside his trance state. Indeed, he was not primarily interested in medicine as much as he was interested in relieving human pain—and in his vocation of photography, at which he was good enough to win regional prizes.

The absurdity of Cayce's impossible gifts—which seemed to take him twice a day into some unthinkable optimum state paralleled only in accounts of ancient seers and prophets of Greece and Israel, China and Babylonia —was stretched to the ultimate of incomprehensibility when he found he could offer similar discourses on nonmedical problems. With the same detail and usefulness as in medicine, he produced findings for vocational and marital guidance, located oil and mineral deposits, predicted earthquakes and major storms, and described epochs of past history as if he were an eyewitness to ancient clothing, language, conflicts, and customs. Many of his reports were difficult or impossible to verify from known information, but those which could be tested produced a profile of such accuracy as to suggest that he was using the same scanning capacities which he used in medical counsel. (The present writer's *Edgar Cayce on Dreams* surveys the major types of Cayce's trance productions, and reports some of the lawful regularities which they seemed to exhibit.)

Faced with this dazzling parade of helpful information, Cayce clung to his sanity by viewing his trance-guidance process against the background of the lives of prayerful men in the Bible, which was central in his personal faith. He also kept his sense of humor and stuck to his fishing, his friends, and his family life. But the mystery of his trance performances stayed with him to the end of his life. Even when responsible business and professional people in New York thought enough of his work to develop for it in Tidewater, Virginia, a complete hospital and a modest university (both of which closed in the Depression), he was not relieved of the mark of strangeness he had to bear, nor did he find it easier to keep his personal balance.

Yet in time his balance became for many of the thousands who met and knew Edgar Cayce a compelling feature of his gift, matching in impact even the startling dramatic accuracy of his clairvoyance in prayer-induced altered states. The balance showed in his trance discourses, which he called "readings," following American folk usage about those with clairvoyant vision. In these readings, the accuracy and intimacy of his inspections were never used to hurt or humiliate others, or used to allow one man to take advantage of another. And though often firm and at times even fiery in tone, his counsel in readings was frequently tender and incredibly patient as it offered people choices to foster their gifts and growth. Further, his trance counsel offered no personal edge to Cayce. Indeed, Cayce was warned by his own trance source (which he thought of as impersonal and "overshadowed" by divine mercy, and which he simply called "the information") that he should not think too highly of himself, since he was but exemplifying laws as old and real as those the great monotheistic religions had long taught regarding the divine aid to men of faith.

Cayce awake also kept a remarkable balance, although he was an impetuous, emotional, and complex man. He refused offers of wealth through commercial promotion, collaborating instead with a small research and educational society established to study his work. And he welcomed the efforts of his family, along with friends in small meditation and study groups, to keep him pared down to size, as well as to pray for him. That he could negotiate such personal balance, despite attention from followers which sometimes approached idolatry, gave him an impact which was as great as any of his optimums. This impossible man remained a possible person. This outrageous counseling facility remained an outgoing tease. This seer figure in a seerless culture remained a believable father and friend.

Just what went on in Cayce's altered state, as he lay in quiet-speaking unconscious trance twice a day for forty years, eludes any adequate formulation of optimum psychology. But Cayce's impersonal trance source had its own view, glimpsed in the instructions which "the information" stipulated that Cayce should be given when daily he slipped into his altered state: "Now the body is assuming its normal forces, and will be able, and will give, such information as is desired of it at the present time." Cayce in his strangely altered consciousness was using his "normal forces," his true and fitting optimums. What was this concept of "normal forces," and how might it be used to illuminate the optimums of others?

When asked such a question, the trance-speaking Cayce replied that there was in fact only One Force in all of

38

creation, which was God. However, man experienced that One Force in two modes, which gave all of his existence a kind of doubleness, such as that which marks play. There was first the divine expression in the soul of man, ever stirring him to new becomings, in each man's long journey to become a full and conscious companion of God. And there was secondly the stream of structured becomings which each man encountered in the souls of others, as well as in Nature and in realms of creation and beings beyond earth life; all of these were expressions of the same God, offering himself to man in rich variety which man might properly call "the Creative Forces"—provided that he remembered that there was finally only One Force.

The proper relation between man and the many expressions of God which met him on his soul's journey was that of being a "co-creator with God," which meant man's undertaking every activity in such a way as to work productively with his fellows, and with the Father or Source of all. Co-creating was beginning to use one's "normal forces," whether in giving counsel as did Cayce, or in making beauty as did an artist, or in making money as did a businessman, or in making justice as did a legislator, or in making bonds of mutual joy as did lovers. Wherever men were able to relate spontaneously and nondefensively to one another, in productive ventures which enhanced the being of each and did not distort nonhuman creation, they were moving towards their optimums.

Speaking from his altered state, Cayce described human optimums in any activity in terms very much like those which describe the best of play.

But the trance-quickened Cayce saw levels in man's efforts at co-creating with the divine which was all about him. Any individual who studied his experience with care, said Cayce, would find himself confronted by what could be called "stepping-stones" and "stumbling blocks," as he sought to use his "normal forces." The stepping-stones were talents and interests and opportunities which made it easier for a man to fulfill the two great ends of human existence: giving service to others, and attunement with the Creative Forces. In the view of the Cayce "information," these stepping-stones came from both the present life and previous lives—for, like Plato and many another religious teacher, Cayce in trance expounded a theory of reincarnation. Whatever abilities a man chose and developed for the fuller life of his fellows, in harmony with the spirit of the divine which he found in attunement by prayer and meditation, these would remain his stepping-stones to his optimums as a co-creator.

By contrast, stumbling blocks were those fears, doubts, compulsions and hardships in any man's journey which impeded his fully creative relating to others, and to Nature and the rest of the divine creation. The stumbling blocks—roughly what modern idiom calls "hang-ups," but also including physical sufferings and blocked opportunities—were derived from one or several lives, as were the stepping-stones. Whatever abilities and positions or advantages a man chose and developed without sufficient care for the needs and growth of his fellows, without the loving-playful spirit of the divine—these would remain his private temptation and sometimes torment, barriers to his life as a co-creator with God until he overcame them with the aid of divine law and grace.

The first human task in the journey of the soul to full and conscious companionship with God, as co-helper in making and changing universes, was the development of each one's stepping-stones—those richer and richer talents and values by which one might work effectively with his fellows and with the cosmic order of things. The second task was the turning of stumbling blocks, which emerged along the soul's journey as the product of individual and group sin and evil, into stepping-stones. In this second task, one did not simply ignore or reject evil but transformed it, piece by piece, with the divine aid found both in and apart from his fellows, until his very problems had become his promises, his hang-ups had become his helpfulness, his curses had become his blessings.

Translated into the metaphor of play, what the trance-speaking Cayce outlined was a distinction between high play and low play. Such high play would be co-creating with one's fellows and the rest of the Creative Forces, from the footing made easier by the stepping-stones. And low play would be falling over one's stumbling blocks, which slowed down all games of love, work, study, or worship.

A distinction between high play and low play is useful. It is similar to the distinction drawn by recreation workers between "high games" and "low games," where the high games are more complex and susceptible to greater creativity and involvement by players. And it is similar to the familiar Catholic distinction between high mass and low mass, where the high mass is sung and is therefore richer in its creative potential of symbolism. Or setting apart high play from other play may be likened to the Jewish distinction between High Holidays and other festivals of the faith, where the former are especially definitive for the believers' relationships with God.

In such a view of two levels in play, the first and crucial feature of high play would be productivity.

In high play there is no tuning out, no dropping out, though one may need to turn his back, even at the risk of death, on outworn values and associations. The player takes a man-sized productive risk with his fellows. He creates something and puts it on the market, or trades it. He plays not only for runs, but for the best form that he can muster, and counts the hits and errors. He proposes marriage, and is through playing around. He grabs a sword and swings, though he knows it may be turned to impale him. He goes after a whale, shouting with the crew, "A dead whale or a stove boat!" He begins a love affair outside his social circle, risking his social standing on a slender thread of mutuality. He propounds a theory and knows he might be wrong. He enters a room to be still before God, not at all sure he can face himself, let alone God. His high play is productive play; it has form and worth. He knows his effort may be rejected, but the player lays it on the line before his peers.

The point of talents, opportunities, and all other step-

41

ping-stones, said the Cayce "information," was finally service to others, productive service. Man, the divine partner, was truly himself only as he brought into being new worlds of joy and growth with others.

Yet to remain high play and not slip into compulsion, productiveness must remain open to puzzlement, to astonishment, to surprise—all essential to the spirit of play. Wits must yield to wonder, points to pondering, dollars to dauntedness, victories to visitations. The high player must risk and take his risk seriously; yet he must let his risky act surprise him into a new appreciation of the play and players. He must offer himself, and yet be willing to find a new self, or a new other person in his opponent or playmate. His stakes must be translucent to something as big as the whole game; his final delight must be in playing, as truly as in winning. For high play is known in the easy swing back and forth between doing and prizing, between making and musing. Opponents on a battlefield salute before they kill each other, and mean both acts. A hunter refuses to cook an animal in its own milk. A conductor stops a rehearsal to walk all the way to the third-chair cellist so he can shake his hand for one phrase played soaringly with the ensemble. In the free and unpredictable swing of high play, each glance of delighted appreciation quickens the skilled risk on the next play, and each apt swing awakens a happy grin in the sweating players.

In the view of the Cayce source, "attunement" was essential to keep service from being ineffective or even deadly. A man who sought to be a co-creator with all the Creative Forces of the divine had to step back to seek guidance and rapport with the overarching and indwelling One Force, which worked its way in everyone whom he engaged, and in nonhuman creation as well. Service required attunement to guide and perfect it, lest service turn to power and manipulation in the name of doing good. Service and attunement were twin actions in all co-creating with the One which had called man into being.

The distinction was much the same as that drawn by Cayce's contemporary, the Jewish philosopher Martin

Buber, who argued that all human behavior alternated between the potentially creative deeds of I-it relations (Cayce's "service"), and the potentially creative openness of I-thou relations (Cayce's "attunement"). Each, said Buber, required the other for humans to reach their optimums. The Cayce source traced the same distinction in Jesus' command to serve others by loving them as oneself, but not without loving God with all one's heart, strength, mind and soul.

What is the mind-set in high play which embodies both service and attunement?

However the player may describe his intent, or forget to describe it, he appears bent on reconciling opposites, two or more good things which are in conflict for him. At the simplest level, such reconciling of conflicting values in high play is making a move so that other good moves may follow it. Reconciling opposites may mean getting a man to second base with a sacrifice hit; or plotting a curve on canvas so that other curves may support it and masses and lines may counterpoint it; or hiring a competent minority person so that everyone in a business firm knows that productivity rather than exploitation is the name of their business game. At a more sophisticated level, reconciling opposites means honoring medium with form, so that plastic is not used as imitation wood, nor a woman made to love as a man, nor a funeral made to enshrine death instead of life. In the hardware of living, reconciling opposites means finding the implications of the Bauhaus slogan "Form follows function," so that the shape of a chair suggests and contributes to its use in sitting, without losing the appeal of its angled design.

The full elegance of high play appears wherever one value is fused with another and conflicting value, so that more and greater values will follow and yet preserve the original values. William James took a mind-bending gas to get the feel of this process; he reported that he found two opposites bodied forth in his imagination, and the greater soaking up the lesser without obliterating it. The person in high play constantly feels out such a process.

43

At the most demanding level of high play he is groping to reconcile the greatly prized ultimates of human existence, whether these be service and attunement, freedom and destiny, justice and mercy, love and wisdom, or some other unwilling but necessary twins. In a word, then, high play is creating. It is not merely originating, because the novel is not necessarily fitting or freeing or fun. It is that kind of creating which is fully productive in time and in space and in personhood (or as the entranced Cayce put it, over and over again, "in time and space and patience"). High play is pruning stately trees to yield ripe fruit, which will nourish plump babies who grow up and outstrip the skills of the gardener that started on the trees.

When the high player asks himself what he has been doing, he discovers that his best playing is not only to possess a person or a piano or a poem, but somehow to give life to these. Holding is not all of living, and having is not all of being. Only as what he touches becomes or produces more than when he found it has he been at high play. He may ask himself why he should not define high play as piling up trophies, counting amorous conquests, displaying paintings or horses or autos or degrees. Are not these the stuff of life's great games, the focus of soul-splitting effort which lifts ordinary play to productive high play? They may be, indeed. Yet from time to time there occurs to the person engaged in high play an intuition of an answer to his question. He glimpses a process so much larger than sportsmanship as to dwarf it. He gets a sense of the becomings of things and of people, a hint of a groundswell of ultimate being which keeps happening to itself in all kinds and sizes of events. He is brushed by a wind which blows all things clean and into full size. He has an idea of an everlasting and dumbfounding unfolding which all his play may be about.

He finds what the Cayce source called the Creative Forces—the One Force happening to itself, on every hand.

Alongside—or is it inside?—player and opponent, artist and art materials, statesmen and people, lover and loved, pray-er and prayed-for, psychiatrist and housewife patient, buyer and seller, loser and winner, griever and gone, there seems to move this shy, dancing, immensely playful Something which Cayce called the Creative Forces. As a kind of Third, it originates and bets on the other two who engage in any game. As Third, it is what Buber called "the Eternal Thou," addressed whenever man whispers "thou" in honest attunement to child or chair or chorus, and then in the next moment beckons these to his service of others as his "it." As Third, it hides in its folds the stranger not yet known and protects his welfare. It carries the child which the lovers will have, the farmer whom the generals forget, the immortal poet among the oppressed. It cannot well be described, but once glimpsed it cannot be ignored. For it is the background of the enchanting doubleness in all true play. In Cayce's view, this Third which was also One, this flow of Creative Forces, was engaged wherever man found that which was near at hand, yet elusive, to be surprising him and signaling him, awakening him and challenging him, alluring him and accosting him, in his high play.

The person who finds such a stream of becomings, with or without drugs, may say as did the housewife under LSD, "I found God"—although what may be seen of such an experience is only that a woman has found herself and her husband and children, all fallen at once into hopeful patterns where daily opposites begin to be reconciled in uncontrived designs. Such high play appears to breed more high play. It generalizes well. Getting its drift, as a captain feels the tug of the unseen Gulf Stream on his craft, the player may journey on more and bolder voyages to his optimums with others. He ventures high play not only in his recreation, but on the job. He tries it in his marriage and in his politics. He risks it with his youngsters, or with his parents, or with others who are both well-known and strangers to him. He notes it in the worship which stills him, and in the sweat which melts off his defenses. He learns that he can count three in any situation, seeking to make all his games and struggles three-handed, even when he cannot for the life or death of him figure out where the Third, who is also the One, is sitting. He can learn to begin each new game, each new trial, each new adventure, with the assurance that there is locked up in it a whole series of outcomes, each of which will discharge an unguessed lively game for all hands. He can play hard, even fiercely, and for life-or-death stakes, without trying to rig or foreclose the game at hand, provided that he has the feel of his optimal action as a co-creator with the Creator.

Or he may settle for low play.

What is low play? Low play is surely not the absence of all play, seen in psychosis or crippling neurosis, or in frantic fear or mind-splitting doubt (in the Cayce view, fear and doubt were the primal sources of all mental illness). Nor is low play just functioning, for it is possible to live an adequate life, meeting the bills and the relatives and death, while engaging in little play at all.

Low play ought to be conceived as the entranced Cayce described it, just under high play.

Low play is the spell which mimics high play, yet forestalls it. Low play is make-believe believed, so that belief in the truth will not follow. It is the hang-up. The trance-heightened Cayce insisted again and again that active human evil ought to be seen as "just under good"—not poles apart from goodness. Where a man did not rest in indifference (which was another kind of evil, more challenging to the forgiveness of both God and man), but spent himself in active pursuit of a wrong goal, his effort required viewing, said Cayce, as just short of his optimums. Such a view would show how close is the hang-up or negative karma (a term borrowed from Sanskrit to represent predispositions created by an act or stance) to positive karma. It would show how close are stumbling blocks to stepping-stones—which they may become.

The closeness of low play to high play is not difficult to see. Certainly risking continues in low play. People play for stakes that matter to them, put up big wagers, make their moves. But their action is narrowed to a few pitches, and their risking becomes a single consuming strategy, rather than a playful way of life, the way of a co-creator with the One. In low play, a business or political title becomes all that matters. Winning one woman is the universe. Keeping a good name is salvation. The world is one white whale for Ahab to find and kill. To be sure, the targets in low play may change, and one may think he is truly playful when now he wants a house and last year it was a car, and before that it was his roommate's girlfriend. But the style of low play is rigid, the compass of effort constricted, the goals felt as overpowering. The player's version of service is simply victory for the right side, in which few opposites need be reconciled.

Likewise, ecstatic appreciation or attunement appears in low play, when defenses are dropped. But in low play the marvel of co-creating is sacralized, set apart for certain times and places. One is happy to be married on his anniversaries. The job is important at the retirement dinner. College is worthwhile at commencements, or at specific coercions of or by the administration. A painting is good when critics say it is. The breezes of mystery and delight blow in certain rooms on certain days, in low play. Religion is for Sundays, love is for bed, chemicals are for parties, politics are for elections. In low play the swift, easy flip of high play from service to attunement, from making to marveling and back again, is frozen into lurching slow motion. The player lingers too long on his prowess, or too long on his pondering. He engraves his own image on whatever he makes, or he looks longingly at the sky; but he notices nobody in the room with him. He inflates his products with near-cosmic significance, and tells himself what services he will render to his fellows when he acquires a certain post, or a certain total of members or dollars. Or he forgets about service in the cult of attunement and retreats to misty realms of art or psychology, of religion or the occult or drugs, atoning for past lapses into activism but putting asunder what high play joins together as a marriage "before God and this company": doing and deliberating, making and musing, working and worshiping, service and attunement.

What fills the mind of the person engaged in low play is not reconciling good and lusty opposites, but winning; he does not seek being, but possessing. As for the Third, he may sense that Something is there, over against him. But his low play consists in squeezing the Third into the two, which he makes Two. "We Two," he says, "will make such lovers, and all we need is each other." Or he announces, "There are just the Two of us in this operation, and I must be in charge, for the good of the company." Or finally he sees only Two in politics: his side and the Reds. Or his side and the Blacks. Or his side and Whitey.

Because low play oversimplifies co-creating, it does not generate ever-widening playfulness. The player tends to stick to his thing, to beat his one drum, to love loving rather than a lover, to fight for the perverse pleasure of being fought, rather than for clean victories and defeats. Low play accumulates force and builds in intensity, but it does not enlarge the areas and kinds of play. Captain Ahab focuses more and more intently upon Moby Dick, but he does not free his crew to chase the white whale; instead, he brings forth his own smuggled oarsmen, so that he can get the whale himself.

What fosters low play and keeps it alive?

First, low play limits responsibility. If spouses can simplify a marriage into either duties or pleasures, then they can avoid the marriage's demands for them to grow. If employees can simplify work to climbing the ladder of pay and position, then they need not improve their skills or revive their imaginations. If politics can be simplified to what the government in Washington, or the little commune, must do, then citizens or members need not propose much, nor make their proposals work for many. In low play it is easy to slide into an image of fidelity, or industry, or "being well-liked" along with Willy Loman, hearing only the collective voice which chants the praises of the image and ignoring the responsibilities of harrowing opposites locked up in the image—ignoring for example the fact that being a man's best friend means being his firmest enemy, when he is unworthy of himself.

Second, low play endures because it has a remarkable way of mimicking high play. It keeps at hand a hint of exactly the high play which is needed. Stumbling blocks are very much like the stepping-stones which an individual *could* have. Destructiveness is like sacrifice, and like purification through fire. Lust is like ecstatic self-giving. Masochism is like humility. Overstimulation is near to vital alertness. Withdrawal is near to a refreshing retreat. The lure of novelty is not far from the loves of true creation. Dissociating with drugs is not unlike the disorienting in valued mystical states. Arousing lovers is like quickening the primal divine spark in another. Dependency is close to acknowledging the true doubleness of co-creating with the One. Pregenital types resemble particular forms of true genitality. The list is long and the point is clear. Low play is the spell by which life tries to rescue itself when it is betrayed. It is the process of making the prince a frog if he won't be a prince, but giving him princely tasks and powers and decisions for his frogginess, until he awakens to his full nature once more. Such low play is what the trance-attuned Cayce described as the operation of negative karma, whether from the present life or earlier. He saw this karma as a process which brought the soul to meet itself, not for punishment, but for specific growth.

Third, low play persists because it offers the co-creator, himself an authentic spark from the Creator, the lure of almost Godlike power over life, rather than Godlike power with life. In the Cayce view, sin was precisely described as "selfish aggrandizement"—the holding of life's true goods for oneself, rather than the sharing of them in service guided by attunement. The drive to be becomes in low play a drive to be what one chooses; man plays God rather than playing with God, met as the Creative Forces. Low play joins potent power drives with the equally potent chemicals of appetite, as Freud so clearly showed when he described the contamination of the super-ego by the id. Instead of freeing the appetites to fuse with vision and burst the person into successive new selves which he may share with others, low play uses one flavor of appetite to conceal another. Anger is the drunk of the sexually anxious person. Sex is the drunk of the chronically angry person. A drug binge may substitute for either drunk.

Finally, low play lingers where men forget to be usefully ignorant and curious. Like the ducklings "imprinted" by judicious exposure at just the right points in their young lives to follow a laboratory experimenter as though he were their mother, children live through well-timed experiences, as Leary has nicely observed, which tell them at the right points that success in living is wealth or popularity or thrills—and the low play propositions seize them as Universal Truth. In the Cayce view, each man was especially susceptible to certain kinds of such imprinting, based on false values which he had sold himself in present or previous lifetimes. For this reason, said the entranced Cayce, there was no dodging the need to "study self, study self's experience"; for only by careful introspection, analysis, and decision might the grip of low play be broken, and the playful wonder and tentativeness reappear which mark the high play of the co-creator with the One.

Through these and other motivations, low play as hang-up appears to weave endlessly in and out of high play. While it would comfort many to think of themselves as High Players, and the useful effort has been made in many a culture to train novices, proficients, and adepts in the true spirituality which is high play in all activities, still the disciplined ones have seemed the surest of all that low play is never far from anyone. Nobody who received Cayce's impersonal trance counseling was admonished more abruptly, over the years, than Cayce himself. The Buddha had no more than wakened to his full optimums and the Four Noble Truths under the Bo tree than Mara the tempter to low play appeared, assuring the Buddha that nobody would understand when he tried to tell them what he now knew. And the old prayer runs, "Lead us—not into temptation." Doubtless the same One will do its doings and sing its songs in men's low play as in their high play. But between pain and play, or more precisely between pointless pain in low play and the pain of pointed stress in high play, there appears a choice worth making.

The choice between high and low play may be traced in four activities or games of daily life. In each of these games may be found the alternatives posed by using drugs to turn on the mind.

First, there is the parent game.

Any two people may play this game, though the roles are nominally those of a child and one adult of either sex. Often a child may be parent to his father or mother, as playwrights and novelists have shown. Certainly most lovers and married couples play the parent game, alternating roles of parent and child with each other, as Missildine has deftly displayed in his work *Your Inner Child of the Past*. Further, a large part of psychotherapy turns on this game, wherever the therapy requires instituting, recognizing, and dissolving a transference; Eric Berne has brilliantly depicted the plays of the parent game, in and out of psychotherapy, in *Games People Play*. Workers and bosses, students and teachers, disciples and gurus, patients and doctors, consumers and tradesmen, underlings and overlings in every field find some version of this game inevitable. The frequency of everyone's dreams about his parents and childhood testifies to the importance of this game.

The point of the game was well summarized in the pithy saying which appeared more than once in the Cayce readings: "Every tub must sit on its own bottom." Part of every human journey to optimums appears to be growth away from dependence on parents and parent substitutes (or child substitutes), toward self-dependence, in a state which Fromm describes as having one's own fatherly conscience and motherly conscience, rather than relying on external figures and behavior codes. In this journey to optimums, the Oedipus arrangement between parent and child which Freud described appears so often as to suggest its candidacy for the mantle of original sin. Perhaps no human being grows to adulthood without trying to buy life more cheaply than it is for sale by negotiating a private deal with a powerful adult—preferably an adult of the opposite sex who can be worked upon sexually as well as in power plays (both of which methods are familiar to a person from other lives, in the Cayce view which brought Cayce near to Freud). When the effort at bargain-rate existence does not pay off in full potency for the child and the adult, as it never does, then each player produces his version of the ultimate "quarrel with the universe" which seems hidden in every man (from karma, in the Cayce view). Crying out, "I am more beautiful than you know"—or more "wise" or "powerful" or "holy"—he storms at the gods. The child-player, whatever his age, rails at the Olympian deity which he wants the adult-player to be, and the adult-player weeps in disappointment over the filial Holy Child which he expected to find in the other; both are disappointed, because they have shrunk the parent game to Two.

Played as low play, the parent game is two-handed maneuvering which may vary in intensity from irritated bickering to the ferocity seen in divorces, or in intrabusiness warfare. The child-player cries out, "Somebody turn me on," and the adult-player responds, "Let me turn you on," neither grasping that human beings can never quite do this for one another except as co-creators with the One. For a while the low-play exchange of intimacies and favors seems to make all hands happy, but then there appears that subterranean dimension to the game which Gerald Heard has called the demand for "reparations." One or another player makes the claim, "You owe me more than you are giving me, because of all that I have done and been for you," and the claim may develop to that hopeless demand which blocks the life flow in paralyzed marriages: "You owe me all of my past, and I will make no move until you pay it all up." In such contests both sides have lost track of that line which nobody can cross uninvited, the line which divides "hurting" another from "destroying" his personhood, and divides "helping"

52

another from "creating" him as a person. Both sides in the parent game ignore the line because they cherish the illusion of their godlike powers over others, even with the staggering guilts which such powers would entail. Warning against all such low play in the parent game, the impersonal Cayce trance source insisted, "Since the time when Christ took upon Himself the sins of all, no man pays for the sins of others; each meets at last only himself." The point made was that while men are involved in and burdened by each other's sins, they are not as souls finally crippled or demolished by the sins of others—only by their own. A complete mural of reincarnation and karma was required for the entranced Cayce to depict this view; the result was a vista of creation which laid immense stress on the necessity for each man to take the responsibility for his own life, and his own pain, with the aid of the Creative Forces.

When the parent game turns into high play, it may be beautiful to see. The mutual pity and self-pity between child-player and parent-player, even between adults, may turn into honest high play compassion. The craving of each player to be sparked, to be stimulated, to be believed in, may yield to accepting responsibility for his own life, and to the growing recognition that the One is quietly helping to build that life as it builds all lives, though it will not be badgered as a parent, nor patronized as a child. Parent and child who have used each other, and hated each other for the using, may stumble into the grace to labor without exploiting, and in time choose each other as full companions. When that happens, the spell of low play is lifted, as perhaps it was lifted for the pious son whom Jesus told to let the dead bury their dead, or lifted for the woman moaning over her dead child when the Buddha told her he would restore her son to life when she brought him seeds from a village home which had never known death. Each who has sought in the parent game to confer on others authority over his life may be found to have the seeds for true authority in his own being—when

53

he discovers for himself how authority means author-ity, the capacity to help author another person, as co-creator with that person and the unseen One.

Not a few take drugs in the parent game. They may seek, at an unconscious level, to break with parents or other authority figures upon whom they have been too dependent. Legal and social taboos on mind=altering drugs make them useful for modest but—in the case of the milder drugs—defined rebellion, though in some circumstances more risky than those seeking emancipation may realize. For some who rebel through drug use, as older generations have with alcohol, the act is weakened by the very process of oral ingestion, which but reinforces their expectations of being fed life's goodies by parents and parent substitutes, such as institutional authorities. They engage in low play. But even for them, and certainly for others, the effort to find some risk-taking venture which calls forth individual boldness and self-reliance may be the stirring of high-play optimums in the parent game—a stirring which may call for nurture in more productive modes, rather than for prohibition of drugs alone.

Similarly, those who bristle with anger and fear at all who take drugs often do so in the parent game. By attacking others, they may seek to strengthen their sagging identities through identification with the ways of the fathers and with authority codes, which are made to substitute for their own mature inner parents, or motherly and fatherly consciences. Their holding firm may prove deceptive to them, producing less authoritative ego strength for them or others than it does low play egoism. But it may also mark the birth of a truly humanistic conscience in the fearful person. One who has driven and stretched himself to painful limits in work and play, under a torturing conscience, may be unable to take his eyes off drug users less anxious than he, until at last he finds new kinds of acceptance and forgiveness which introduce him to his own optimums in the parent game.

The second game in which high play and low play appear in daily life is the romance game.

While it might be expected that this game requires a man and a woman, it may be played by a child and an adult, as Freud showed, or it may be played homosexually. And while it might be supposed that the romance game is reserved for leisure hours, it appears in low-play forms in the worlds of business and education and other institutions, wherever roles are defined in terms of personal liaisons and loyalties, rather than in clear job descriptions, chains of command, and briefing and debriefiing sessions. Shaw has skillfully described such low play between a minister and his adoring flock and secretary in *Candida.* There may be more of high play in the long run, welcoming romance in daily life, when a man runs off with his secretary than when he makes of all his employees and associates, male and female, his half-sexual playthings, now in and now out of his good graces.

The point of the romance game is twofold: polarity and passion. On the one hand, the romance game displays the implications of the claim so basic to all of psychoanalysis: men and women are different, both biologically and culturally, and can best work as co-creators by recognizing and using their differences, without over-emphasizing them. On the other hand, the romance game provides an entry to ecstasy, to delight and abandon, at its every level from the admiring and confirming glances of strangers to the full-mouthed kisses of lovers (or of members of a work-encounter group), and on to that ridiculous and temporary but rarely dull dance of delights called intercourse. In the Cayce view, polarity and passion were part of handling the primal energy which was the birthright of every person; even the highest tasks of thought and social reform and artistic creation, as well as of worship, required vitality which was sexual in origin, and subsequently was polarized into male-female opposites (in what Cayce traced to the work of obscure "cells of Leydig" in the endocrine system of the body). Following the ancient Hindu teaching of *kundalini,* the snake of divine energy which rises from its symbolically coiled base within the gonads and stretches up the spine to open its cobralike hood over the head of a man, the trance-speaking Cayce saw all of man's creating as requiring chain reactions among his endocrine glands. Whether an individual's creative potency would reach its optimums, or would sluice off in uncreative or destructive acts and drives, depended finally on the purpose of a man's acts—his desires for service and attunement with the Creative Forces. But the proper functioning of any high creativity required man's passions, which served, said Cayce, to "awaken" each person to greater and greater potentials in his relationships with others, as well as to give him energy for his deeds. When these passions were aroused and used in fully responsible tasks, they would carry the rich qualities of human existence—just as men and women romantically joined in dreams often symbolized not only the union of their quickened desires but of justice and mercy, work and celebration, form and imagination. In such a view, romance was not a mere pastime, to be played as one wished. There was no appetite which did not require completion by creative responsibilities; it would be a mistake to assume that the waves which swept the body in orgasm would not call forth drives to parenthood, homemaking, community making, and vocation. Full sexuality belonged in the covenants, burdens, opportunities, and delights of marriage, where the potent snake of creative energy in each partner could uncoil without throwing body or mind into unwanted moods and compulsions.

Low play in the romance game proceeds by conquest, rather than by full enhancement of the partner. The lover is gowned and jeweled, but not crowned. Devotion becomes idolatry and love-making mere technical skill. Sex is reserved for appetite, in low-play dualism of flesh and spirit which is foreign to biblical thought, while spirituality means rising above passion rather than creating in and through it; such dualism is mocked in the Latin chant at the end of *Who's Afraid of Virginia Woolf?*, where the romance game has not yet become sacramental, "an outward and visible sign of an inward and spiritual grace."

Yet low play in the romance game may slip into high

56

play. Men and women may step beyond stylized encounters to the adventure of helping those of the other gender to recover their separate savor. They may do it in the high play of flirting, or in the fiery high play of lovers, whether on the stage while acting roles or in that performance as true as fiction: real life. High play in the romance game puts passion at the service of polarity of gender. Perhaps in our culture, for example, only a woman knows the fullness of desire to entertain others in her home. When she turns that desire into high-spirited occasions, she sends away her guests as if protected in a charm, for she has dipped them in the extended womb of her home as surely as the mother of Achilles protected him by dipping him in the Styx. Full, mutual, playful passion between man and woman arouses spontaneously to celebrate and advance the times of a woman's entertaining, as it does also her nursing or nurture, or—when she turns to her own masculine side—her sword, her theory, her plan. Perhaps, too, in our culture, only a man knows the painful fullness of desire to build a venture of his own, whether by carving out a kingdom of creativity at the office or plant, or by developing his own spare-time garage or kennel or real-estate office. When a man can turn this desire into high play, he quickens the sense of potency in everyone who enters his office or workshop, as truly as David's kingship marked the men and women of Israel for generations after him. Full mutual passion between man and woman arouses spontaneously to celebrate and advance the times of such building, done not only at home but at the office, wherever a man calls upon all of his brains or muscle or leadership or judgment, or when he turns to his feminine side in tenderness, forgiveness, and nurture of others (qualities which killed the storied King of Siam, when they arrived too late in his manhood). Whatever the time, high play in the romance game can welcome that surprise of ecstatic delight which engages the unpredictable One. When lovers no longer present themselves as actors of roles assigned to certain stages of courtship, nor spoil an embrace by announcing how good it will be and proclaiming its potency afterwards, then high play may transpire in that space where there is no space, between bodies.

Clinically, it is not difficult to show that some take drugs in the romance game. They may, for example, seek an unconscious substitute for sexual experience, by pursuing the thrills of a forbidden ecstatic pleasure, without risking the responsibilities of full personal intimacy. Such drug use is low play. But drugs are also used, though often without sufficient care for their side effects on body chemistry, in quest of naturalness in romance which avoids stereotypes of rating and dating, prowess and potency. In states of mind where speech and gesture are not so predictable and standardized as in film rituals, something of lost poetry may creep into sexuality and humanize it towards optimums. Such use searches for high play in the romance game.

It is also simple to show that some who blindly oppose all exploration of drug experience do so in the romance game. They may react out of sexual anxiety. For a drug, like semen, is a small quantity with a very large outcome, not always desirable. Those who live under truce with their own sexuality, unable to welcome it in high play of the romance game, may view drug users with fearful dismay. Yet in their fascination with the seemingly illicit pleasures of others they may be pushed by currents of their own optimums to lift sexuality and the rest of the romance game beyond its usual function for them as medication —for their anger, their sleeplessness, their meaninglessness, their loneliness. By such a process, hang-ups lead to serious reflection, and stumbling blocks become stepping-stones, in the romance game.

A third game where high play may be contrasted with low play is the work game.

While this game traditionally pits man against man, and man against the environment, it may be played just as intensely and competitively by women or by children, wherever tasks are undertaken toward defined goals of success. It may be played in the form of war between lovers, despite and even during their romantic truces. The

58

courts where the work game is played, often in deadly seriousness, may be the deceptively serene walks of a campus, or the antiseptically impersonal halls of a hospital, or the upholstered comfort of professional offices, or the stately vaults of a religious sanctuary, as truly as the familiar places of farm and factory and field of battle; the game may even be played at the silent breakfast table of a family, where the struggles are more poisonous because players pretend there are no competitions or trophies. In point of fact, the beginning of high play in the work game in any setting may be open acknowledgment of struggle, so that skirmishes may be held where they matter, and not for invisible reporters or the honor of the ancestors.

The point of the work game may be found in the Hindu traditions of the four wants of man. There it is claimed that even as a man must find and live out "desire" or *kama* in the romance game, lest he inject into his work or his worship illicit and distorting overtones of passion, so he must take his turn in the work game by striving for "success" or *artha,* before he goes on to "service" or *dharma* (and, in the achievement of all of these, reaches at last the "freedom" of high play *moksha*). For if community service, as service of the divine, be attempted without the firming and trimming of ego strength found in the work game, then the service will be prostituted to personal successes. Ecclesiastics will build churches where they should have built people, politicians will build empires where they should have built mines, and educators will build departments where they should have built theories. Recognizing just such peril in omitting the work game but investing other games with success strivings, William Sheldon, the somatotyping psychologist, has proposed that no man be allowed to talk theology until he is fifty years of age—and presumably has taken his licks in some version of the work game.

The centrality of high play in the work game for the thought of the trance-heightened Cayce could be seen in the phrase which he most often used to close his vocational and existential trance counsel for individuals, which he called "life readings." Quoting from the New Testament, he encouraged those whom he had analyzed in their talents, style of life, and deepest ideals (in part on the basis of what he saw as their previous lives) with these words: "Study to show thyself approved unto God, a workman not ashamed, rightly dividing the word of truth and keeping self unspotted from the world." The image of a workman was not mere rhetoric, for it reflected the deep concern of the Cayce source for every man's best use of his creative energies, his birthright from the Creative Forces. Only as a man or woman engaged in tasks demanding that person's fullest creative potential would he or she enter the best of co-creating with the One. Such work of course required study and discriminating thought, as well as advance planning and follow-up evaluation. It also required practice and disciplined skill. And, above all, it required focus on accomplishing some constructive good, rather than a purpose of self-enhancement in the public eye, or in accumulation of funds and power; these last would cause one to become "spotted" by low-play values. In the Cayce view, man was by nature a creator, of the same order as the Creator whose inward image he wore. There was for man no deeper longing than to fashion things and worlds in loving concert with others, as well as to procreate and nurture children, and to co-author others into their hidden greatness. This was man's divine birthright. When the social order impeded such creating, leaving some groups disadvantaged in the use of their divine workmanly potential, then the social order must be changed in each political and economic and cultural institution, and every man must make himself responsible for advancing such changes, beginning in his own round of life. Ultimately every person had to ask himself the question from the Genesis account which the seerlike Cayce put untold times to his counselees: "Am I my brother's keeper?" In this view, there was no private work game, no purely personal success story, when high play was the prize.

Competition in the work game is the ring of real metal

on real metal. When competing players can honor opponents, casually but not indifferently, and can salute a good play from any quarter, then the struggle can be the merry high play which sends Prometheus running from the gods with his stolen fire, though he must shortly face some liver pecking by an eagle for his pains. But when the work game is played to exploit customers and belittle competitors, then the players may end in the predicament of being walled-in by their own devices, which they must then dismantle in greater or lesser grace—perhaps by deprecating their own absurdities, as admen making TV commercials may lamely lampoon their own art.

The work game is played in the strategies of dealing with things, as well as with men. The player may farm or mine or fish, or he may paint or market or build memorials. As the Cayce source pointed out, the biblical injunction of God to man was, "Subdue the earth." But as the Cayce source also noted, the first part of the same injunction was, "Be fruitful, multiply." And this command could not be kept if man played the work game merely to overpower Nature for her pollution-producing oils, or for her potency to make mushroom clouds in nuclear fission. Where power-over replaces power-with, then low play is at hand, and the same skill which sends men to the moon may also send them poisoned air, water, and food. Western man has long held to the convention of splitting the universe into a moral segment, where man is answerable for his attitudes and actions, and a natural segment, where man might tinker as he liked. For the Cayce source, this division was untenable; just as the story of Noah's time suggested, human evil would in time bring direct consequences from Nature, as an expression of the One. In modern times the fruit of wars and social injustice would be devastating earthquakes, until man finally learned that he dealt with but One Force in all his doings. What the Cayce readings called "vibrations," as the metaphysical base in both Nature and the psyche, would be found to connect deeds and stones, thoughts and

61

electricity, social order and natural order, far more intimately than yet realized in his ecological speculations.

Played as low play, the work game sets up an awful din and smoke of battle, a clanging of slogan and ideology, and a haze around products marketed and groupings formed. Yet even from out of low-play versions, high play does spring up. Two men shout bids at the Board of the Stock Exchange and learn to relish each other's adroitness, though they are opponents for the same dollar. Two housewives campaign for community office and manage to debate issues despite heavy pressures from their cohorts to mount personal attacks; winner and loser alike present their respective husbands with remarkable women, newly enrolled in the lists of high play. Husband and wife storm at each other of a Saturday morning as if to exterminate each other with sound—and then turn to and clean all the kitchen shelves in suds-slopping high play together. Gandhi leads Indians to the sea, where they can make their own salt not taxed by the British; in so doing, he illuminates high play of the work game at its finest, where players evoke from players the final ground of each.

Clinically, some take mind-altering drugs in the work game. They may, for example, use drugs to calm their flaring hostilities towards others who do not appear to recognize their potentiality and their achievements. At times their effort is vitiated by their bitterness against authority or outsiders, so that the drug-induced tranquillity is but a lull in a battle obscured by the smoke of self-deception. Such drug use is low play. But for others, achieving deep and alert quiet for the first time in their lives, the use of drugs as catalysts may stir them towards optimum efforts of imagination and skill, such as the human family has often sought through its myriad devotional practices, and proclaimed in ideals of peaceful men working together in just societies. Drugs used to enhance such visions and drives are used for high play in the work game.

Clinically, some who oppose all mind altering with drugs

do so because they have lost, or failed to develop, potency in the work game. They may then find in attacking drug users the thrill of conscious or unconscious cruelty as substitute potency. They may be only too willing to test the life quality of those who seem to affront them by driving drug takers to the wall, trying to discover what inward strength and identity they may have. But cruelty begets irritability, and irritability begets general exploration, and exploration begets knowledge. By some such devious process even the harshest stances may contribute to the emergence of optimums, when the mind which cannot transform itself in any better way tries to release itself in rage and remorse at others, in hurting alternated with hiding, until it finds new ways of being human.

The fourth game which contains high play and low play in daily life is the religion game.

While it might be expected that the religion game would be limited to the encounters of priests and other dignitaries with their people, interrupted by occasional sorties from prophets, it may in fact be played by many players. Lovers who celebrate the pleasures and initiations of love as the ultimate human value play the religion game. Businessmen who assure consumers that their products will bring the greatest of inward joys and prized relationships play the religion game. Statesmen who wave banners of the common welfare and the final dignity of a people play the religion game. Whenever the followers of athletes and opera stars, pundits and psychics cross the line which divides buffs from devotees, they play the religion game. Parents who say to their children, as lightning flashes on their Jovian brows, "We don't do that," or "We must," play the religion game.

The point of the game is not the performance of faith, nor the working of true spirituality; these are no less than high play in all games. Rather, the religion game is the vehicle by which co-creating itself is taught and celebrated and acted out, or hidden and eviscerated and pretended, in its higher and lower forms. It is a game without which human life is cheap and meandering, a journey on an uncomfortable treadmill, and also a game in which license is sometimes found to murder and burn and coerce. Yet this game manages to set forth a dead carpenter from Israel, a dead philosopher from North India, and a dead adviser to Chinese rulers, so that the sayings and deeds of these men are sung in scores of tongues through generations on generations of those who gladly walk in the shadow of such companions.

Played as low play, the religion game is two-handed, just man and his unconscious with its transpersonal foundations, however trapped and bedecked the bearers of that unconscious. In this form, where young and old compete to cast spells on one another (and too often succeed), the religion game merits the contempt offered it by Marx and Freud alike, as well as by religion's own blazing prophets. For the religion game is indeed a subtle game. There are many players for whom it passes understanding that some Zen Buddhists hang Buddhist scriptures, the Three Baskets of faith, on holy tablets directly adjoining the toilets of monasteries, where the traditional words of the faith may be read and appreciated, but not without a warning stench. Players of the religion game as low play were upset by jaunty disciples of Jesus who gathered wheat grains as they walked through a field on the Sabbath, just as they were upset by the Jewish Essenes who avoided the Jerusalem national shrine in favor of their retreats and friarlike healings. For it has always seemed to many pious minds that the religion game must be played to overpower mankind with a telling image or tradition, a potent rite or institution or leader. That such images and doings and leaders may be used to awaken and strengthen men towards their optimums as co-creators with the One, but only as men are required to make the force of them their own, eludes those who cannot play the religious game as high play. They find it impossible to join the Zen teacher who says, "If you meet the Buddha, kill him," or the Rabbi who says, "It is necessary that I go to the Father." For too many in too many ages, the religion game has been proclaiming Harvey, the six-foot rabbit around the corner. Surely the man who cannot see invisible man-sized rabbits is a man poor in spirit and in soul. But the man who can only see such rabbits, and not human faces, is poorer still. He knows little of the religion game as high play.

The Cayce trance source, his impersonal "information," warned Cayce and his associates again and again that they should not make of his work a "cult, schism, or ism." Cayce was to be seen as using laws available to all men everywhere; such laws were not new, but were the substance of biblical faith and of many another monotheistic faith, and could be known even in their misuse in idolatrous cults. Above all, the ideas in Cayce's trance readings were never to be presented as though from divine or special authority, nor should an emphasis be placed upon the uniqueness of their origin in his trance state—for this would be showmanship, not co-creating with others. The point to be made about Cayce's trances was only that they embodied processes at work in everyone's earnest "attunement" to God in prayer and meditation; not uniqueness but generality was important about these altered states, available as needed and safe, for every man. What Cayce and his associates were encouraged to trust was simply offering principles and processes, ideas and actions, which they themselves had tried to live out and understand. Others could be invited to experiment with these same ways and to note the consequences, nothing more. The best response to the stimulus of Cayce's work would not be simply to quote him, but to live out in one's own life whatever he found of value from Cayce for his service and attunement; only such living-out would give the best of Cayce's contributions more weight than novelty. Yet at the same time, those who responded to Cayce's aid and example were encouraged not to take lightly the methods and resources of men of high faith. In the view of the Cayce source, souls which were growing in human bodies, or "in the earth," had great need of the traditional sayings and doings, explored in company with the like-minded and dedicated among their fellows, which would remind them of the Source of their lives and of their far goal of being companions with the One, as well as of the best of their co-working with God in past existences. Exemplifying such dependence on the forms of faith, within the traditions and rites and works of organized religion, the Cayce readings themselves drew heavily upon the Bible to illustrate and express all of their serious concepts. The method used was more than one of proof texts; it was an intimate living and thinking in biblical thought forms, suggesting how the ways of the people of Israel and of the New Testament could be made a living Way again for modern man in all his games. This view put a premium on high play in the religion game.

The marks of the religion game as low play are not difficult to find. One of them is overseparated sacredness. When the spirit of baptism is found in stone fonts but not in the baby's bathtub, low play is there. Low play is at hand when the spirit of confirmation is known in churchly robes and rites, but not found where the elder takes a teen-ager on a trip and gets him to talk. It is there when the spirit of penance is known in the confessional box or the secret closet, but not in the shouted admission to a marital partner or a fellow employee that one was wrong, dammit. Religion is played as low play when ordination is reserved for priesthood, but not known in extra time freely given on the job to coach a new employee. It is low play when matrimony is known by vows and rice, but not by sharing good news and bad from the daily paper and the daily routines of spouses. It is low play when certain breads and wines have a spirit never found in the serving of sandwiches, and when the oil of unction is differently applied than is a cold shower to a loved drunk.

The religion game as overseparated sacredness has many precincts. It may be played in the paneled board room of a corporation which is used for decision making too far from the assembly line, or in the commencement rites of a faculty whose members march neatly robed in ceremonies but never speak seriously to each other across departmental lines or on off-campus issues. It is found amid the shiny motel furniture of lovers playing sex for holy apart from its bonds, and in the shiny, sidling seduction of spouses trying to make up in bed rituals what they lack in final respect for each other. Separated sacredness may be known in the frantic rush to take a vacation somewhere, or the demand to keep a therapist's hour for too many months, or the clinging to children who should be long gone from the home.

Further, the religion game is played as low play whenever the private authority of absolutes is offered, whether from a psychic or a philosopher or a social reformer or the Bible. High play is the delicious and bewildering play of reconciling opposites, on the ball court or in Congress or in a corporation office. But absolutes need no such reconciling, for they are presented as completed truths. Whenever a pattern or form or idea is presented as true and final, without specifying the criteria by which another might examine or appropriate or reject or improve it, then truth belittles giver and receiver alike. Truth and beauty so offered become low play which wipes the faces off the heads of all beholders. And similar to playing the religion game with absolutes is playing it with numbers and size, where quantity is supposed to validate quality. As high play, the religion game is intrinsically selective, just because it is play with matters universal and free for the creating of all, and therefore matters of gravity. Its ancient rites and teachings offer worship, which is a term shortened from worth-ship—worth not easily found in mass endeavors, but surprisingly accessible wherever even two or three are gathered as co-creators in the name of the One.

But out of the low play, and alongside it, the high play of the religion game appears again and again. The man who has lived by scruples does something unscrupulous —and then must learn to forgive himself and his fellows in a wholly new kind of play where evil is withholding (in the Cayce view, sin was simply selfishness), rather than misbehaving. The woman who has reveled in religious powers, including her powers in prayer, finds herself confronted by Nature's own answer to spiritual messianism: bouts of sexual fantasy which demand that she define herself as a responsible and creative human being, lest she be carried away as a goddess of love, rather than as a lover of God. The religious dignitary who has conducted services each week in the spirit of a cheerful funeral director, using well-appointed chapel and lights and sound, one day discards the whole low play apparatus; instead, he invites his congregation to go with him on stations of the cross—seven sore spots of poverty and privation and indifference in their community, where the waiting One might still be found. The tycoon who has built an empire and keeps his paneled office as a holy of holies secure against his priestlings finds himself called to a wordless, monasterylike retreat by that old retreat master, illness. In the hospital quiet he discovers how he needs to let others into not only his office but his heart. The father who cannot understand why his adolescent son runs around "wearing my body" and yet behaving so autonomously towards him, comes to see that whatever parents fail to live out in trust of the Creative Forces becomes charged agenda for their children, who must solve these riddles or become frogs. The man and wife who live by shopping rites of buying some new thing for basement, kitchen, den, or yard, find that life has leaked out from their household; they must join an encounter group, where the shouts of fellow members carry to them the still, small voice which once reached busy, big-time Elijah. Those who worship in temples of size, whether of big government or big unions, big churches or big businesses, big campuses or big shopping centers, find that something painfully small eludes them: their own few children. In pain and in hope they must sit and talk all night about drugs with their youngsters; they find that their offspring grow and grow before their eyes, until at sunrise they realize that none but peers have been in the room with the One, from the start of their talking.

Certainly many take drugs in the religion game. They

may do so for mystical visions of the ultimate. Or they may do so, for example, to find conscious or unconscious solidarity with their peers, however individualist they may consider the drug-taking act; they probe an important dimension of the religion game, its offering of life-giving covenants between co-creators and the One. For some, the degree of low play conformity in their taking of mind-altering drugs is equaled only by their conformity in jargon, clothing, and opinions, so that they achieve little of reflection, choice, or growth. But for others, the task of picking their way into new kinds of group sings and experiences, on their own initiative and working out their own style, may give them a bond with peers which is worth having. They begin to see how it happens that when people selectively choose one another for the best that they see in each, and accept each other's knobby peculiarities as well as their greatness, such choosing releases the optimums in each player. They begin to savor high play with the One which is more than mere identifying with each other, or with a cause.

Not a few cannot look squarely and openly at the drug experiences of many in modern times because they cannot bear to face questions of the religion game. They may dread to ask whether they may be missing some of the real meaning of life. What if some of the drug users have found a deep inward stillness, which they themselves cannot touch, except occasionally on vacations, or after tragedy? What if some of the seeming wild ones know more than they about how to be close to others, in relationships which are sexual but much more? And still more threatening to some, what if even a few of the drug users are "finding God," as the housewife said, in strange but rewarding times which free them for generous and playful lives with others? Such questions add force to the door slammed shut on the psychedelic adventure by those who monotonously claim that drug users all throw away their lives—even while the critic tastefully drugs himself on alcohol or anger, on tobacco or caffeine. Yet the fearful person often finds that he cannot ignore his hidden doubts, so that he circles around and around the "drug problem," until he is caught in some dilemma of judging others—perhaps his own children—which requires him to sound his own greatness at last, and to embark on a new religion game of celebrative co-creating in high play.

Whatever the game—parent, romance, work, or religion—the prize of turning on is high play. If there is an alternative to the psychedelic adventure with drugs which makes unnecessary the grave risks which sometimes go with those drugs, the alternative cannot be mere prohibition of chemicals, however needful legal limits and controls may prove. Only opening the way to high play in many walks of life will meet the challenge. And finding that way requires taking account of the puzzling experience of altered consciousness.

CHAPTER THREE

ALTERED CONSCIOUSNESS: UNSANITY AND INSANITY

The widespread modern use of drugs to induce unusual states of perception, imagination, reasoning, and motivation puts a premium upon understanding the varieties and degrees of altered consciousness. Melville's novel *Moby Dick* provides a display of altered states and their consequences.

Captain Ahab calls all hands aft and fires them to chase the white whale. He drives into the mast a gold coin, the prize for the first man to glimpse the spout of Moby Dick. Yet he knows that money alone will not bring them to risk their lives with him in the oared whaling boats, chasing the huge albino creature so feared for his malevolent attacks. So he calls them to raw human adventure, to the peril of their dangerous trade, to pride in their seagoing skills. Throwing them challenges until they shout back in a spontaneous litany of battle, he overpowers by his fierce gaze even his practical first mate. Then he seals the crew's pledges to hunt Moby Dick with his own ritual of exaltation, which he climaxes by pouring a chemical—the ship's fiery grog—for each crewman to drink from the upended harpoon butts, held by the appointed whale killers of the ship. To a man, the whalers step with Ahab over the line which separates mere whaling for a living from the extravagance and glory of optimum states. They are ready for high play, as they show in the skilled high spirits of their next whale chase, and as they show when at last they throw away their lives with Ahab in the climactic encounter with the white whale.

Yet the same Ahab who can so lift his men to high play becomes the one to fall into fixated low play. When Moby Dick is engaged, Ahab stops short of the exalted gift of authoring others towards their own nobility, which is the potential of leadership in any walk of life. Instead of sending his high-spirited crew after Moby Dick, he blindly lowers for the whale himself, seeking personal revenge against the creature who had once bitten off his leg. His compulsion costs him his ship, his crew, and his life when his consciousness alters to give him not greatness but madness.

Modern researchers on altered consciousness have emphasized how close to each other are optimum states and states of mental illness. Writing in his excellent study of LSD entitled *The Beyond Within,* the psychiatrist Sidney Cohen has suggested a distinction between "unsanity" and "insanity" as two states with radically different personal and social consequences, yet with features so similar that the two states shade into each other. Both unsanity and insanity may be glimpsed in altered states brought about by diverse means, each represented in *Moby Dick.*

There is sensory deprivation. Melville describes it as a spontaneous change in consciousness which occurs to seamen swaying high on the mast over a glassy sea, hour after hour while their ship is becalmed. Today's research methods reach the same state by suspending subjects with ttached breathing apparatus face down in tanks of water, here nothing moves or changes for hours. When robbed f external stimuli, the mind eventually spins powerful ntasies as though they were reality. Whether it does so keep the brain busy (since the brain appears to function est with at least a minimum of stimulation), or in a eakdown into early stages of insanity, or as a venture to unsanity which compensates consciousness with eeded archetypal material from the unconscious (material hich Melville called "Platonic vistas"), is not known.

There is sensory invariance. As Melville tells it, such variance nearly undoes Ishmael when he stares too long to the blazing fires cooking whale blubber; after a time, hmael, who is steering the ship, thinks that the craft is shing stern first into eternity. In modern research which eks to understand how brainwashing works, similar re- lts are achieved with lights and sounds under conditions f fatigue. At times the subject's entire world of values may e turned around, resulting even in permanent changes of utlook, as has been discovered not only by those who ractice brainwashing military or political prisoners, but ose who use intense concentration in exercises of re- gious asceticism, often with fasting and fatigue.

There is hypnosis. The South Sea islander, Queequeg, ips into a self-imposed trance in the cold room of a antucket inn, where he sits motionless for a day and a ght with a devotional figurine of wood on his head. odern research has experimentally created and probed any levels of hypnosis, identifying some of its regulari- es, such as the personality types susceptible to deeper ypnotic states. But the essential mechanisms by which nsciousness is altered in hypnosis are still unknown, ther for the states achieved by a stage hypnotist or for e religious trances of figures such as Cayce and his pre- ecessors among seers of earlier times.

There is sleep and dream deprivation. When Ahab rgoes sleep to stalk the decks and sail the seas, he finds oughts and images crowding his sleepless brain with verwhelming force. Modern research on that every-night altered state called sleep has shown that the sleeping mind insists on dreaming, which it will try to do even while the person is awake if systematically deprived of sleep and dreaming—just as it will spend extra time in active dreaming when the person is allowed to sleep at last. If subjects spend as few as eight nights without dreams in a laboratory (where they are awakened when twitches of their eye muscles show them starting to dream), then these subjects begin to report disturbed or even psychotic trends and states while awake, which may include fixations similar to Ahab's on the colossal whale. The same processes which can occasionally generate dreams of remarkable beauty and depth in nighttime states of unsanity, may when disturbed lead straight toward insanity.

There are other states of altered consciousness recounted by Melville which today's science cannot yet follow with experimental duplication. The ragged old figure called Elijah prophesies doom before the *Pequod* sails, and dusky Fedallah later adds further prophecies. The predictions of both prove accurate, but how are they to be distinguished from the ravings of the demented sailor Gabriel, whose pseudoprophecies and curses Melville also sets forth? What happens to Queequeg when he simply makes up his mind to die, crawling into his coffin to remain unmoving for days and beginning to approach actual death? What state of elevation is entered by Father Mapple as he preaches with stabbing prose his testimony on the story of the whale-swallowed Jonah—and then is overcome by silence before God, in his pulpit? How does Ahab move his men into an altered state where they seem compelled to do his will, though they often fear and resent his authority? On all of these processes, with their varied outcomes of unsanity and insanity, current research is uncertain. What is clear to research workers is only what William James reported after his own experiments in taking a mind-bending gas: ordinary consciousness seems surrounded by a variety of states quite different from normal, from which it often appears to be separated by the thinnest of veils.

74

The layman unfamiliar with hypnosis or brainwashing or drug-induced states can glimpse for himself what is meant by altered states of consciousness if he reviews certain familiar experiences which slightly change his perception, reflection, judgment, and motivation—and glimpse how easily these might further alter. Nearly every automobile driver knows those times of fatigue in monotonous driving (sensory invariance) when he begins seeing things on the highway: a leaf becomes a cat, a road branches off the ground, an approaching car appears to weave. At such moments what Freud called the "primary process" of the mind appears to dominate perception, overshadowing the signals from external reality with those inward forms and patterns which normally give needed depth of meaning to external sights. In contrast, there are those times which nearly every driver also knows when he is alertly "on," so that he drives with simplicity and elegance through difficult traffic, unruffled by motorists or pedestrians who threaten his safety or challenge his split-second timing. These two states of slight alteration of consciousness while driving may shade into more extreme states. There are times when the monotony of guard posts flashing past at the edge of the road seems to hypnotize the driver, so that he steers his car off the road to an accident, as though compelled to do so. And there are times when a presentiment of disaster seems to prevent an accident, as though a moment of unsanity placed the driver in a field of awareness larger than his senses alone could offer him. Less dramatic, but equally evidential of altered states, is the capacity of driving a car to elicit fantasy. When the requirements of negotiating traffic lightly bind the surface consciousness, then other realms of the mind may push into prominence, and Walter Mitty glories creep across the field of thought. Sometimes the task of driving provokes a different kind of dissociation which seems to free the mind to recall forgotten tasks, or allows a well-loved memory to quicken with surprising force. Even notable insights may emerge as the automobile rolls along and the driver in his slightly altered state ponders a decision, a fear, or a relationship with someone important to him.

The mysteries of falling in love offer another layman's doorway into altered states of consciousness. He may recall that melting state of feeling kindness toward all creatures, alternated with complete absorption in a lover, which together make romantic love a transformer of consciousness—and also make love blind. Different, though enjoyable with a lover, are those spellbinding moments which he may have known beside a great roaring waterfall, or at a night campfire, or in pondering the slow unfalling heave of the sea, or in sweeping his gaze across creation as seen from a mountaintop. At such times something within the beholder seems to match the outer view with elemental force and majesty, as well as sometimes with subdued fright, in meanings impossible to trap in words, yet suggesting that not all the deep springs of human intention and interpretation are often available to surface consciousness.

Times of great shock, as in death loss, may also strip a personality of its surface consciousness, laying bare the absolutes of a life in an altered state. What is spoken and done in such moments of truth comes as if from deeper realms of selfhood, where dwell an individual's final reality, noble and ignoble at the same time. Despite their pain, such moments of wisdom, which may be accompanied by heroic or selfless action, arise as though from a state of unsanity, generated by extreme pressure on the psyche. To find such states again, once they have been entered, Hemingway and others haunt the bullfights or hunt on the African veldt. And some who are young seek to drag-race, while some who are older venture extramarital affairs, each half-consciously hoping to recover the visions, the collected drive, the deep self-awareness which he found before under shock and pressure. In their own ways, these modern seekers after unsanity reinvent exercises not unlike those used by ascetic monks, as Heard has noted in his penetrating studies entitled *Pain, Sex and Time* and *A Preface to Prayer*.

Exploring cycles in such daily-life alterations of consciousness is part of the business of modern research in optimum psychology. There is a ninety-minute cycle of dreaming and not-dreaming at night; psychologists are asking whether a similar cycle repeats through the day, affecting each person's fantasy and moods, as well as his capacity for sustained attention or fresh creativity. Researchers are also asking whether there are times of day or night when depth and clarity of thought—or madness—come more easily to human beings. Even the old question of monthly cycles of alteration of consciousness, leading to the use of the stem "luna" in "lunacy," is being asked again. And the seemingly arbitrary patterns of the weekly Sabbath, as well as seasonal festivals, are being re-examined for what they may show about the spontaneous ways and rhythms in which the human mind alters in its own psychedelic ventures.

What essentially happens when consciousness drastically alters, with or without the aid of drugs? Present knowledge from laboratory and clinic is so sketchy that describing the changes is like trying to describe an earthquake from the vantage point of having fallen into a crack in the earth. But accounts and comparisons must be ventured, while optimum psychology is developing the vistas which may one day be refined into serviceable theories supported by experiments.

Distorted Versus Reoriented States

Damage to the body may change the function of the mind. Fever, shock, injury, illness, senility, and coma all produce states where perception, skill, and judgment are impaired. A study of these body-based forms of mental breakdown can contribute much to understanding altered states. But the modern use of drugs to achieve optimums of mental function focuses research attention not on pathology, but on alterations of consciousness not triggered by obvious physical damage. These alterations are of two kinds: distorted states and reoriented states.

77

Distorted states leave perception and other mental processes not far from normal, yet in some striking way amplified or focused or narrowed or exaggerated. This kind of normal-made-more in a distorted state is a familiar product of such drugs as alcohol or marijuana, and of mood-changing and metabolism-changing drugs such as benzedrine, amphetamine, and barbiturates. Probably similar are the effects of sustained sensory overload, found in listening to a pounding rock band, or to the pounding of a raging sea or battle; similar effects are found also in the early stages of LSD, where sensations of one type cross over to other sensory circuits, and sound produces color as light produces notes. Drug users often assume that the achievement of distorted states is free of the dangers which attend the wilder changes of reoriented states; in many cases their assumption proves correct, just as was a similar assumption by those of previous generations who altered consciousness with alcohol and nicotine and overeating. But what begins as mere squeezing and popping of the mind, mere damping or heightening of the processes of normal consciousness, does not in every case stop with mere distortion of mental function. Today's clinical evidence is strong that the action of drugs —like the action of changes in sensory input, or of hypnosis, or of sleep and dream deprivation—constitutes but one of the variables which determine how drastically consciousness will change when it is altered to achieve interesting distortions. The same alcohol which soothes one man may make a violent bully of his drinking partner; what varies is clearly not the drink but the drinker. As a consequence, the effort to magnify and titillate consciousness (exactly the effort, in the unusual Cayce view, which first brought souls into earth bodies which they were ill-suited to occupy), whether by chemical means, or by inducing stresses, or by some form of concentration or yoga, may lead at times far beyond the colorful experience of distorted function which was sought—proceeding sometimes to mental ecstasy and sometimes to mental hell.

But it is not the relatively rare extremes of unsanity

and insanity in distorted states which hold the chief interest of optimum psychology. It is rather reoriented states, where both unsanity and insanity are more common and more easily studied. In reorientation of the mind, the change is not merely a change of scope or intensity in mental events; the change presents genuinely new material on the screen of consciousness, or ascribes new meanings to familiar perceptions and drives. Reoriented change may offer new material against a background of familiar meanings: the drug taker or hypnotized person, for example, may see a prehistoric monster which somehow he still knows cannot be there. Or reoriented change may present familiar material against a background of new meanings: the subject may watch a flower dissolve as into component atoms in a way that the senses ordinarily could not disclose, and may develop a fresh intuition of the endless becoming of living things so strong that the intuition changes his world view and self view. Or reoriented change may sever old connections of meaning: in the aftereffects of electroshock and insulin shock, and perhaps of some states of deep meditation, the altered mind seems able to process new experiences in relative freedom from older fixations and stereotypes which have crippled it.

Some measure of disorientation typically occurs along with reorientation, whether before or during the drastic mental changes. In those cases where the disorientation dominates and lasts, in an altered state, so that the individual cannot make meaningful and satisfying connections of meaning for his thoughts, he reports that he is on a "bad trip," whether he got there by drugs or by hypnosis, by ecstasy or by stress. The consequences of such overwhelming disorientation may only be as temporarily upsetting as the feelings which follow being in an auto accident. Or they may be as long-lasting as the recurrent ripping despair of the suicidal child who unconsciously feels he has murdered his father because his father died during a period when the child actively hated him. Not all such "bad trips" of disorientation, great or small, are concluded in one unhappy episode. Sometimes the unpleasant disoriented state of mind appears weeks later, unwelcome and unsought, whether it was originally brought on by chemicals or by hypnosis, by brainwashing or by battle fatigue, by occult exercises to dissociate the mind or by overly emotional sessions of an encounter group (sometimes arranged in the name of therapy or growth).

But when disorientation, however unpleasant, is followed by constructive reorientation of consciousness, the result may be useful unsanity. Whether the desirable reorientation occurs briefly in what drug users call a "good trip," or continues in permanent transformation of personality (which is the hoped-for result of shock therapy and, in some sense, of all serious punishment which is not blind retribution), the personal and social consequences may be great. A fluidizing and reorganizing of the personality appears to take place, so that at the least the individual is introduced to challenging vistas of thought and feeling, and at the most he seems recalled to his real and best self within the universe, as if a spell of unreality had been lifted from him.

Those who are tempted to minimize the weight of drastic states of reorientation, reached with or without drugs, might well review the changes which can and do occur. In the best of reoriented states a new center of mental and emotional life may develop for a subject (William James said it was as if a polyhedron had settled on a new side); new springs of love or firmness or learning now operate stably in the personality where they were barely glimpsed before. New perceptions of self-boundaries may emerge, so that afterward the person sees himself as differently embedded in the human situation than he did before, or finds himself a different kind of mode than he thought, in the flux of matter daily washed and chewed and breathed through him. He may find that he can enter the games of his life with far less defensiveness and proprietorship than before, yet without losing track of his own unique worth in the maze of daily events. New ways of knowing may become available to him, even though these ways may rarely take him as far as did Cayce's "normal forces": through these ways the reoriented person may handle symbols or syllogisms more wisely than before, and he may display better thresholds of perception, longer attention spans, new rates of imaging, and more sophisticated routes to certitude. New integration of his selfhood may emerge along lines which the analyst Neumann has aptly called "centroversion"; he may find his dispersed and conflicting values brought under the hegemony of his deepest commitments and ideals. His long-standing panics and fears may disappear, never to return in their former terror. And the inward meanings which answer to daily-life experiences may seem to unfold for him with greater immediacy, clarity, richness, and better handling of creative tension between opposites.

Taken together, the processes in the best of reorientation make a staggering total. But if their achievement is hopelessly unpredictable, and includes Russian roulette with insanity, they may not be worth the effort needed to alter consciousness to unsanity, with or without drugs. The task of optimum psychology is to make clear what parts of the mind enter into altered states, and how.

The Ego in Altered States

When reoriented, surface consciousness seems plugged in somewhere new, activated by fresh circuits, fed by different computers, tended and guarded by novel animals and angels. Whether the mind has been altered by drugs or by drive, by prayer or by pain, by traumas or by truth, by love or by litigation, it seems to go through a period of fluidizing or "unlocking" of consciousness, followed by a restructuring or "locking in" upon signals and meanings not so prominent before. Such locking in may be temporary or it may be lasting, but it is crucial for alteration of consciousness beyond colorful distortion, whether the result is disoriented madness or reoriented high play. As the critical locking in occurs, it takes place as if in an ellipse, where two poles create the new field of awareness and intention. One of these poles is an unfamiliar center or level in the recesses of the unconscious. The other pole is surface consciousness itself, as it operates under control of what is loosely called the ego.

The business of surface consciousness is to meet experience with signals, skills, and schemes of all sorts, including language and gesture, habits, rites and roles, with which discoveries of the senses can be channeled and fitting responses mobilized. But along with the wares and wiles of surface consciousness—its everlasting cupboards and charts, labels and lists, skills and signposts—there is in surface consciousness a certain toughness and drive, a certain directionality and force for the person's decision making. Modern psychology of optimums calls this aspect of consciousness "ego strength": that which gives the individual his capacity for self-determination, his capacity for responses rather than mere reactions. Research findings on ego strength are controversial, and there is no agreed meaning for the term "ego" itself. Yet personality theorists find they must each postulate some version of ego strength—whatever it is which makes Ahab capable of captaincy, while his first mate Starbuck is not quite able to take command away from him, even when Ahab is wrong.

The trance-speaking Cayce did not often use the term "ego"; he preferred the term "self" to represent the decision-making and event-interpreting part of the mind, as contrasted with the entire body-and-psyche, which he called "the entity." But when he addressed questions of ego strength, he made it clear that from his perspective ego strength was a function of three processes: will, identity, and productivity. Interestingly, the trance-heightened Cayce associated each of these three processes with the operation of a specific endocrine gland, in a fashion which contemporary endocrinology would only suggestively confirm, if at all. Cayce associated will with the function of thyroid and parathyroid glands, the individual's sense of his own identity and uniqueness with the function of the pineal gland, and the person's productivity with the function of his pituitary gland. His point was not that personality is a helpless product of glands, but rather that psychological growth occurs in and with the action of these endocrine tissues. Whether or not future research substantiates these unusual claims of the sleeping seer, his description of altered consciousness as affected by an individual's will, identity, and productivity makes good clinical sense.

The person who has developed many coordinated resources of language, skill, and problem-solving strategies, by an active and non-defensive playing of his life games with all of his resources of will, self-evaluation, and productivity, can respond creatively to the gifts or terrors of his nonconscious realms. By contrast, the individual with relatively low ego strength must put up his defenses as quickly toward his own unconscious as he must toward what he perceives as his often-threatening fellows. The effect of retreating behind such defenses is early to shut off material from outside surface consciousness or to limit such material to shallow contents.

Hindu tradition has emphasized the role of developed ego strength in its teachings of four ways to God, all ways of equal value. Three of these ways require steady, disciplined application of consciousness under control of the ego, in one lifetime or in many, while the fourth route is that of suddenly altered consciousness, such as Western drug users explore. There is the way of knowledge, or *jnana,* by which the individual cultivates not simply book learning but true wisdom and discrimination, until he becomes not only a sage but one whose consciousness can alter at the touch of earnest thought, allowing him immediate awareness of the divine activity in him and around him. There is the way of action, or *karma,* by which the individual cultivates not simply busy-ness but graceful and effective action in all the routines and duties of his station in life, until he becomes not only a productive and creative doer but one whose consciousness can alter in an earnest deed of service, bringing him immediate awareness of and alignment with the One. And there is the way of devotion, or *bhakti,* by which the individual cultivates not simply emotional attachments but deep and generous loving of his fellow humans and other living things, until he becomes not only a happy and radiant lover of the best in others but one whose consciousness can alter in an act of affection or sacrifice for another, placing him in immediate relationship with the Ultimate. All three of these ways, each requiring concentrated use of will, discovery of personal identity, and productive service of others, are meant to issue at last in capacity for spontaneously altered consciousness, to give an individual greater access to the helpful work of the divine, in and through and around him.

By contrast, the fourth path, that of *yoga* or "yoking to the divine" (the stem of *yoga* is the same as that of "yoke"), concentrates directly on altering consciousness, not simply by the physical culture and exercises which have their necessary place, but by moral uprightness and by extraordinary practice of devotional acts, chiefly meditation. Hindu tradition insists that this fourth route is the swiftest path to direct awareness of the divine, and to fullest partnership with the divine creativity, but that it is also the most dangerous of the four ways. For unless the individual has cultivated one or more of the other three paths (presumably in a number of lives), and has built for himself a refined and cultured consciousness, able to handle with ideas, deeds, and love the sudden gift of divine energies, the effect of an alteration of consciousness may be to destroy his sanity, rather than to enlarge and uplift him in blessed reorientation of his selfhood.

Western traditions of individual growth to optimums have paid little attention to the possibility of personality development over many lifetimes, assigning major individual differences to genes and to upbringing instead. Consequently, Western efforts at improvised *yoga*—such as seeking a moment of truth in the danger of a bullfight, or swiftly altering consciousness with drugs—have not always included asking whether the individual is ready to handle a drastic change of consciousness. But even where the question of preparation through reincarnation is laid aside, the question remains pertinent: whether anyone should attempt a drugged or drugless version of swift *yoga* unless he has proved to himself that he can function so well in some path of knowledge, of action, or of love that he hardly needs the extra stimulus to bring him to the heights of altered consciousness. Paradoxically, it may be that the one who least needs the sudden boost to his optimums, found with or without drugs, is the one who can most safely venture to alter his consciousness. Only he is likely to have the mature ego strength, grounded in constructive and steady use of his will for others in response to his deepest intuitions of self-identity and talents, which can handle what develops when his psyche splits open for him. Where the individual has not lived out such athletics of the spirit, his ego turns defensive or predatory, and what he needs as resolute and skilled ego strength for high play becomes mere egoism in fearful or selfish low play.

To grasp the concept of ego strength, it may be helpful to consider a construction of its stages, whether these stages are drawn from psychology, from literature, or—as in the sketch which follows—from anthropology. Using the mythology of the Winnebago Indians, the anthropologist Radin has suggested four stages of ego development.

First is a stage where the developing ego is best known by the person's efforts against persons and ideas and institutions, rather than for them. Whether in the clever or taunting role of the joker, or in the charming form of the imp or droll tease, the ego makes itself known at first as does a bird learning to fly, by beating against the prevailing winds. Where the ego does not proceed to further development of its will, identity, and productivity, it may settle into such hardened personality forms as the devil's advocate, or the blind negativist. But whether in tentative or toughened style, this stage of ego development does not lend itself well to drastic reorientation of the psyche in altered states because of its instability, which requires the ego to be braced against something outside the individual. When the psyche is fluidized, such an ego flounders, or at times retreats in terror before visions of the evils which it has adopted as its opponent.

Second is a stage of ego development at which the growing ego of the child or adult enthusiastically espouses a cause or leader or idea, a book or place or tradition. Prometheus stealing light from the gods is reborn in the person at this stage. Such an individual may be delightfully fresh or a monotonous bore, but he is certainly doing his own thing, though the narrowness of his espousal may rob it of force for more seasoned individuals. While the trickster or habitual objector of the first stage may serve society by challenging old ways which need to be challenged, the light bringer of this stage of ego development may be a genuine innovator, whether in industry or in politics, in faith or in family routines. If he does not use his resources of will, identity, and productivity for further growth with others, he may become a perennial joiner, a spokesman for the ideas of another, as unable to think and act originally for himself as is Govinda in Hesse's novel of spiritual growth, *Siddhartha*. In any case, his ego strength is not adequate for repeated and deep altering of consciousness, because his ego is trained to borrow strength by identifying with unconscious material invested in whatever he espouses. Such identification is dangerous when surface consciousness is stripped away, and the individual may find himself carried off by an inner image of his supposed greatness or exalted vision, which in fact visits him with insanity rather than unsanity.

In a third stage of ego strength, the developing ego is able to carry more than its single banner of Excelsior. Now it can carry as well the weight of institutional and group roles, especially in those times when a rescuing leader is needed for some clearly defined course of action. The helpful rescuer, the dream-interpreting and Pharaoh-guiding Joseph, comes before his fellows with more than a new cause; he presents that sensitivity to person and to events which enables him to mobilize others and to lead them through a crisis at hand. But his ego strength is not necessarily rich and steely enough for the full weary task of governing and guiding and judging when crisis is past. Not every general on a white horse makes a good president or prime minister, nor does the inventive and life-saving Indian scout make a good wagon master. Still, ego strength at this level can offer itself in legitimate candidacy for drastically altered consciousness. Joan of Arc would be a notable example of ego development at this stage which could constructively handle transcendent visions and imperatives. Likewise, Joans and Janes and Jills in lesser walks of life, as well as their male counterparts, may have sufficient ego strength, seen in their daily use of will, identity, and productivity, to profit from swiftly altered consciousness. Often, however, such individuals are already achieving spontaneous high play at their optimums in some path of study or work or loving, so that they may feel little need to abruptly detonate the mind, whether with chemical means or some adrenalin-producing means of sought-out danger.

A fourth stage of ego strength must be attained for full captaincy, whether of an army, a revolutionary cadre, or a household. It is the stage often signaled in the growing person's dreams by the appearance of twins, or of brother and sister together, where the two characters appear to stand for the individual's capacity to see and handle this-side-yet-that-side, in his daily work with others. The leader or mature person who can see so much that he is almost twins may seem at times paralyzed by his vision, or may fail to mobilize his followers who have narrower views. Yet he is the leader prized in sagas of King Arthur and of Confucius, of Buddhist Emperor Ashoka, and of Lincoln and Martin Luther King. Because his ego strength is fully developed and tempered in the productive service of others, guided by his discriminating and resolute will upon a path of knowledge or action or devotion, he is able to bear and to profit by those times when his conscience alters, whether slowly or swiftly. Not only the famous in history but the unsung sturdy parent or businessman, the struggle-tempered youth, or the pain-tempered minority person, may in fact have the twin-sided, twin-pillared ego strength of this level. But not a few think they have it when they do not, and they enter into ventures of altered consciousness to their undoing.

If there is a stage of ego strength beyond that of the mature man of truly binocular vision and binaural hearing in the affairs of his life, Winnebago tradition does not offer it. But such a stage may be that in which the ego is so securely grounded in life-giving processes of willed effort, of chosen identity (grounded in the One Force), and of productive service of others, that the ego allows the individual a maximum of high play, unanxious about protecting his life or position. Such ego strength, both of individuals and of a chosen people, allows the work of what the biblical record calls the "suffering servant"—one who can risk all to co-create with his fellows when given no assured outcome except the playful companionship of the One, which may in due time burst past the defenses and fears of the other players. In some such ego strength Socrates drinks the bitter hemlock without bitterness; unknown Altgeld, the "eagle forgotten," pardons persecuted anarchists; the emaciated but peaceful Buddha gets up from a tree to preach the Sermon at Deer Park; and another man goes to a hewn tree to pray forgiveness on those who nail him there. Followers of such figures may read them as rebels, as light bringers, as rescuers, or as administrators of new dispensations; they read their leaders according to the stages of their own ego strength. But the full force of such servant figures may be as far beyond conventional ego strength as the mind can guess. When these individuals, or tempered small groups, confront altered states, including the ultimate alteration of dying, they appear to find in the strange states less threat than promise. But even Socrates handles his daimon with care, as does the Buddha his ascetic trance, and Jesus his baptism-quickened temptation.

One way to look at Ahab is to see him as a man who has reached, in the ripeness of his productive years, that full and seasoned ego strength of the twin stage, which makes easy for him the mastery of his ship and crew, as it does mastery of his body, which he does not allow to rest. But Ahab, in his strength of seeing both sides, standing as twin with silent Fedallah, is a man struck by an accident which sets him off balance. He suffers an amputation by a whale's bite, which answers his dignity of office and fairness of vocation—his ultimate identity so far—with blind cruelty.

Ahab's riddle then becomes whether he can take the final step of ego strength into that sturdiness of conscious identity grounded in the One—a selfhood which can encounter life's cruel absurdities and yet remain playful, which can be hurt without asking for play-destroying revenge, which can serve even when done a disservice, which can spend itself even on one leg in ennobling rather than manipulating others. Ahab tries to solve his riddle by turning all the developed resources of his consciousness into overpowering his Object, the tormenting whale, in a game of Two. In just such a spirit, perhaps, Paul and Judas alike responded to the force which tormented them by seeking to destroy it. But Paul had the fortune of being struck blind and wise when his consciousness altered on the Damascus road, while Judas walked as Ahab walked.

What happens when consciousness is reoriented appears to depend heavily on what sort of man is there to receive the gifts of gods and demons, of Spirit and spite. When consciousness is of the highest order, tutored in the way of knowledge or action or love, then when it meets the deep and varied streams of the unconscious, it may be said of the man whose mind alters as it was said in the Psalm, "He shall be like a tree planted beside the rivers of water, that bringeth forth his fruit in his season; his leaf also shall not wither, and whatsoever he doeth shall prosper"—though not necessarily in his generation. What is in those "rivers of water," outside of surface consciousness, from which consciousness draws so freely when it alters by reorientation?

Levels of the Unconscious in Altered States

Nearest to surface consciousness is a stream of ideas, impulses, habits, defenses, memories, fantasies, and other material which enhance the practical work of the ego. This stream might be called a problem-solving stream. In it are two currents, one of contents having to do with the body, and one of contents having to do with the mind at work with persons and culture.

That part of the unconscious which continuously works with surface consciousness to meet the needs of the physical body (the entranced Cayce called it the "body mind" or "body conscious") may be seen at work in the spontaneous food imagery of the hungry, as well as the sex imagery of the aroused, or the threat imagery of the alarmed. It may be observed as it generates the hypnagogic images which seem to appear in the mind to aid falling asleep, or staying asleep. And there may be further dramatic evidence of this body-serving stream in the research currently under way on somatic dreams. Such research studies how far the body seems to signal to the mind, in what symbolism, its current needs in diet, exercise, eliminations, rest, and even medication or surgery —both in dream material and in the fantasy or memory or other material supplied by the unconscious in waking life. In the view of the Cayce source, a much larger portion of dream material was engaged in such monitoring and advancing the care of the physical body than most modern dream theorists suggest.

Woven in with the flow of body-serving imagery is a second problem-solving flow, having to do with effective personality function in daily work, daily relationships, daily tasks of adjustment. The imagery of this current is operations-serving imagery, constantly offering to surface

90

consciousness an array of hopes, plans ideas, principles, memories, and associations which may be used to tag, arrange, and improve the practical operations of the psyche (the entranced Cayce called this flow the "mental mind," or that part of the "subconscious" which was most responsive to the needs of surface consciousness). Glimpses of the operations-serving stream may be found in the back of one's mind at even the commonest events —as when one dimly senses that the stranger just met is like Uncle John (and dreams that night promptly produce Uncle John), or when one dislikes a jacket for its hard buttons which dimly betoken his own defenses, or one delights in an autumn-hued tree which reminds him of those climbed in his boyhood's confident spirits. As Freud and his successors have skillfully shown, the events which occupy surface, waking consciousness echo almost endlessly in nearby underground chambers of the mind, where the winds of the unconscious muffle some echoes and amplify others. The exact contents of this operations-serving flow are of course affected by the style of the person, with his typical defenses, temperament, amplitude of responses, idealized models, and overt values and controls (Cayce in trance traced seven major modifiers of this flow, which he named poetically after the seven planets, exactly as did the ancient Stoics, centuries before him). When the wraps of social office and convention are taken away from the personality—as in role playing, projective tests, and unstructured situations for encounter groups—then the material of the operations-serving flow shows itself promptly, confirming hints already given in slips of the tongue, lapses of memory, spontaneous word choice, and other indicators of the themes with which an individual takes hold of life.

What happens when the result of one or more alterations of consciousness, achieved with or without drugs, is locking in on the problem-solving stream?

When the locking in occurs at the body-serving flow, and the fixation is reinforced by deeper currents in the unconscious, then the new personality structure may be a prison, even as it seems to offer tasty sensate pleasures. For the price of pure animal indulgence as a way of life appears to be pure animal defensiveness and sometimes cruelty. What begins as healthy abandon to basic biological drives, so often needed to balance and refresh an over-controlled personality, ends as ennui, possessiveness, jealousness, irritability, when the personality is locked in at this level. Why this should be so has puzzled the human race as long as it has had poets, asking in their own days and tongues how the serving of animal impulse, so dangerous for humans to ignore, is yet so debilitating when made central for human existence. In the view of the impersonal Cayce source, the warning was put in biblical language that to "live unto the flesh" would bring a man under "the law of the flesh," making him vulnerable to less-than-human panics, passions, and rages from the animal kingdom.

If the locking in occurs at the operations-serving flow, especially when reinforced by deeper currents in the psyche, then the individual tends to become a prisoner of his own devices, as farce so neatly caricatures. His healthy pretense becomes unhealthy conviction, his style of life is unrelieved by contrast, and shallow narrowness rules, where the individual is caught in his own cleverness. His helpful imagination, so quick to suggest for him tricks and treats all through the day, becomes his trap, as when one is caught on a carousel and the pleasure ride turns into a swirl too sickening for play. Common speech has it that such a person "spins his wheels," generating ideas and poses and critiques of others which are not practical or true to his personhood. The warning of the Cayce trance source was that the surface and near-surface "personality" of each person would have to be brought into alignment with his deeper "individuality," both before and after altered states, or he would find himself ineffective in whatever he tried, and alienated from others as well as from the rest of the Creative Forces.

Well below the problem-solving stream of the unconscious, and flashing through it as if in particular crevasses and in periodic geysers from within, there ranges a second flow of unconscious material which is often quite different from the flow nearest surface consciousness. Here the memories are unfamiliar or long-forgotten, the emotions less identifiable as one's own, the styles of perception and behavior sometimes markedly different from those of the surface self. The drunk who suddenly becomes playful or sexy or violent, when a certain level in his glass has been passed, displays all too well the existence of this counter-current within him. He shows the action of the second major level of the unconscious, the compensatory level.

This level functions to correct consciousness in two ways. It may rebalance surface consciousness when the plans and schemes of the ego have carried the personality too far on some track in its zigzag course of growth and productivity. Or it may work to stir up and heighten new values not yet fully grasped or used by surface consciousness. In either case, it appears to serve the personality purposively, though sometimes clumsily. In the Cayce view of the psyche, it was not true that the farther away from surface consciousness, the more primitive would be the material found; indeed, the entranced Cayce pointed to a structure at even greater depth which he called the "soul" of man—the *scintilla dei,* or spark of God. Ultimately the compensatory layer of the unconscious, which Cayce called "subconscious," functioned—as he saw it—as much in response to the "superconscious" realm of the soul in man as it did in response to his surface concerns. The compensatory layer was also the carrier of deep trends or patterns of karma, established in many lives, and ready to be worked out toward creativity as the ego established itself in its use of will, identity, and productivity.

Compensatory material is relatively easy to find in any markedly altered state. It appears to form much of the stuff of those slightly altered states called dream and fantasy—as Freud suggested when he stressed the wish-fulfilling role of dreams (the entranced Cayce broadened the function of dreams to be "life-fulfilling," and included guidance and judgment in dreams, along with enactment of wishes). The popular notion of the compensatory level of the unconscious is that it contains only discards, dredges, repressed traumas, and unworthy impulses left over from waking consciousness. All of these contents may quickly be found in material from this level, together with other contents which are surprisingly fresh and useful for the individual. But even the remnants do not have the disorder of a garbage heap, or the aimless destructiveness of an underground fire. To the careful observer of this level, the unpleasant or unworthy appears to be saved up and deployed for specific purposes of counterbalancing surface consciousness. The controlled perfectionist may keep a smoldering hatred of his parents and teachers, so that one day he may sear off part of his own cruel conscience with the force of that same hate. The snob keeps at the compensatory level just the sexual tides which can undo him, and return him to the human family in quite a glow. And the libertine keeps at the compensatory level memories of honor and dignity in the family circle which can one day flash to consciousness with the healing force of person-respecting ideals—for he has repressed his conscience as truly as another may have repressed his passions. The manipulator retains at this level such longings for friendships and open intimacy as may surprise him when they turn his dealings with others into love. And the practical man keeps at this level a love of learning and wisdom which he may betray to himself only in the solemnity of the Sabbath or a crisis, when its force surprises him.

Taking compensatory material at face value appears to be the most common mistake in responding to drug experiences, or intensive encounter-group experiences, and certainly experiences of the devotional life. The surface self announces about the discoveries made at the inner level, "This is the real me"—and turns a half-truth into a dogma. For when the compensatory side of the personality is shoved into consciousness without discrimination of the intent and value of its currents, and without a balanced integration of its contents into the entire selfhood, the result is only a new one-sidedness which must in turn be compensated. The counsel to "Do your thing" is not adequately observed if the counsel is reduced to "Do your compensatory thing."

When the locking in which follows reorienting alteration of consciousness leaves the surface self fastened upon the signals from the compensatory level, the consequences for the personality vary from doubtful to disturbing. What begins in enthusiasms and freedoms, found by breaking through to this layer, ends in uncertainties. The formerly authoritarian man now wallows in his new permissiveness and cannot give effective orders, while the self-indulgent person relishes his new disciplines until he begins indulging himself in extravagant disciplines. Reification of the compensatory is perhaps the oldest and commonest temptation of the enterprise of altering consciousness. Such exaggerated emphasis is made easier by the psychological processes of this level which so often dress compensatory qualities in the form or aura of the opposite sex, so that a man sees his compensatory self in his neighbor's attractive wife, or a woman sees her other self in her competent doctor, or both come under the spell of members across the room in an encounter group. High and low moods, bursts of activity followed by indecision, fascinations, and compulsions, masterful but offensive inflations—all of these betray the unstable footing reached when the compensatory level of the unconscious is made the new being by an abdicating ego. The characteristic result is neither insanity nor unsanity, but chronic low play. Warning of the need to discriminate among contents of the unconscious, the Cayce source insisted that each individual must learn to discriminate between an "idea," which might grip him from within and seek to direct his behavior, and an "ideal," which would be found to come from much deeper in the psyche, and to grow into consciousness by a process of awakening matched by "application" in daily life, rather than to emerge by a process of dramatic compulsion.

The next level of the unconscious, beyond the compensatory, is one glimpsed more rarely in markedly altered states. It is the charged ground of individuality within the person which Jung called the "true self" and the impersonal source of Cayce's discourses called "the soul." Just such an inner realm is suggested at the end of *Beowulf,* where the long-sought treasure is found in a cemetery, inside a ring of fire. When consciousness alters to allow access to this level of true individuality, the entrance seems found through graveyards of low-play ambitions and schemes, private glories and weapons. The altered mind's journey to this level requires it to pass beyond the endless busywork of the problem-solving stream which runs nearest to surface consciousness, and to pass through the ring of fire established by the compensatory flow—that fire which waits to give heat to schemes and needs of surface consciousness as well as to melt and refine consciousness at critical times. Stopping at the compensatory flames yields much warmth and vitality, as encounter groups and lovers know, but not necessarily the full treasure of personhood.

This third level of the unconscious contains what might be called the "life form" of the person, or what Cayce called the "individuality" developed over many lives, as contrasted with surface "personality." The realm of the life form is well protected in the psyche, and not to be entered lightly. Approaching it in an ecstatic experience, Moses saw a bush which burned psychedelically without being consumed, and took off his shoes in awe. For Moses, this was the place and time of discovering the rest of his vocation when he thought he had lived his active life and retired to herd the flocks of his father-in-law. Similarly for each individual, this region of the unconscious contains whatever values serve the individual as his source of vocation and true personhood; here he finds his crown, his scepter, his particular sword, which none can use as can he and none can quite take from him. Legend has depicted such values as charmed until the individual claims them; they are his final talents and commitments, all that he trusts and honors and can rightly handle, whether small or great. Perhaps this level is signified in tales of gold beneath a river, or of a heroic sword embedded in stone, which only the rightful claimant can remove.

Because of the force of its contents, the life-form level holds greater threat to sanity than does the compensatory level. Rushing inward, with or without the aid of drugs, the person whose consciousness is altered to expose this depth may perish in his own flames, or find himself unable to leave the magic of the charmed circle. Legend has it that he must draw his sword or wear his crown for particular conscious tasks; he must use his new resource for the service of others, building their becoming as truly as his own. Failing such purpose, or even losing it briefly, he may experience during or after altered consciousness that seizure of insane force from within which the author of the Exodus account suggests, when he tells how Yahweh fell upon Moses and sought to kill him, directly after appointing Moses to rescue the children of Israel. In psychological terms, such peril of insanity suggests that growth in permanently altered consciousness ought to proceed at the pace of one task at a time, one new quality at a time, allowing each new development of individuality to be integrated into conscious daily life with the aid of the productive ego. For it is from this level that the ego finds signals of its proper identity, which can serve to govern both its will and its productivity. As the inner fire parts —in altered consciousness brought on by LSD in loving therapy, or by the heat of battle, or by argument or lovemaking or holy processions—each may discover how he carries within him, from cradle to grave, a certain heraldic crest of life-giving concern; each may see how he is always a particular seedling oak, even in his acorn-hard stubbornness.

The Cayce impersonal "information" stressed again and again that the "superconscious" realm of the life form in each individual would be found to have specific content, specific themes and values, which the soul had chosen when it entered a given earth life. "No soul," said the Cayce source, "enters the earth by chance, but always with a specific purpose, a specific lesson, a specific way in which it has chosen to glorify God in that lifetime."

If consciousness is locked in at the life-form level, the consequences are varied. An individual who attempts to seize what he glimpses at this level without working it into his life may find his mind addled in insanity. The man who correctly envisions, in an altered state, the great love of which he is ultimately capable may find himself incarnating his vision in a dubious course of promiscuity where he is a love god instead of godlike in his loving. The woman who correctly glimpses the finely wrought treasures of intellect which can be hers may find herself caught in disputations and preachments which block her appointed intellectual growth with a screen of words. Perhaps all the gifts of goodness and greatness which are found at this level, and which constantly work to quicken and enlarge and unify the entire psyche, may destroy as truly as they may ennoble—whether gifts of forgiveness or fantasy, of humility or holding fast, of wealth winning or wisdom. The critical difference between destructive and constructive locking in at the life-form level seems to be determined by how the ego handles its will, identity, and productivity. A mere filching of inward treasures leads to engrossing fixations and repeated calamities until the entire psyche seems bent on correcting itself in a mighty cathartic suffering—as Lear and Ahab show. However, if the surface consciousness be anchored in the inner place of treasures (in the inner "homeland," as the psychologist Binswanger calls it), so that the person may build and love as a co-creator with others and the One, then the life which results may be beautiful to behold. It may show joy and peace and security which are not shaken by the anger of men or the gods. Once the call from the life-form level has been heard, however, once the inner vistas seen, the individual must make his play, try something constructive; for the psyche seems branded by the encounter, and all its games seem tightened. Better not to start to grow at all, warned Jesus, than to proceed to this level and then look back for simpler days and ways. For this is the realm of the best of unsanity. Yet it is never far from insanity.

Are there levels of the unconscious beyond the level of the soul's individuality? Beyond the personal layers of the unconscious, are there impersonal layers which are the foundation of personhood as water is the foundation of each individual snowflake? The Cayce source suggested that the "superconscious" realm of the mind could reach not only to the soul of the individual but beyond it to "universal realms," where the individual could "make attunement" with the three primal orders of creation: matter, mind, and Force.

Not a few whose consciousness has altered under drugs, or under ecstatic elevation, have reported coming upon a river of animal forms, of vital processes, of blood and birth and death, which has such vividness as to overwhelm them. For some, the gift of such an experience is good, giving them a sense of the striving flow in all nonhuman creation which justifies what Schweitzer called "reverence for all life." They would understand why one old Buddhist and Hindu exercise has been the attempt to pierce this impersonal flow by identifying the self with specific birds or fishes, or by contemplating a corpse, in wordless concentration which may be aided by unconscious ESP. But for others, the experience of seeming to enter, through altered states, the near-mindless, yet ever-striving world of protoplasm is horror, an encounter with blind struggle which unnerves them, when human defenses seem helpless to stay the relentless progression of death and disease, and of being eaten by other creatures. Some may even reach beyond the nonhuman world of protoplasm, in their altered states, and tell of their astonishing perception of the action of light, the bounding of atoms, the quivering tug of gravity, the unthinkable swift polarities of electricity. Their words and drawings may fail to reproduce such intimations, but the experiences seem to leave their mark on the beholders, either prodding them to new stature as part of the cosmic processes or sending them in headlong flight from realms which they cannot understand or control, in games where they are not potent players. Such experiences of protoplasm or of realms of pure physics and chemistry seem to indicate an impersonal, "universal" level far beyond surface consciousness, such as Cayce called "matter."

Beside the imagery of creatures and things may run an equally strange flow of impersonal patterns which seem to show the altered mind unveiling itself—exactly as suggested by the term "psychedelic," or mind-manifesting. Reminded of the biblical account of a time when "the morning stars sang together," journeyers into altered states sometimes report finding that design and order seem to spring forth in everything touched or seen or heard. Some connections are musical, some structural, some spiral, some linear, some parallelograms, some make warp and woof, some are so complex as to make the perceiver think he has wandered witless into pure science fiction. To be sure, these dancing mental forms may be linked to the viewer's life-form treasures. The circle of closure may dominate the view of one who has too long held himself back from others, and the line of lightning may repeat for one who has wondered whether striking out on his own is worthwhile. In such a stream of Hegelian becomings and counterbecomings, in such a world of Platonic archetypes strung in chains and swinging free, the beholder may find glory if he can use it—as would a composer who can suddenly breathe chords with each lift of his chest. But if the beholder is merely rummaging in the far reaches of altered consciousness, he may run from these dizzying patterns and counterpatterns as the essence of insanity, and perhaps be correct in his surmise about them. For the drawings and ramblings of the demented suggest that only a little too much of that which gives form and pattern to sanity, and inspiration to unsanity, is needed to push the person over the line to utter disorientation—where lightning reverses all compass needles, as it did on the whaleship *Pequod*. To reach such an impersonal realm in altered states, for good or for ill, may be to find what Cayce meant by the primal order of creation called "mind."

Yet a third kind of impersonal material, also beyond the charmed circle of individual selfhood, appears in the account of those who have altered their consciousness by drugs or by some other yoga, or have found it altered for them by crisis or injury or heroic effort, or as the gift of a lovely spring day. Formless and yet giving direction to the play of forms, matterless and yet seeming the drive in the dance of atoms, Something breaks upon their consciousness which is like light or word or void, or pure unbodied intention. It may have the character of personhood, so as to seem to call the beholder by name, and yet be so different from a person as to make conventional personality a belittling of it. It may be felt as loving, incredibly loving and helpful to all that moves through time, and yet may be felt as having such force as to remind of Otto's phrase, "God's love is only His quenched wrath." Encounter with this flow, far beyond surface consciousness, may produce ecstasy. But the ecstasy is likely to be a state well beyond relish, containing its own version of the cry of Isaiah in his time of altered consciousness: "Woe is me, for I am unclean, and I dwell in the midst of an unclean people." At times the compensatory level of the unconscious may contain elements from this more distant layer, glimpsed or hinted in the warmth or mystery or strength of the opposite sex, so that many who strike upon currents in the compensatory level of the unconscious think that they have encountered this more distant, impersonal stream which Cayce called "Force," or the "One Force," or the "Creative Forces." But the compensatory level of the unconscious rarely contains the full, blinding, dangerous light and might, securely grounded in consummate goodness and patience, which made Job speechless in his psychedelic time.

What happens when altered states leave surface consciousness locked in upon one or another of the impersonal streams, beyond the fire-ringed circle of life-form individuality? If the connection is made by an immature, unbalanced, or predatory ego, not guided by its life form and not bent on productive service of others, then some form of insanity appears to be assured, though it may be temporary. Perhaps the impersonal streams of matter, mind, and Force may be fused into one obsession. Or the overwhelming inner image or imperative may tip in one direction—as Ahab found a whale, Nietzsche found a superman, and Bar Cochba found a Messianic Age. It would be reassuring to believe that such delusions strike only the weak-minded. But as Melville suggests in his tale of Ahab, it is often the strong or gifted who find repeated access to the impersonal levels of the psyche—though their strengths and gifts may be known only by their unpleasant imperiousness or neuroses. At the same time, those who have too often let their individual evil be strengthened by the action of impersonal inward forces may also be men of considerable social value, when at last they find their way—with visible and invisible aid—to reorganizing their will, identity, and productivity.

Saul the bigot becomes Paul the builder, Moses the murderer becomes a rescuer and teacher of his people, Luther the scrupled becomes strong, Augustine the self-indulgent becomes the self-transcending visionary, and Gandhi the violently ascetic becomes the apostle of creative nonviolence. The ex-gunman makes an excellent lawman, not only because of his conscious skills, which are so essential if the psyche is to reach its optimums of productivity, but also because he has found at least how the action of his inner individuality can transmute the obsessing impersonal force into a radioactive stream to fire daily life. The same far forces of his unconscious which can raise up a monster can also quicken a lively and lovely and loving soul—when the person is stretched to his optimums on a line which reaches all the way to the souls of his fellows, sought for the games of high play.

The biblical tradition that man may see only the back of God carries with it the threat of destruction, should men seek to encounter the impersonal Force without living vessels of thought and purpose and action to contain or channel the Force. But it is not necessary to look to long-ago Israel to find people who have glimpsed what seem holy things in some altered state and then spent their days in well-meaning trivialities, as weightless as their original vision may have been weighty. Insanity is never far from unsanity. Yet sadder still may be those who never seek the far levels for themselves but who ask for the Nameless only as it is reflected in the souls of others: teachers, authors, leaders, gurus. For though the Dark Light of the One may offer swift or slow destruction, it may also offer that disorientation which is followed by reorientation that makes it storied in the human family. Ahab may have truly sensed, by means of the eerie white whale, Something alive and yet alien to his surface life, Something portentous and yet ominous to all pettiness of spirit, Something like his daily strivings and yet capable of upending him to incredible new becomings. But Ahab alone on the ship's bridge cannot sustain his vision or find for it a noble action with his shipmates. So he reduces his response to a chase, not always sure who is chasing and who is chased, or Who is the Hound of Heaven.

CHAPTER FOUR

THREE WAYS OF ALTERING
CONSCIOUSNESS FOR HIGH PLAY

Three modes for altering consciousness toward high play may be viewed in three scenes.

Racing to catch the first whale of the voyage of the *Pequod* in *Moby Dick,* Stubb drives the men of his harpooning boat by alternating fierce exhortation with comical encouragement for them to relax as they row. Like the other officers of the ship, he has his own style for getting his men to pull so furiously as nearly to split their oars when the great creatures come up from sounding, to seek fresh air. Somehow Stubb's lashing yet absurd playfulness, as he chews on his ever-present pipe, puts his crew ahead and allows them the first kill. In high spirits as his men tow the whale back to the ship, Stubb undergoes a change in consciousness. He insists that a steak be cooked for him from the tenderest part of the whale, though it is now late at night; he rouses the ship's old black cook to prepare his treat. The exaltation of the chase has stirred something lordly in Stubb, perhaps compensatory to his small stature and feisty but guarded ways. He orders the cook, who has served him his whale steak, to preach to the sharks that snap and tear at the whale carcass beside the ship. Stubb is hard on the grumbling old black while cutting and tearing at his own piece of the whale; it is not clear whether the officer on the ship or the shark in the sea excel in rapacious delight. As Stubb's consciousness is altered, it moves to unaccustomed grandeur, showing more of low play than the high play of driving the men in his boat.

A handful of young adults plan a three-day festival of folk and rock music on a rolling farm at Woodstock, New York, more than a century after Melville wrote his sea tale. They hire the best musical groups and soloists in the country, and for months they send the word through youth circles that a happening will take place, a first. They provide toilets, concession stands, and police to handle as many as a hundred thousand people. For they are sure that they have an idea whose time has come: calling to one place the people of the new youth culture to celebrate the music, peace, and togetherness which stand as opposite poles to the youth-outraging war in Vietnam. As the cars from every part of the country begin to arrive, it quickly appears that many more will attend than expected. Roads to Woodstock are so jammed that drivers must abandon their cars on the highways, for as long as a week. Ticket taking breaks down and the festival becomes free, producing for the backers a deficit of a million and a third dollars, but also producing for them great joy over the spirit which develops amid hardships of the week. The crowd runs out of food and water, and few are prepared for comfortable sleep in the fields. Rain turns the grounds to universal mud, and soon private toilets and bathing facilities become impossible to find. Police, who know the rioting of beer-drinking youth in Florida each spring, are prepared for the worst. Astonishingly, a peaceful climate prevails; not one black eye is reported for the festival and police are unusually friendly and helpful. While some of the townspeople in nearby communities profiteer from the sale of water, not to mention food, most are generous to the stranded youth. But above all, the throngs, who now number between four hundred thousand and a half million, begin to show patterns of people helping one another. Every scrap of food and cup of water is shared with strangers as readily as with friends; clothing, towels, coats are shared in the pouring rain. A laughing, steady, open camaraderie develops, which the singers and masters of ceremonies keep rolling along; the mood is infectious as the hours turn into days. Men and women alike slip suitless into the few murky pools to wash off mud, and a few stalwart individuals starkly disrobe in the rain, enjoying the music in their own fashion of openness. Yet no sex orgies develop; the whole impossible happening is too much fun to be sidetracked into private kicks. The crowd polices itself, with volunteers aiding the appointed garbage collectors, and a thousand people, strangers to each other, willing to stay afterwards to clean up the incredibly littered grounds where one American in every five hundred had stayed at Woodstock. Similarly, the crowd polices itself by keeping out the pushers of such hard drugs as heroin, or closing down sales, while allowing the sales of marijuana and LSD in every knot of people. The event is clearly a drug event, with as many as ninety percent taking some form of drug during the week; a tent is set up to handle those having bad trips on chemicals. Yet the happening is not one of tuning into private drug worlds, but rather one of sharing. The drugs are passed freely and generously among strangers, in thousands of spontaneous incidents, and a mood develops over the throngs which the backers call "high vibrations": strong peacefulness, determined goodwill, and great delight that the music-centered festival could take place in a world wounded by riots and burn-scarred by napalm. In the months which follow, Woodstock becomes a byword wherever youth gathers in numbers for a purpose, so that the mention of it helps to quiet a restless throng of protesters. Many of the youth who met on that New York farm are not surprised to find themselves met in numbers to equal Woodstock's masses, not long afterwards in Washington. Here it rains again, as they march and wait and sit, listening to some of the same musicians, but now in the hush of grave purpose where drugs are little evident. Not marijuana joints are now lit but candles, one for each American serviceman killed in Vietnam. For these youth are proclaiming their Woodstock-fed hope that the times could change, that people could change, that modern consciousness could somehow alter towards daily life lived in optimums.

Ishmael describes his own crowd scene in a chapter of *Moby Dick*. The whalers of the *Pequod* have come upon a great rarity: whales gathered not in pods of a dozen or so but in a vast milling armada of thousands, stretching clear to the horizon in what seems acre on acre of living flesh. The harpooneers from several ships deal death to as many whales as they can, leaving markers to identify their catches. Ishmael happens to be in a boat towed by a whale at breakneck speed into the very center of the herd, where it seems uncertain that Ishmael and his fellow oarsmen will get out alive. While their comrades out on the edges of the great herd are struggling to slay whales on every side, Ishmael and his small crew must be still, lest they be destroyed by the blind animal panic of the great creatures around them. Then they discover that they are in something like the eye of a storm: a peaceful center of the great sprawling, turning field of whales. Here mothers are suckling their young and the waters are quiet; in the deeps, whales can be seen coupling, replenishing their kind. The vista is one of profound intimacy and peaceful play in the very center of turmoil which stretches to all horizons. Staring at the unexpected sight, Ishmael is reminded of the best of his own high play.

And thus, though surrounded by circle upon circle of consternations and affrights, did these inscrutable creatures at the center freely and fearlessly indulge in

107

all peaceful concernments; yet, serenely revelled in dalliance and delight. But even so, amid the tornadoed Atlantic of my being, do I myself still for ever centrally disport in mute calm; and while ponderous planets of unwaning woe revolve around me, deep down and deep inland there I still bathe me in eternal mildness of joy.

Three ways of altering consciousness appear in these three settings. The first scene shows consciousness altered in the exaltation of chase and victory, as Stubb catches and eats from his totemlike whale; risk and appetite meet in the transforming chemistry of autointoxication. The second scene develops its own kind of altered consciousness, in desperation turned to sharing, under the gentling influence of music and several kinds of drugs. The third scene shows an outward shock of contrasts awakening an inner sense of depth and meaning, where neither violence nor appetite tells the whole story of a quickening to high play. Each features its manner of unlocking consciousness, followed by a distinctive locking in. What directs and guides the freeing and locking in of each episode?

Six Nondrug Factors Affecting How Consciousness Alters

A frequent mistake in evaluating the action of mind-altering drugs is the assumption that the drugs are chiefly responsible for the mental effects which follow their use. Research has shown otherwise. The drugs serve to unlock the mind, just as does the heat of chasing whales. But where the mind goes and what new circuits it adopts, temporarily or permanently, appears to be significantly affected by six nondrug factors.

Stress. The trance-speaking Cayce's view of the biochemistry of altered states was one not out of harmony with contemporary research findings, though certainly not as yet verified by experiments. In his view, all unusual states of consciousness not derived from bodily injury were created by the endocrine glands, pouring their chemicals into the bloodstream in various combinations which affected the operation of nerves and brain. Two kinds of stresses could be seen to affect these endocrine glands and their associated states of consciousness: physiological stresses, and psychological stresses.

In the Cayce picture, any kind of ill health or medical disability, including fatigue, could markedly affect the endocrine sequences stirred up by drug taking, or by whale chasing, or by methods of quiet yoga. Poor diet produced poor chemistry in the bloodstream, as did poor eliminations, while pressures on nerves from strained and knotted muscles inhibited circulation of the all-important blood chemistry. Consequently, any attempt to alter consciousness drastically while the body was under stress of poor function was a foolhardy attempt, for the result might be not only unrewarding but dangerous to sanity.

Because these same endocrine glands were immensely responsive to thought and emotion, psychological stress must also be taken seriously, in the Cayce view, by those seeking to alter consciousness. Some stresses were the normal tensions of developing new levels of selfhood for full co-creating with the Creative Forces; these stresses, found in productive efforts at service and in attempts to achieve loving attunement, would be helpful in springing the mind to its optimums. Choosing definite ideals meant that one was choosing definite stresses, as he sought to reach those ideals with his fellows and the One.

However, attempting to blow open the mind while the body was in the grip of strong emotions was not the wisest or safest procedure, even when these emotions were the products of healthy stress. Anger, grief, fear, sexual passion, all would stimulate the critical endocrine activities, and when combined with drug action, with or without the hazards of bodily fatigue and illness, could produce results which were at the least disturbing, and at the most catastrophic for the altered mind. Not raw emotion but the focused drives of earnest effort for high purposes, guided by attunement in meditation and prayer, offered the safest springboards for altered consciousness in the Cayce view.

Further, the Cayce trance source pointed out that not all psychological stress was the stress of healthy growth or healthy drives.

Many individuals show the stress which comes of standing with their faces averted from real life, in rigid determination to proceed on their own terms or not at all. Their manner and speech shows that they can define what they are against but not what they are for, because they respond to each new event and person with an habitual *Nein* before *Ja*. Their fundamental negativism (which may be unfaith in its basic form of lack of trust in life and in themselves) can produce immense stress; it can shower upon the individual the very monsters he defies when his consciousness is sufficiently altered to allow his inner animals to roam in imagination. Likewise, those who are not so much against what they dislike in others as against themselves (and the two forms of negativism support each other) are vulnerable to disturbing material when their internal conflicts surface in altered states. And those who repeatedly violate the simplest rule of morality—not to do that which always puts them out of sorts and at odds with themselves—may join those who violate another basic precept: not to do that which they could not share with their most respected associates. Both are likely to fall headlong into chasmlike splits within them, should they achieve markedly altered consciousness. Similarly perilous for altered states is cynicism, no less real when hidden under gushy flattery and manipulation of others. Indeed, any enduring stance of devaluing others or oneself is a primary danger signal in the trip to altered states. Stubb's devaluing of the cook left him vulnerable to inward inflation, while those at Woodstock and in Ishmael's whaling boat were not as subject to distortion from stress.

To attend to the factor of psychological stress which Cayce highlighted, the person contemplating radical alteration of consciousness might do well to ask himself the first questions of balance from psychotherapy: If a man, is he secure in his work, good at it, proud of it, and paid enough for it? If a woman, is she secure in her loving and being loved, good at sharing it, proud of it, and intrinsically rewarded in her bonds with young and old, male and female? While these questions might be different in other cultures and should not be used to stereotype either men or women in this culture, they can serve to screen some of the stress in contemporary culture. Certainly it is possible for reoriented consciousness to lift frozen and stressful low play to high play, often by disclosing to a man or a woman the very qualities which he needs enshrined in his low play. But when the signs of great stress of self against self are present—including the dry and controlled voice, the uptight walk and gesture, the damaged sex life, the invasion of unwanted moods, the alienation of close associates—then the effort to alter consciousness promises maximum risks for sanity. A neurotic housewife who is pitifully against herself and others may move through LSD therapy to a remarkably undrugged and creative state, provided that she has a therapist to help her who is a genius in the puzzling arts of healing the mind. The same housewife, without his aid in an optimum setting, could take the same drug to the destination where her stresses had already pointed her: the calamity of insanity.

In the Cayce materials may be found yet another warning against taking drugs under conditions of stress of body and mind. This was a warning which showed up in guidance given on how to use drugs needed as medication, whether such mind-altering chemicals as those used for anesthesia, or drugs with smaller side effects on the nervous system. From the point of view of the Cayce source, whenever any drug was taken which might strongly affect endocrine action, there was the possibility, heightened under stress, that the individual could be left vulnerable to what this source called "obsession" and "possession," as forms of insanity. These terms, alien to most of modern psychiatry, were used in deadly earnest by the trance-attuned Cayce, who saw the drug-stimulated person as potentially vulnerable to two kinds of unwanted invasions of his nervous system. There was the invasion of autonomous "thought forms," similar to what medical psychology calls "complexes." And even more dangerous, there was the invasion of low-grade discarnate "entities"—souls who had once lived on earth and trapped themselves into lingering around the living, where they sought to gratify their appetites and power drives through action on the endocrine systems of those left vulnerable to them by stress, injury, and drug use. This possibility, which seems bizarre to many moderns who discount survival of any aspect of consciousness beyond death, was offered by the Cayce source in the same way that it was offered in New Testament accounts of some types of insanity. Should research ever verify the Cayce picture, that picture would help to make sense of the suddenly violent or self-destructive behavior of some drug users, which puzzles investigators of the action of mind-altering drugs. And it would certainly heighten the warnings, familiar in traditions of yoking and yoga from East and West, not to seek sudden altering of consciousness under conditions of severe or chronic stress in body or mind.

Set. Laboratory and clinical investigators of the effects of LSD and other psychedelic drugs early discovered that what happened to an individual in a drug-altered state was strongly influenced by what he expected and wanted to happen, at both conscious and unconscious levels of his intention. They called this factor "set," borrowing the term from the psychology of selective perception and broadening the term to include the motivation which affects perception. In drawing attention to set, the researchers took an approach similar to that of the trance-counseling Cayce, who insisted that after stress the most critical factor affecting alterations of consciousness was the individual's "ideal." By this term the trance-speaking Cayce meant more than a conscious goal, and more than an unconscious "idea" which might compensate a narrow or mistaken goal of surface consciousness. He meant the deep commitments and values of the person,

112

operative at both unconscious and conscious levels; he referred to the individual's real working norms in daily life, which might be different from what he outwardly professed.

Set has not only conscious and unconscious levels, but long-run and short-run aspects. In the long run, set is whatever one prizes as having ultimate worth for his life, whether power, passion, position, possessions or piety— or some combination of these and other values. When the long-range set is narrow or shallow, rather than toward co-creating in high play with the One, then the mind turned loose in an altered state tends to jump at once to compensatory material which might broaden or deepen the set. The individual sees what he could be, and often—to his dismay—what he now is; such compensatory material may be reinforced by currents from the far impersonal realms of the mind. A selfish set may produce swings into animal horror, mental spinning, and episodes of uncontrollable Force; by contrast, a set for high play may produce vital animal drives, mental beauty or clarity, and spiritual Force. Short-run set is the attitude towards the experiences of altered consciousness itself. To enter the experience as a series of events to be dominated by force of will may produce "bad trips," where the struggle throws adrenalin into the bloodstream. Or to seek altered consciousness for thrills, or for escape, or for narcissistic visions, may throw the mind to strong compensatory material, especially where the momentary set is in conflict with the deeper long-term set of the individual.

Probably set, or what Cayce called "the ideal," is the one factor most worth discovering, and if necessary improving, when the attempt is made to reorient the mind in altered states, whether by whaling, by inhaling, or by silent contemplation. Using dreams, self-inventories, sensivity training, and projective methods can contribute to exploring the potent factor of set; but because set is so subtle and personal, there are no tricks or shortcuts for its evaluation. The individual must ask his closest associates, as well as his own dreams and his reflections before

113

the One, to press upon him such question as these: What are you trying to prove? Who are you trying to be? What do you hope to share? Why do you try it this way?

Setting. Every effort at altering consciousness towards its optimums takes place in a particular locale, with specific objects or stimuli, and with particular companions or none. Stubb's whaling has a different setting from Ishmael's whaling in the center of the whale armada; Woodstock is not the same as Washington. Because the unconscious works so largely by means of symbols, as every night's dreams disclose, the effects of setting upon alterations of consciousness are much greater than a layman might expect, though well below those of stress and set. In addition, what both the Woodstock backers and the entranced Cayce called "vibrations" in people, places, and activities may contribute larger effects than even contemporary research workers might suppose.

Early researchers on LSD noted with surprise that the same drug given to the same person produced startlingly different effects in a bare and antiseptic hospital room, where doctors poked at the subject of an experiment, and in a tastefully appointed room among loved and trusted associates, where good music and objects of art or nature were available for the loosened mind to fall upon. Comfort proved to be helpful in achieving useful and safe altered states, but beauty was more important, and vehicles for sharing love and honesty were more important still. Similar discoveries about the effects of setting were made by growth groups and encounter groups, seeking to alter the mind without drugs in retreat locales as well as in classrooms, medical offices, and homes.

There is the physical setting to consider, with its connotations of closeness to or alienation from Nature—and therefore connotations of whatever there is in the person which is able spontaneously to be itself. The physical setting may also offer hints of desired self-transcendence to the altering mind, through providing the play of light and shadowed areas (which Otto emphasized in his milestone study of altered states, *The Idea of the Holy*), as

114

well as providing high and low levels, and opportunity for going in and coming out. Specific objects can contribute to the physical setting, not only in their relative formality and informality which suggest ways of control or abandon (or that marvel of altered consciousness which is abandon that shows its own inherent controls), but also in the richness and immediacy of tensions of opposed values—found in art works, furnishings, and hangings. One graceful piece of sculpture, with its inherent tensions of proportion in planes and curves and masses, may be worth more to the altering mind than general comfort or sensate pleasure; the loosed consciousness can engage the form to move itself into new depths and directions—just as it can with music which is not mere background chords and jingles, but structured composition and performance. Music as part of setting seems especially able to free or constrict the consciousness altered with or without drugs (the Cayce source urged the use of historic religious chants, to aid and accompany the movement of consciousness in meditation). How the music acts appears to depend in part on its physical impact or "vibrations" as it strikes the body, and in part on its symbolic elements —its sentimental or bravura quality, its climbing or pounding, its counterpoint or lucid simplicity. Choosing an artistic or musical setting to feature intensities of sensation, or to feature the emotional color of altered-mind experiences, may drive the changed consciousness into the more sensate corners of the psyche, yielding throbbing beauty or unbearable ugliness or both—according to the set and stress of the person whose consciousness changes. Speaking of setting, the trance-counseling Cayce often warned that music should be chosen carefully, since "music can span the distance from the sublime to the ridiculous" in its direct action on the mind.

However, the social setting is probably more important than the physical setting, in affecting the altering mind. The social setting includes representation of the polarity of male and female, so basic to symbolizing human values that it appears in some part of every night's dreams.

115

Critical in the social setting is the character of the trust and bonds among participants in a venture to alter consciousness, for these bonds employ high-play co-creating or low-play mutual using. To many individuals in their time of changed awareness, one human face seen across the room may be more meaning-laden than any art form, especially when that face carries reminders of mutual love and of a cherished purpose for coming together; the face of a friend may shine with meaning and promise such as that told of friends who met on the Mount of Transfiguration, in a psychedelic but drugless experience. Yet another dimension of social setting is provision for signaling back and forth whatever is experienced in altered states, whether this is done in words or perhaps in an embrace or a symbolic gift—carrying the force which made Stubb feel that preaching for the assembled sharks was required, at the time of Stubb's heightening.

Finally, there is the issue of transpersonal fields in the setting, added to physical and social fields. At the present state of research, no adequate instrumentation is available to assess the transpersonal aspects of setting; indeed, there are few models for even thinking about whether a venture in altered consciousness occurs in the presence of angels or demons, or with the blessing or interference of the disembodied departed, or with the help of some field or current of divine energy focused upon participants by their work and their loving meditation together. There are those who attempt to alter consciousness towards reorientation by encounter-group methods of stimulating exchanges, or by drug methods, who would consider the very question of such transpersonal fields and forces to be folly. On the other hand, there are those conducting similar ventures who feel that they know only too well the Ahab within themselves, ever ready to take over the divine; they are unwilling to voyage into new realms of consciousness without sustained and heartfelt seeking of the One. The perspective of the trance-heightened Cayce was that the most important resource of setting, for altered consciousness, was not Nature, not sound and sights, not social

116

ease, but the invisible field of force or "vibrations" created by serious prayer and meditation among those with a set to be productive co-creators with the Creator. Over a period of years, the strangely attuned Cayce traced in detail how he saw such a field formed by a group of seekers, and how he saw it move and change in response to divine aid, lifting its real but invisible Force field to more and more helpful impact upon the minds and endocrine operation of individuals in the group, through action which included ESP but also included what men had called the Holy Spirit. By cultivating this aspect of setting, Cayce explained, those who sought permanent change towards their "normal forces" would find their own natural energies enhanced by forces beyond their own, coming freely from the divine, and focused for them by that Companion of every man whom Cayce called "the Master" or "the Christ." To leave Him out of the setting, in Cayce's altered-state view, was to attempt to play with God with human consciousness, rather than to attempt high play with God.

Shutoff. The remarkable ability of the unconscious to select and mute its offerings to surface consciousness, protecting the ego from more than it can handle, was sketched by Freud in his epochal treatment of censorship in dreams. Later research has followed Freud in disclosing not only how such censoring operates in lapses of memory, as Freud showed, but also in the forgetting of each night's dreams, where selective repression rather than lack of dream vigor or clarity may be at work. The factor of shutoff in altered consciousness remains elusive and yet dramatic, where it shows. Psychotherapists such as the present writer, spending long months on the dreams of individual clients, have noted, for example, how carefully dream themes appear to be worked up in nighttime productions, now vigorously developed for a time and now muted in favor of other themes. Particularly noteworthy is the tendency for runs of dreams which work to build the dreamer's confidence and self-esteem to alternate with runs of dreams which take him apart to reveal his weaknesses. An observer of this process is struck by the seeming self-regulation of the mind, as it gives to its parts and levels the material which each can handle—except when organic damage is present, through illness or injury or drugs, including alcohol. Even in the mazes of psychosis, where the personality runs out of control in its own grand or petty style, there remain hints that the psyche is trying to right itself, to shape and direct and focus itself, through the flow of inward imagery and meanings which meet the outward signals from the senses. And not only from psychotherapy, but from other ventures of East and West to help the mind to grow itself, the evidence accumulates that significant psychological change occurs in stages, rather than all at once, so that the self-regulating work of the mind is important to its growth and balance. All of this evidence points to the factor of shutoff in altered states.

Many items suggest to investigators in optimum psychology that body and mind have their own rhythms in reaching optimum states, including timely shutoffs. Maximum creativity in a task of high complexity may require at least ninety minutes for sustained optimum performance (just as dreams run in ninety-minute cycles of brain-wave states); research may one day show that modern worship and modern classroom periods, like much of psychotherapy and perhaps some lovemaking, may operate in time units shut off too early. Further, maximum creativity of task or insight does not appear to be easily sustained for more than a few hours in any one day, except under crisis conditions (Cayce, for example, found that he could only achieve effective trances twice a day, in midmorning and midafternoon, as a rule). And full creativity appears more difficult to reach after the best energies of the day are spent—suggesting why many prayer groups and encounter groups have difficulty generating steam on the leftover coals of the day's fires (Cayce urged those who wanted the best fruits of meditation to try it in the early mornings, or even at sunrise). Failing to shut off the effort towards maximum creativity, at the right points, often turns productivity to sudden irritability. Strong emotions

118

also appear to have their own aspects of shutoff in cycles which build to peak and release; terminating them too soon, or prolonging them too far, has often-noted effects on sex, anger, grief, and religious ecstasy. All such matters of sequence, duration, and degree in timing point to shutoff as a major variable when consciousness alters.

The Zen master seeking the altered consciousness of *satori* for his trainees may keep them long hours in cross-legged meditation. But he also uses shutoff to get them out gardening, and one day sends them back to the everyday world of politics and children. Not unlike him in function, perhaps, are the self-regulating capacities of the psyche to pace itself as it grows, stretches, or withholds itself for future effort. However, any drastic approach to altering consciousness, whether by drugs or a war dance, by sensory ecstasies or ascetic silence, may remove or distort this same self-regulating function of the psyche. The whirling dervish does it in a dance, and the mind-whirling drug taker does it in a chemical trance, but both play a risky game if they do not take careful account of the factor of shutoff when they seek altered states. In particular, those who use drugs to blow the mind, without reckoning on how the drugs damp or remove the self-directing shutoff capacities of the mind, do so with insufficient care as to which door to the unconscious reads insanity and which unsanity. Whenever the native wisdom of the body as Cannon called it, is discarded chemically, and the native wisdom of the mind in timing and spacing its changes is impaired, then the need becomes imperative for experienced and sensitive guides to altered consciousness, who can provide the required shutoff and starting again (as the psychologist knew when to urge the housewife under LSD to be quiet and listen to music for a time). But such guides are not easy to find. A psychiatrist who knows sex may not know what Otto called the "numinous" or the holy, stirring in irrational depths of the mind; and a retreat-master who dwells in realms of the numinous may have lost track of sex in the clouds of his incense. A civil rights leader may know disciplined force

119

but not the force of subjective disciplines, while an artist may know the might of symbolic forms but not the forms to advance the action of the Almighty. Consequently, the Cayce counsel to those who sought the best of altered consciousness was that they ought not to place their trust in any external guide, not even Cayce, though instruction had its place. Rather they should follow the innate timings offered by their own souls, in balanced activities of growth, service, and attunement, where they would discover that by working together they could find help in timely shutoffs and beginnings. They could find aid from the Other Force, which "ever seeks its own," answering to its counterpart in the soul of each man; this was the aid of the Christ, the one guide whose aid would not distort or mislead any man. He might seem difficult to find, but in fact He was never far from any man's "superconscious," which would use ESP and more to place him in helpful relation to the Other Force, the elder brother for every man. Such attunement would afford the safest handling of the critical factor of shutoff, in the quickenings towards optimums which were the birthright of every soul.

Sharing. When consciousness alters, the factor which often determines whether the effect is a momentary novelty, or progressively deeper transformations of personality, is sharing. Those encounter groups which make a lasting difference to their members encourage a variety of spontaneous actions by which members may herald and reinforce a breakthrough or a lift to optimums by one of their number. The range of sharing runs from a blow to an embrace, from a dance to a shout, from a silent prostration to a spontaneous ceremony, and often includes the signaling to oneself and others which considered or impetuous speech affords. Such groups, whether they use drug or drugless methods, find that they need times of quiet and reflection, but they also need times to do something with and for another. For sharing not only conveys, it consolidates. Sharing not only reports an experience, but it frames a meaning in larger meanings of tradition and group concerns. When self-pity needs to be lifted into honest concern for oneself and others, when bitter anger needs to become courage to turn wrongs into rights, when sexual desire needs to be personalized into loving, then the process of sharing becomes critical for the best altering of consciousness. Each stage through which the altering mind passes may require its own kind of signaling and feedback through sharing, whether in contrition or release, in joy or forgiveness, in remembering ancient values or recognizing new ones. Especially gratitude, that gift of the gods, appears to require sharing in order to reach its full force, in a process which Cayce called "lifting the vibrations" in a group. Sharing, said Cayce, could transform a potential for change into an actuality, it could add understanding to a nameless quickening, and it could turn the energies of a freed mind towards service of others; for these reasons, the trance-speaking Cayce encouraged members of study and meditation groups to write down their daily-life experiences of growth and bring them to meetings, as well as to report on what occurred to them in group sessions.

By emphasizing timely and loving sharing of experiences and insights, so that these could be raised to yet higher levels of meaning and decision making, Cayce underlined a grave problem in drug-induced experiences of altered states. The stronger drugs, which can go beyond distortion of the mind to useful disorientation and re-orientation, act to set individuals moving in their own private cycles of becoming. Dorothy and the Tin Woodsman and the Cowardly Lion and the Scarecrow are only dimly in one another's presences, and most of the time on parallel roads to Oz—unless compelled by the magical troubles of a Woodstock. The mutual enhancement and engagement, the resonation of discoveries in a group—which appear to be important to forward the growth of the mind blown loose by drugs, as truly as when altered by pain or great love or exhilarating creation—are hampered when participants are absorbed in their subjective worlds. For this reason the assets of speed and hope which

121

are offered by the stronger psychedelic drugs must be balanced off with their liabilities, which include limiting conscious and creative sharing at the highest levels of alertness—except where individuals momentarily touch each other from their separate worlds, or where a sensitive doctor and a nurse dedicate themselves entirely to sharing the experiences of a housewife on the way out of her neurotic maze.

One critical part of sharing, whether fostered by a group or by an experienced guide, is that feedback to an individual which reinforces him as he reaches what psychotherapists call the "transpersonal control point." This point is a kind of footing within the individual from which he produces the truth about his life and relationships, while unforced, unafraid, and unforcing. Those who prize conscious group interaction enough to be unwilling to lose it or weaken it with strong drugs, or with strong emotions cultivated for their own sake, treasure the capacity of group members to be priests to each other at moments, when they may confirm and bless and clarify what they see unfolding in one among them.

Wherever helpful sharing is needed in the work of altering consciousness, it may be done with memories, with phrases worn by happy use, with family photos held before the deeply reflective gaze, and with references to treasures of story, legend, scripture, theory, or joke. By whatever means, the sharing in speech or act or speechlessness appears to be what Cayce described: the quickening of a flow, the nurturing of a process of change, rather than a trick of displacing consciousness with novelties from the unconscious. Altered consciousness at its best is a becoming, not a mere coming out with wonders. It is a delivery of a human being, not a display of powers. Ishmael dumbfounded in the center of the whale armada understood what could be shared and what could not, while Stubb called too soon for a sacrament of whale steak and preaching to the sharks.

Serving. As sharing with others determines whether the altering mind proceeds to moments of ever-greater depth and weight, so the factor of serving others with the fruits of the experience determines whether the consequences of changed consciousness will be temporary or permanent. To Cayce in trance, productive service in co-creating with others was the necessary twin to any deep attunement or inner quickening to the pulse of the soul and the beat of the One Force. Without such service, attunement even to the level of the "Christ Force" would yield little fruit, proving only a passing diversion, soon doubted or forgotten.

But rendering service is not simple. It was service of others which Mara the tempter sought to forestall in the awakened Buddha, and the wrong use of surging power and identity which tempted Jesus in the wilderness, after he had chosen to have his consciousness altered in the baptismal waters of the Jordan. If a truth be propounded in supposed service before others have found the question and have glimpsed the start of an answer (which comes folded in all true questioning of ultimates), then the truth belittles in the very act of offering life. Further, if words are used for service when action should be the vehicle, whether with a broom or a crusade, then service reduces the effects in the altering minds of all who participate. Or if the service be trivial, as when group members settle for the comfortable companionship of cleaning up a meeting room together, but will on no account take one another's children on vacation trips with them, then any alteration has limited impact and duration.

How and when the co-creating service shall take place are finally derived from the chosen and mutual set of those who seek to grow together. There are no tricks which can turn a narcissistic set into a generous one. Especially important is the set of service towards those not of the ingroup. Centuries-old traditions of the altered state sought in penance require generous action to round out the process of contrition, especially action with the weak or sick or confused, who cannot be expected to exchange gifts with the giver. In this perspective, the altered mind is seen to stifle itself if its service is reserved for the closed circle of the ingroup and does not spread its offerings to business, to politics, to sand lots. Altered consciousness appears to have the peculiar quality of presenting the mind with values which may only be kept as they are given away—especially given where there is no bargaining for return favors, but only in co-creating effort with others.

Whether the acts of service which consolidate the effects of altered states are done with intimates or with strangers, these acts need to include both conceptual and physical efforts. As therapists know, an individual may propound truths about transferences and complexes and life styles, while nothing within him changes until at last he actively gives himself to others in new ways. Then everything about him seems to change: his face softens, his eyes gain depth, his voice moves freely through its registers, his skills click, his memory clears, and a full person steps forth from the shell of protected possibilities that was there before. In the same way, when consciousness is altered not for recovery but for optimums, the critical question of permanent change is to turn insight into investiture, to transform lovingness into love. In such a process of co-creating service, the most important chemical may be saline. It may be sweat. Without the fixing action of honest, perspiring effort, the gains of altered states may be temporary or even delusory, suggesting vistas which are mirages rather than miracles.

How may the six factors of stress and set, setting and shutoff, sharing and serving, be combined into activities which generate high play? Three modes of activity deserve consideration in any survey of routes to optimum states: those which feature autointoxication, those which feature drugs, and those which feature an undrugged quickening.

The Drugged Experience, A: Autointoxication

The method which Stubb uses to catch his whale and lift his spirits is autointoxication. It is the same method which Ahab uses to drive his men across the seas of the globe to catch one albino beast. It is the method by which much of society's work is done. Yet not only whales but whalers are slain by it when the method fails to reach its goal of high play.

The stages of this method for altering consciousness are familiar. The eye of a man falls upon something which holds his interest. He then turns himself over to coveting that object, whether it be a woman, money, an office, an art form, or a whale, trusting that the claims are sound which assure him that thus individual greatness is won and society served. As he allows his object to dominate and ravish him, he is faced with mounting conflicts and decisions. New disciplines and skills and ego strength are required of him. His chase will make a man of him or will break him. If he is fortunate, the pressure he feels to possess his object will at some point evoke his optimums. For a period he will know high play, enjoying every minute of the chase and finding himself generous to competitors as well as solicitous of the high quality of his games. Something like the One will range itself beside him, though he may not acknowledge its presence except to note that he is having the time of his life, and so are those around him.

On the other hand, if he is not so fortunate he may early win the object of his desire and find himself in a flat and tasteless state, wondering why he drove himself so hard—until his eye falls on something new and he begins again the feverish cycle. So he may live out his days, now and then wondering how others may be happy with less than his lot of books or of flesh, of cars or of votes, of palaces or of pews. If one of his chases is not successful, his lot may be better. After he recovers from his dismay, he may find that his next whale is a white whale. Then all his pent-up longing for a more authentic life is invested in a monstrous struggle, and he either slips into high play at last or goes down with a notable splash. If he does not alter his consciousness, he at least alters the affairs of those around him.

There appear to be two styles of the method of autointoxication, one style of the superego and one style of the id: crisis, and craving.

In the style of crisis, the games of parent or romance, work or religion, are played under the impress of a superego image of success (not necessarily what Cayce called an "ideal") which the player feels compelled to attain. He must go from salesman to sales manager, and then try for the presidency of his firm. Or the woman must move from suburb to suburb, picking the best shops, advantageous friends, and churches or synagogues in each locale. The instruments for this style are available in every walk of life; the simplest restaurant contains its structures of ascending grades, from busboy to headwaiter, allowing for the beckoning, imperious call: "You must make something of yourself." And if the game be not upward, but inward toward acceptance by the group which dominates the driving superego image, then there are available a faster and a slower set among the waitresses—or among bankers or publishers, artists or plumbers, athletes or admen. Whether the stakes are great or small, victory is defined in the same way: "You are what you hold and can control." Not only property, but subalterns, lovers, competitors, devotees, all offer themselves as trophies.

This style of living by crisis, of placing personhood under pressure and pain which at its worst may reach self-terrorizing, succeeds at times in achieving high play and magnificent optimums. There come moments of blessed release, after a particularly trying shared effort, when the whole mad scramble is joy. Those who have worked for a Madison Avenue advertising agency, as once did the present writer, know the times when a good program is developed and sold to a client in emergency speed which calls forth the best of each person at the firm. At such times high play is attained which carries into the next job and the next, while the painful pressures keep producing moments which are diamonds out of materials of coal.

But at other times the method of crisis only arouses defenses, so that nobody works at his best, but each grows

126

more irritable and guarded in his game. Then a retreat from crisis must be made to some island of play; the island may be a hobby or recreation where the tough games are simulated, but under conditions which assure each player a few victories. The island may be social manipulation in party, convention, vacation, or love affair, until the social side of life is swallowed up in the work game of the firm. Or the player may turn to the other version of autointoxication: craving.

Where crisis insists that living is escalated position, craving insists that living is satisfied appetite. Romance is the basic model, with all of the requisite stages of falling in love, courtship, quarreling, landing the love object, and further trials and tendernesses—even when the romance is with a Buick, a split-level house, a growing expense account, a Mattel walking toy, a trip to Europe, a great campus for one's children, or a four-seasons hideaway. In the style of craving, the hardware of life is to be consumed with the same tender craving as are people. And the people are to be handled seductively, rather than in terms of competence and authentic roles, romanced in business just as truly as they are in school, church, golf foursome, or encounter group.

There are times when the flirtations and courtships with things and with people demand every fiber of sensitivity and originality from the players, so that they step over the line into high play. Owning a house may lead the new owners to try to decorate it, developing their tastes to levels which they never knew while camping out in city apartments. A love affair which starts out shallowly enough may reach moments when the players truly choose to love, across difficult personal and social barriers, and for a time know love by choice, rather than by dull habit. At its most rewarding levels, the autointoxication of craving yields a person on fire with sensitivity and alertness to a set of values—whether of beauty, truth, goodness, love, wholeness, or holiness. In the demands of romance the fire may be charmed into a steady glow which supports all the risks of high play. The result is much the same as when crisis so scalds and sears a man, as Ahab was burned from head to toe by lightning, that his personhood is left pruned and spare, and he is able to step freely into high play, secure in his grace and vision and generosity.

That autointoxication is drug using hardly needs laboring. If drug using be pragmatically defined as introducing a chemical agent into the human bloodstream in sufficient quantity to alter markedly the functioning of body and mind, then the endocrine jolts squirted into the bloodstream by crisis and craving are not different than if introduced by needles. Insofar as most urban adults spend a good portion of their lives laboring under autointoxication from adrenalin in the style of crisis, or under autointoxication from sex hormones and related chemicals in the style of craving, then most are chemical addicts of one sort or another. Further, each person develops his favorite internal drug antidotes. Anger may be used to damp frightening sexuality, or to force catharsis and intimacy not available in a better way, or to substitute for ego strength in a critical pinch. Sexual arousal may quiet subsurface rage, or offer assurances of masculinity or femininity not found in productive work and service, or masquerade as esthetics. Self-pity may soften those who crave mercy in their crises, or may bring on cathartic tears which temporarily dissolve shells of pretense.

How frequently sought and readily available are the chemicals of autointoxication must be apparent to anyone who can recall wandering dazedly through sales exhibits at an auto show or an art show, or who can recall frantically buying last-minute Christmas gifts that he did not like to give to someone whom he did not like. Few are those who have not fallen victim to catalog fever on coming across a Sears Roebuck catalog during a rainy spell on a vacation trip. The mounting frenzy of a civil rights crusade, the consuming gossip and strategy ploys of a struggle for power in a church or corporation or campus, all show how bountifully Nature will reward with her drugs those who seek them as their means to altered consciousness.

With each person a walking drug factory and pharmacy, not to mention being his own pusher and junkie, it is not surprising that the question of how to handle LSD and related chemicals for affecting the mind is one of the most charged in modern times.

The autointoxicated venture towards high play magnifies material from the compensatory level of the unconscious. At its worst, the process produces players who lurch from one compensation to the compensation which compensates it, whether in crisis or craving or both. Careful examination of dream and waking material from the compensatory level shows how readily it associates itself with figures of the opposite sex, who are ever the bearers of life's hidden values and of new becomings. Because of this association, a man driving himself to autointoxicated heights of power or learning suddenly has an affair with a feminine associate who seems the incarnation of helpful understanding. And the woman priding herself on the autointoxicating beauty of the children and furniture which she owns suddenly lands in an affair with the leader of her Great Books group, who seems the incarnation of enduring values. But the dynamics of such linkage are more than sexual, for they affect all autointoxication, where goals of position or possessions or learning or piety may be as captivating as any passion. Hinduism has traditionally called the contrasexual image from the compensatory level *Maya,* the alluring divinity of appearances who traps men at the same time she awakens them from their sloth or fixations, by casting her lovely veils over cars and careers, kingdoms and theories, romances and friendships. (While Maya is conventionally represented as feminine, there is much evidence to suggest that masculine dynamics fulfill the function for women.) Not a little of Hindu tradition revolves around how to deal playfully with Maya, so as to attend to her beckonings without becoming her prisoner. And the problem is certainly not one limited to India. Interpreting some sixteen

129

hundred dreams submitted to him while he was in trance, Cayce repeatedly pointed out the work of the contrasexual Maya-like figures in dreams, offering both helpful and destructive forces in the psyche. For Cayce the limits to autointoxication could be found in the biblical phrase already quoted, with which he closed his vocational and personal-growth counsel to many: "Study to show thyself approved unto God, a workman not ashamed, rightly dividing the word of truth, and keeping self unspotted from the world." The last phrase was definitive of the limits of ambition and desire and service in any walk of life; it did not refer to keeping sterile virtue, for Cayce commended primary human drives as "awakening" the individual to successive becomings, when these were rightly sought and shared. Instead, the phrase was used as a precise warning against becoming "spotted" by autointoxi-cation, by what Cayce so often called "selfish aggrandize-ment" in the essential processes of being a productive workman with others, and a co-creating student of the truths of living and the ways of loving.

While the method of autointoxication certainly works to alter consciousness to its optimums, at times it has built-in drawbacks. In set it not only reifies the compen-satory, but tends to make coveting the trophies of play more important than honoring playing and players, leaving the winner master of an empty and lonely ball court. It is not the characteristic set of this method to struggle as hard for worthy goals as did Ishmael in the great herd of whales, yet ever to find that calm center where the deep self or soul disports itself in eternal mildness of joy. Rather is artificial stress so highly valued as to make it part of the set. A great man is a tense man. Therapy is good when it provokes powerful conflicting emotions. Living is being romantically pained. Growing is getting ready for great crises to come, while ignoring the burial of spontaneous selfhood under present routines. When stress is so featured, then alterations of consciousness produce gross swings into unwanted regions and currents of the unconscious. Stubb the conqueror of a whale is inflated and petty. Ahab the superb captain is avenger, rather than the instrument of a rollicking good crew. The tautly stretched psyche springs hard and erratically when released into altered consciousness, with or without drugs.

The aids to timely shutoff from autointoxication are few, for recreation itself becomes infected with styles of crisis and craving, as the boss is taken golfing to make points not on the score card. To many players in the risky sport of autointoxication, the only effective shutoff is illness or disaster. Not a few modern hospitals may be monastic retreats. Not a few wood-paneled therapy rooms may be groves where Socrates walks again with his lifegiving questions. Not a few divorce courts may be the places of commissioning to divorce from the whole round of things, before the Grail is altogether forgotten. Not a few offices where business failures are sealed may be places where a will to fail has carried forward a will to be real with others, somehow. But there also remains the possibility of shutoff from autointoxication with drugs, whether alcohol, or mood and tempo changers, or mind benders.

All such drugs may offer speedy shutoff from the drugs of autointoxication when taken in the company of those truly chosen, rather than dragooned by social pressures. Chemicals drunk or smoked or swallowed may afford some degree of honest sharing, from levels below surface consciousness which are not unduly stained by compensatory material, at those moments when defenses melt and predatory stances release. Indeed, the very act of taking a chemical becomes a ceremonial act, a symbol of stepping out of thruway traffic, even when the only drug used is nicotine—made more precious by the knowledge that the user gives up a minute of his life for every minute he offers this incense to an unknown Author of nonrush, noncontrol, nonexploiting.

If indulgence in strong doses of body-produced chemicals in autointoxication is so chancey, is there in fact a better chemical route which leads straight to high play in full optimums, on a real-life yellow brick road to an emerald city?

131

Part of the appeal of taking external drugs, whether mild or strong, is repudiating autointoxication. Somebody views the work game played as war with bombs and burned babies, and decides that others are mad who think they are sane while fighting their shadowy games of dominoes. He may light up his joint of pot if not his draft card. Somebody watches the manipulation in intra-corporation politicking and decides that it is more weird than science fiction, as well as less productive than farming by hand with comrades in an informal commune. He may "drop acid" of LSD as he drops seeds into the earth. Another may gaze at commercials which nobody believes, strung in lights against the sky and flashing soundlessly and soullessly to everywhere that autointoxication thrives; he decides that such make-believe is sick, and that he might better gather with his peers to make music or hand-tooled leather jackets, or even make protests which are original and serviceable. He may prefer to "freak out" with drugs, rather than be a freak. In each such situation, taking drugs becomes a shared ritual of asking out, denying the method of autointoxication. As such, the ritual can be more potent than any vacation of the driven, more vital than the welcome relief afforded by illness, more solidarity-producing than psychoanalysis. The research work of Katz and Pahnke, giving LSD to those dying of terminal cancer, shows that drug-induced experiences under optimum conditions can strip off artificial life goals of autointoxication from the dying, leaving them with remarkable tolerance of excruciating pain, and able to face with relatives, in creative ways, the fact of their certain and near end.

There are stages in psychoactive drug experiences, just as there are stages in autointoxication, although the drug stages are not as familiar or defined, in part because drugs give so much leeway to each individual's unconscious. In the action of such milder drugs as marijuana, and in the first stages of LSD, alterations in perception and reasoning and motivation may occur almost at once. Surroundings look different, and often more interesting. Under optimum conditions of set and stress, setting and shutoff, people may not look so threatening, not so much like things. Colors may dance, sounds echo delightfully in the mind, touch may be amplified into tactile drama, sex may be more fun and less of a production. But if stronger drugs or larger dosages are used, or milder drugs joined to severe stress, then the farther reaches of reorientation may be entered. A period of disorienting fluidizing and unlocking, of spinning and exploring, may be followed by a locking in at successive levels of meaning, where the content of the drug-triggered experience is more structured.

If helpful signaling and sharing occurs, and if music and companionship lead into rhythms of shutoff followed by startup into further adventuring, then the regions of the compensatory unconscious may sometimes be explored, in all of their brightness and fright. In more rare experiences, where ego strength is joined with stout and unselfish set, the realm of the fire-protected circle of individuality may be entered, and perhaps not so blindly as in the rush of autointoxication which sometimes allows the same entry. In such drug-aided moments, one may try on his inner sword and helmet and hold to light his royal jewels. More rarely yet, the waves from impersonal regions which Cayce called the "universal" may wash upon the margins of consciousness, bringing fear or refreshment or both, depending upon the capacity of the ego to interpret and endure and share what is happening, as well as upon the extent to which access to these far forces is guarded by entrance through the life form, in a set towards service of others. Whether the total journey adds up to growth or to trauma, and whether it later spontaneously repeats itself when no drugs are present, depends upon many variables. But the stakes may be very high indeed, in a journey to unsanity or insanity which may sometimes transmute a life and sometimes remove it permanently from all play.

Because of low-play patterns in the culture which do

not feature co-creating with others, or partnership with the Creative Forces, but instead feature narcissistic novelties of subjective experience, taking drugs to influence the mind is often approached, unfortunately, in a poor set. The drug experience may be sought in the mode of the very autointoxication which it mocks; a drug user may find it easy to crave the thrills and risks which accompany drug use—the more so because the ideology of his drug-taking group tells him that his craving is the one which is against all craving. In such a set, his drug-induced alteration of consciousness may become but one more romantic venture, to be savored in all its nuances as would be autointoxicated experiences of power or sex, position or creeds. Or it may become a venture in crisis, because the use of drugs often risks severe social and legal penalties, and the use of certain drugs sometimes results in drastic mental illness. Then the question of set subtly changes from "Why do you take this drug?" to "How come you don't?", with attendant pressures like those which make an executive climb the ladder to social success, or make a suburbanite anxious to belong to a better-rated country club. When images of self-worth are challenged by such approaches to drug use, then the chemicals of autointoxication join those which are ingested. The combined results are sometimes powerful, but because artificial stress is introduced, the potentially calming effects of psychedelic drugs, and their best release of the healing materials which the unconscious is ready to offer, are distorted by less pleasant or useful contents. For the set of the drug taking has secretly changed to that of the surrounding culture and seeks its own play of appetite and stereotyped successes in self-alienated stress.

The greatest hazard in taking nonaddictive mind-altering drugs may not be chemical at all (grave as some of the chemical risks may prove to be), but cultural. It may be the danger of taking drugs in conformity with surrounding cultural patterns of autointoxication.

By themselves, and under ideal conditions of setting and shutoff, sharing and serving, pure doses of such drugs as LSD can introduce and reinforce a remarkably unintoxicated open gaze at the world, at the self, at fellow humans, and even at the One, just as could the older and milder drugs of communion. But when these same psychedelic drugs are taken in the anxious appetite for colorful experiences as such, and to meet social pressures to belong and to achieve, they may produce miseries beyond those of autointoxication. For the drug user playing with crisis and craving is mixing internal chemicals with ingested chemicals. And he is hiding from himself the fact that his set offers him no new social or personal beginning at all. Adrenaline is a poor solvent for LSD, as clinical reports show. Anxiety plus strong drugs is more productive of poison than peace. The resultant disturbance to endocrine function, and to other body chemistries, may be as grave as the trance-quickened Cayce suggested. Or as Paul suggested in his New Testament letter, when he warned that those who took the chemicals of communion in a poor set did so to their own destruction.

The effects of setting must also be considered in the drug-taking route to optimums. Because so many of the more potent drugs are illegal, there is often little opportunity for the user's social experimentation to achieve the graceful and peaceful settings which are so helpful when consciousness alters. The presence of Nature, even at her muddiest and wettest, seems to have been no small part of Woodstock's drug-heightened success, despite the calamities of food shortages and blocked transportation (which offered stress, but not the self-against-self stress of cultivated crisis and craving). And the agency of live music, performed in great spirits before a multitude that must have looked like assembled mankind, appears to have contributed to the setting, as did the knowledge that those who made up the social setting had come because they wanted to come, often from long distances. But how are such conditions of setting to be duplicated in a darkened apartment or a dormitory room, where any knock on the door can lead to penalties as great as prison? No psychological expert is needed to discern that the materials

135

for paranoid imagery are at hand, despite pillows and mattresses and recorded music, whenever buried stress and poor set join in a setting which leaves drug users so vulnerable.

The problem of timely shutoff, or rhythms and cycles, in drug use to alter the mind, is a knotty one. The tendency of panics to build, when the self-regulating of body and mind is impaired, is familiar to those in the drug subculture, as are methods of "talking people down" from bad trips, and sequences of unforced action and leisurely reflection, to help prevent the worst effects of drug-damaged shutoff. But the problem of substituting outer controls when inner controls are distorted remains as pressing for drug users as it does for those who love to immerse themselves in gripping episodes of autointoxication. Similarly, the problem of finding effective means for sharing haunts the method of drug taking for optimums. Drugs which are strong enough to reorient the mind are also strong enough to set the users into cycles of subjectivity where they are often of little help to one another. The mind blown open by drugs, like the mind blown open by pain or by great love or by exhilarating creation, offers its treasures. But accepting and holding such treasures requires more than a bow and a nod. Things must be said and done, shared and celebrated in the company of the faithful, if momentary inspirations are to be turned into life-changing revelations, and if breakthroughs between individuals are to lift beyond momentary novelty to enduring regard and cherishing. When the company of seekers is stoned, or even separately bemused, the going is harder.

Serving others after the drug-induced journey towards optimums, however, may be less problematic. To be sure, the work of co-creating service in shared sweat, which so often fixes the action of the best mind-altering times, may be obscured by the passivity of the drug-taking act; its form may suggest to the unthinking that human greatness comes by swallowing or inhaling, without the complementary acts of feeding another or handing him his incense, or helping him make the tools and times to do his thing. And insofar as the clandestine nature of drug taking, enforced both by social constraint and the need to protect the altered mind from jars, makes the drug trip seem more like a vacation than real life, it sidetracks service of others, including those who cannot give back. Perhaps those who combine their drugs with making music for others have a better prospect for skirting the bogs of triviality or the quicksands of insanity than do their more passive drug-using peers. Further, LSD taken at a wedding of loved and work-sharing group members is different in its effects from LSD taken where nobody loves anybody, or knows anybody, or takes on anybody, beneath the level of social pleasantries. Drug-stimulus levels may be lower where resonation of effects is richer and higher. The cure to drug abuse, where it exists, may lie as much in deepening structures of community within contemporary subcultures as in any action for or against drug taking as such; Judaism has shown that its solid family ties and festivals make it possible for Jewish families and friends to control the excesses of alcoholism which other ethnic and social groups cannot so effectively handle. It is often the alienated, essentially lonely person, one who cannot share his mind-opening discoveries of daily life with cherished adults or peers, who pursues instead greater and greater stimulus by drugs or other methods of assaulting his nervous system, to make up for the missing resonation of his deep becomings.

Surely something remarkably undrugged and precious crowns the best of the drug-induced experiences of optimums, as it does the best of the autointoxicated experiences. But if systematic drugging to reach for high play proves at times to impair endocrine function, as Cayce warned, and offers built-in handicaps of suspended shutoff and limited sharing and serving, is there a drugless route to high play? Is there a way to join Ishmael in poised alertness at the center of a sea of creatures, where he finds eternal mildness of joy in the midst of great whaling?

The quest for an undrugged passage to high play with others may be as old as mankind. While India of earliest history was offering to the devout the apparently powerful psychedelic drug of *soma,* after which it named a Vedic god, and offering the autointoxicating *ashvamedha,* a ritual sacrifice of hundreds of horses on the plains, it was also cultivating the grounds for a psychology of meditation— one that emerged in the Upanishads and has colored Hindu piety ever since, and that also has been carried through the entire Orient by its missionary offspring, Buddhism. And while Israel was offering its people the intoxicating wines of nationalism, in postexilic days of the heroic exploits of the Maccabees, it was also generating that Hassidic purity before God which contributed to the service brotherhoods of the Essenes and other covenanters, later honored in some features of early Christianity. In succeeding centuries when Christian rulers boldly marched in the intoxicating Crusades against equally bold and auto-intoxicated Muslims they were all overtaken in the Renaissance which followed by men of great faith and talent who brought forth new co-creating in high play from Christian monasteries, and from Jewish and Muslim halls of learning and piety. Whether today's intoxicating crusades, which have visited two world wars upon the planet and divided civilization with invisible curtains, may also be covering a nascent movement of quiet renewal in which men may again find their way to cultivating wholly undrugged high play, unborn historians will have to report.

If there is a mode of altering consciousness without drugging from within or without, what is it like?

The entranced Cayce described a process of heightened co-creating which could be found in any worthwhile human activity: work, recreation, study, worship, loving. Part of the energy for such arousal of shared creating would come from man's natural endowments as a soul in a physical body, calling upon resources of matter, mind, and spirit (or Force) which were each person's birthright. But part of the energy in any such shared quickening came from beyond the individual; it came from his fellows, and it came from his being "overshadowed" by the divine, in his earnest efforts at high play with others. The divine Force would be found, then, helping each man in two ways: in the mysterious good Force of his own ever-unfolding soul, and in the Creative Forces which each man would meet in his companions, in nonhuman creation, and in the transcendent "Holy Spirit," focused for man's needs by one like himself, "the Christ." In the Cayce view, these were not poetic concepts or terms but lawful realities, as sure as the forces of gravity or of molecular or electrical action. These realities of abounding creativity would take an individual through stages of altered consciousness as surely as would the action of drugs, or of crisis and craving, but would temper the stages to the needs of the individual. Five stages, not clearly defined but rather overlapping and coalescing, can suggest what Cayce saw in his own altered state as a chain or cycle of levels of high play: disorientation, lift, an "on" state, focus, a kickover effect, and a state of readiness with release. While the trance-counseling Cayce did not use these terms, he repeatedly suggested the usefulness of such constructs for those who would "study self, study self's experiences" in the effort to become co-creators with the One.

The first stage of undrugged high play appears to be disorientation, bemusement, surprise, humor—a regrouping of perspectives. As Mary sings the Magnificat, she sings of how her baby, yet unborn, will make the lowly high, and some of the high become low: things will go topsy-turvy in the new day of the powerless infant which she carries. Her notes of high play in a psychedelic but drugless experience should be heard not as vindictive or as unhappy social protest, but as that bold and mischievous disorienting which begins whenever the One is loosed among men, and there will be hell and heaven to pay. When the Awakened One, the Buddha, begins to preach, tradition tells that he recalls fasting until scratching his

139

belly scraped his fingers on his spine; this was one of his quaint images to suggest how ridiculous he found his own autointoxication methods when the first humor of undrugged high play hit him. Wherever high play with the One begins, even in a vast herd of whales, it has the taste of wonderful absurdity, of things changing delightfully into other things. Consciousness starts to unlock, so that it may go somewhere, and with Someone. The mood is not anxiety so much as surprised interest. Moses is astonished at the psychedelic bush and finds that rush, that lift of excitement and bewilderment, which says to him what the Voice says, that something is astir which is not all of his conscious doing. Such a first stage of high play is not, however, reserved for figures of note; it may come to anyone as a touch of whimsy, a prized memory, a note of hope, a hunch to try a new tack—whenever something outside of surface consciousness seems to say, "So that's how it is!", in cool animation. It may come in the breathings and sighings of lovers, during their moment of teasing or a full kiss or eloquent silence together. It may come in the press of strenuous work, whether rowing whaleboats, or running after children, or pounding term papers, or getting out a stock order or the vote. It may come in a concert, in petting a dog, in a quiet prayer, or in the time of dying. The first stage may be marked or fleeting; it may have specific content or be only contentless good giddiness, a signal of more to come.

The second stage of high-play quickening is often a lift. Something as much physical as mental transpires. Whether directly after the first stage or hours later, there comes the flow of good spirits, the sense of abundant potency, the readiness to take on what comes, even defeat and failure. The high play lift is not manic, not enthusiasm, but runs deeper and steadier than these. It may be emotional, with its own notes of joy or awe, of fear or wonder, or its sense of vital drives ready to function. But it need not be emotional, remaining instead deliciously cool as it unfolds into infectious high spirits; to call it a "peak" experience may accidentally mislead some into thinking

140

that this stage features intensity of affect, rather than heightened aliveness with others—which may be hushed as well as excited. So surprising and so steady is this lift, like the surge of the ocean beneath a craft, that many a person pauses at this level to see what is happening to him; Moses did so at the bush. So unaccountable is the feeding of live signals into the background of consciousness, at the lift stage, that it is like welcome and potent background music, setting the body to swaying and the mind to soaring (perhaps readiness for the lift experience makes background music so appealing to both young and old, however different the musical modes). The thought which may often accompany the lift, in any task or walk of life, seems a delighted and startled, "Here we go again —but where?"

The third stage of the high-play cycle appears to be a focus stage. Here energy and activity are tugged in a defined direction, which may be clarified by sharing, and by reflective comparison with the deep inward set, which it does not violate. At this focus stage Moses begins to sense that what is quickening within him at the psychedelic bush is not guidance to finding some lost sheep, there on Mount Horeb, but something about finding the lost people of the Hebrews. Yet the focus is not necessarily upon outward events and activities, for it may come as a quickening to love, to endure, to pray, to humble oneself, to repent of one's evil. It would be mistaken to conceive this focus as being taken over, for such imagery better fits the action of the compensatory unconscious than it does the full quickening of high play with the One. A kind of heightening of personhood appears to go on, sensitizing the individual to whatever is needed of him for his fellows, and prompting him to wake up to present reality—often at this stage including the reality of his own mercilessly exposed evil. The biblical language of being "called" by the One is not inappropriate for the focus stage, provided that the process be not conceived too literally, and the call be understood as a beckoning to be, just as readily as to do or to know. If such a call is answered by a sturdy and tempered ego, pledged to author productivity with other creators, then the next stage may appear. If not, the action subsides, and the energy and quality of high play aliveness disappears to wait for another day, or slips into low play where the game is more confined and the pressures from within more grim and compensatory.

If the specific focus is found and welcomed by conscious choice, then the "on" state may develop. For a time, action comes effortlessly and fittingly. Other people are found and met in their real force and character—even by strangers who glance at each other in a grocery store. Skills at daily tasks are marshaled in elegance and grace, in good timing. Ego and nonego currents in the psyche seem to meet in a dance of forces which appears equal to any task or burden. If the uses made of the "on" stage of co-creating are constructive and taxing, and do not put the person at war with his best self, then the stage may endure for a time, perhaps even for days or a week or so. Usually, however, the stage is more temporary, leaving only promising traces on the day following its appearance. The "on" stage is so startling, and yields such confidence and elation, that many a person entering it succumbs to inflation, allowing whatever human quality is being aroused within him to swell to godlike proportions—as did Stubb's unconscious at the time of his eating his freshly caught whale steak. Such hubris soon brings forth from the unconscious its own compensatory reproach and loss of potency, made more embarrassing by the inward certitude —such as that of shorn Samson—that the powers of being and knowing and loving were nevertheless present in an "on" state, for a time. How the "on" gifts are shared with the like-minded, and in what kinds of service to others, contributes much to determining whether the cycle of high-play stages moves yet higher or stops here. Moses is "on" with Pharaoh, and again at the Red Sea. But his way is lonely in the Sinai desert, even in the midst of his people; when he finds he cannot share his altered vision and purpose with them, he breaks a set of mountaintop tablets in dismay.

The stage which next follows, if the action of the "on" level has been carried forward under a set for high play in which others join, is a kind of kickover effect. It is as unnerving as it is also rare. Often it comes as a flash of insight or joy, or a burst of strength—such as blind Samson knew at the end; or there arrives an unexpected level of skill beyond even that of the "on" stage, perhaps with a Zen readiness to take on whatever comes from any quarter, or a Cayce plunge into realms of unknowns made suddenly clear. This kickover stage, unlike that of the "on" time, cannot be described as less than a gift from beyond the ego, and from beyond the personal levels of the unconscious; its characteristic content is some direct awareness of the divine at work with man. While it uses compensatory material, and material from the fire-ringed circle and beyond, it is so refreshing and autonomous in its turns and potencies and melting joys that the response of the thoughtful man is to say that he has been met—as William James put it—by More than himself. He may call it his daimon, as did Socrates, or the action of Krishna, or the Ancient of Days, or the answering of nameless Nirvana to the Buddha nature within. In the Cayce view, the puzzling, astonishing effects of this stage came from the Spirit of God, often specifically known as the Christ Spirit, seeking "its own" within the soul of man. At the kickover stage, singers sing notes which they cannot reach, demonstrators are prepared to die without bitterness, and a housewife ending a session of LSD in love finds her husband and the One. To be sure, the kickover may not yield outward action at the moment; it may seem only to loosen much-needed tears, or contagious deep laughter—though these may prove only the beginning of its effects. It may provide transfixing assurance that the God-delighting soul disports itself in mildness of glee, just below and within all games of high play. The temptation to inflation at this stage is now doubled, if not stronger, and fanaticism or selfish authority hover near to that true authoring which gives others ground on which to take their tallest stands. Entering this stage of blessed being, though briefly and sometimes in company of pain, one may there-after force the meaning of his life into the wrong frame-work, and set about chasing his white whale with demonic force. Yet the kickover is likely to be so strong and so good, compared with even the best of the "on" states, that the journeyer into altered states finds it difficult to be negative or destructive so long as the effect is present —an effect which he may be quite willing to describe as being "filled with the Spirit." Fortunately, the kickover stage in itself does not seem to last many hours, and usually not more than minutes to an hour and a half, so that the temptation to misuse it or overanalyze it is less-ened. But even Moses slips once from high play to low play, in the midst of an altered mind state, and tradition tells that it cost him the privilege of entering the Promised Land with his people. He found, as others have reported of the kickover time, that forces were at work which af-fected not only his creativity but that of others all around him, including his enemies in battle; as others have, he mistook these forces for his own potency rather than the doing of the One Force.

If each stage of the cycle of high play has been re-ceived and answered responsibly by commitments and actions of the ego, and shared with others, then the final stage of release and readiness may proceed. The work of this stage is partly a cleansing and refreshing action, ex-tending throughout the body and mind; it takes the cramp out of the life style, and offers an equanimity of forgiving and accepting others which is as unforgettable as it is im-possible to contrive. As if some inner chemical had washed clean the springs of motive (which Cayce said was in fact the case, in the cleansing of endocrine glands), this final stage makes it difficult for those who enter it to be mean or petty, at least for a time. And if the entire undrugged cycle, rare as it is, be repeated often enough, then the entire dynamics of the person appear to undergo change which makes the release and readiness enduring and vital. Force is still there in the formerly angry person, but now that force shows itself as boldness, courage, nerve, and the brass to break down another's crippling defenses. Tenderness is still there for the person formerly swept by waves of low-play lust to consume others, but increasingly the passionate tenderness becomes sensitity, honest caring, ecstatic abandon, and the delight in maleness and femaleness which so refreshes those who have lost their flavor. In the Cayce view, such transmuting action from the high play cycle was authentic, not delusory, and was precisely what men of faith called the unearned gift of "grace" from God. The afterglow of the final stage is typically poised and ready peace, as of the momentarily sheathed silver-handled sword, which may yet cause pain to bearer and others, rather than the pleasant euphoria which accompanies the "on" state. With the peace, however, comes a peculiar readiness; there seems tucked away in the back of the mind a sense of greater inventiveness than before, which assures that something helpful will turn up, at the next time of need. There is also, in the readiness, a sense of direction about one's life, even though that direction may not yet be verbalized. And not surprisingly, the other person's inventiveness and proper, destined direction seem also perceived more clearly than before. In this afterstage of the cycle, it does not pass comprehension that good could come out of anyone's seeming evil. The soon-to-die Moses, blessing his people, tells them to send for no saviors, and the dying Buddha says the same. Both appear to have long since learned what there is to trust in everyman, once he chooses high play as a co-creator with his fellows and the One who created all.

Reviewing these stages—of disorientation lift, focus, coming on, kickover, and cleansed readiness—more than one person will be inclined to observe that all of this is merely sexual activity writ large. Perhaps, he will say, Freud described such high-play turning on in the first place, and orgasm is microcosm of everything important. Surely sexual experience may be found to accompany, pace, and express stage upon stage of high play, for sexual experience can be full loving, and what high play exceeds love? But on the other hand, those who think that the stages of heightened creativity just described are merely attenuated passion are due for a shock when they enter its higher levels.

For while the full cycle of stages of high play is indeed an experience, occurring to individuals as a series of events in time, its peculiar nature is not felt as "an experience" —as a thrill, as a pleasure to be consumed, as a series of sensations to be heightened. As this cycle is discovered and cultivated, it is apprehended rather as a *circuit,* a *closure,* a *coming into relationship*—with others, with the universe, with one's best self, with the One which has no second. Exactly this sense was conveyed by the prayer which Cayce urged hundreds upon hundreds of his counselees to formulate in their own words, and to use so often that it became their living daily intent: "Lord, let me be a *channel of blessings* to others, this day." Any quest for intensities and colors of experiences in altered states pales before the felt quality of this incredibly good closure; that is why the term "cool" so aptly describes those at home in, or wanting to be at home in, the undrugged cycle of fullest high play. With regard to the interesting boggling of consciousness, with regard to the mounting and heaving of feelings and perceptions and states and emotions, they become in time alertly unanxious. Not insensitive, or ungrateful, and certainly not incapable of wild joy. But equably unanxious. Climax is not the point. Closure of a circuit is the point. Becoming a channel for and with the One is the point. This turning on is a turning about and taking on, not just quivering or marveling. Seeking the turning on of high play as one more novelty in an overstimulated life will only stunt it or shut it off, as those who have brushed against it and lost it can testify, when to their dismay they found that they could not repeat their experiences won in autointoxication or drug taking.

Is the undrugged quickening of high play always safe? Surely not safer than the human mind and heart. Like any other altering of consciousness, it is profoundly affected by stress and set, by setting and shutoff, by sharing and serving. That undrugged greatness may falter even

146

at the time of exalted stature and co-creating service is no surprise to readers of either Moses or Melville. Indeed, the crash of those who have been lifted up is often noisier than the crash of those who played it safe. Yet for those who have traversed its startling stages, the undrugged quickening remains a breath-stopping adventure in aliveness with others, suggesting the truth in Cayce's claim that the unseen partner of this game is no less than the One.

Because the undrugged cycle of high play relies on the self-quickening of the total mind, answering to the needs of others, and steered by the ever-strengthened ego, it is free of the built-in handicaps of autointoxication and drug ingesting alike. But it has its own shortcoming. Since the name of this game is awakening, it often requires waiting, and waiting some more, for the next full arousal of delighted becoming with others, even when the individual ego is doggedly active in the best it knows. The undrugged venture is often painfully slow. Are there activities which might free it to move more swiftly towards the optimums of all players, in Woodstock, Washington, and whaling alike?

Five activities which turn attention inward, giving the lead to the unconscious, deserve attention alongside five activities which turn attention outward, giving the lead to consciousness. Together, these two kinds of efforts may constitute a balanced program to clear a channel for that turning on which is high play, at the top of the "normal forces" of each player.

Part II

FIVE INWARD APPROACHES
TO HIGH PLAY

CHAPTER FIVE

FASTING AND MEDITATION

Fasting

Edgar Cayce was finishing a three-day fast. In recent weeks he had grown increasingly grumpy, irritable. He had wondered aloud whether continuing his strange prayer-induced trances was worth the effort. It was now several years since the Depression had brought on the collapse of the spacious and well-staffed Cayce hospital which had been his life's dream: a place where trained physicians could conduct the wide range of therapies which his readings prescribed. Now he could see that the hospital might never again be developed in his lifetime. And he could see that prospects were equally dim for reopening Atlantic University, sparked by his work and off to such a good start under the presidency of a professor who had been Republican candidate for governor of Virginia—until the Depression emptied the classrooms, dispersed the faculty, and halted the football games, yearbook, and research on his readings.

His trances were still yielding sound medical, vocational, and business counsel, or so people told him. Yet even his readings had seemed a bit wooden and mechanical lately, limited to the bare facts of each case put before him in his altered state. Then there had come a dream which suggested that he should fast, as he had in days gone by. The reading which he had sought on the dream urged him to take the suggestion seriously. So for three days he had not eaten, but dressed in good clean clothes each day and gone out to fish and pray, returning to his study for quiet times with the Bible, which he knew largely by heart after these many years of studying it.

Now the fast was over, and it was time to go back to work—if going unconscious could properly be called work. Twice a day he must seek in trance both factual information and deeper personal guidance for individuals often hundreds of miles away, most of whom he had never seen. He must steer them to physicians who could cure them, to schools where they might study, to businesses where they could work, to communities where they could live and serve, and to study groups and churches where they could share their pilgrimage Godward. He knew that he could expect warm appreciation from many whom he helped (often including a photograph which they would send him to mount with the hundreds already on the wall of his study). And he could expect a small but steady stream of investigators, such as those who had come from Harvard and elsewhere in the past, always urging him to continue, after they had studied him at work. Yet recently he had been asking himself whether his was a living which a man could rightly perform before his two growing sons. And he had been wondering whether his was the living which he owed to his bright and lovely wife, who had worked so long with him to develop the photographic studios they had given up.

Yet now that the fast was over, it proved to have its way with him, as always. Nothing of his circumstances changed, but soon he was in ridiculously good spirits, teasing his secretary and welcoming visiting friends. His trance sessions took a jump towards their best levels; they began to offer not only full detail on the cases offered to him, but to break into unexpected discourses on the nature of a disease being diagnosed, or on the customs of the ancient Romans or Chinese, or on the events in Europe which would soon culminate in a World War. Whenever he did such optimum work, he was told, he would simply read off the questions held by his wife on a typed sheet of paper, and would readily correct the spelling of medical terms by his secretary taking shorthand across the room, though all the time he lay unconscious with his eyes covered from the cheery sunlight of his study. At such times of the best of his "normal forces," his trances would sometimes offer breath-taking sketches of the human drama, reaching from original creation to a distant time when all souls who chose to do so would be conscious companions with God in daily co-creating the universe.

But at times such as this he knew without being told that he was "on." Whether in or out of his strange altered state, he felt within him the same sunny spirit, the same loving patience, the same abounding goodwill, which often seemed to melt people while they listened to his trances, and made them sure that the same Cayce spoke when awake as when unconscious.

The process of fasting to which Cayce was turned by his dream was one of the oldest and most widespread practices for altering consciousness by chemical means: a kind of drug taking in reverse, to achieve mind-altering effects upon the bloodstream. Muslim faith has had its month of Ramadan, during which believers fast from dawn to dark each day, starting and stopping when they could barely distinguish a white thread from a black. Primitive cultures have had their mind-altering fasts, such as the vision-seeking totem fasts of the American Plains Indians, extending for as long as two weeks of solitary vigil. The shaman figures of Tibet, of the Arctic, of steaming Africa, each have had their periods of fasting to change consciousness and transact business with unseen holy powers. India's use of fasts to alter the mind had extended far back beyond the Buddha's famed excesses of fasting before his enlightenment, as well as reaching into modern times when Gandhi sought peace for his people by fasting to alter his consciousness and their goodwill. The more Apollonian or serene of the Hellenistic mystery cults also had their fasts, and Christianity had moved with ease among their followers, by drawing on its Jewish heritage of fasting by prophets, priests, and kings alike—a fasting held by them in restraint which later Christian monastics did not always observe.

The original psychedelic drug of the human family may have been the blood chemistry produced by halting food and drink under the gentle but firm pressure of a high set. Historically, such fasting has been directed fasting, joining devotion to the divine with the fluidizing effects of the abstinence; the pioneers of altered consciousness in many cultures apparently discovered early that while fasting by itself may help to unlock the mind, other elements will determine where the mind goes and stays after it is unlocked. Historically, too, fasting has been presented as dangerous. The special danger does not seem to be its threat to health, though of course there are times when illness or the necessity for strenuous labor suggests avoiding a fast—just as there are other times when fasting with high purpose seems to speed cure of illness, or to make certain labors more efficient. The danger in fasting lies rather in the vulnerability of the mind to stress from negative emotions while the body is registering its initial displeasure at not being fed. Especially when fasting is first attempted, and more so when it is tried without group companionship in graceful and peaceful surroundings, fasting produces tendencies to troubled stirrings and dark moods while the organism adjusts to its new state. If the mind is not well-directed—though gently directed—toward the highest values during times of abstinence, it may easily settle into self-pity, or black angry moods, or corrosive sexual fantasies. To be sure, pity or anger or desire may be exactly the kind of vital drive which an individual needs—in order to balance and renew his life; such feelings may spring forth naturally from the compensatory level of the unconscious when fasting loosens the tight grip of consciousness. But in order for such energies to be integrated into new personhood, where the opposites of nature and culture reach vital reconciliation, the altered mind needs to come under the sway of what Cayce sometimes called the "other self," the individuality of the soul, as well as under the sway of the answering One.

Effective fasting for altered consciousness, then, is directed fasting, as the Cayce trance source always counseled. Not eating or drinking accomplishes little by itself, although there are times when fasting is bracing for the person who chooses to keep so busy as to forgo nourishment. The best fasting is undertaken in a set of high play. It may be undertaken in order to prepare for some approaching task or decision or relationship which needs that full openness and engagement and spontaneity which make men co-creators. Or directed fasting, done in conscious awareness of the One, may be sought to handle heavy personal strain, as from shock of grief or broken dreams. It may also be undertaken to cleanse and unify the whole complex sprawling body of one's personhood, so that he may approach whatever next befalls him in collected wits and swinging spirits; such fasting is part of many a traditional retreat. Or the fasting may be taken up when reason and strength and the rest of conscious resources fail, in time of illness or calamity or great opportunity, so that one must kneel to seek resources which he surmises are available to him, but upon which he does not ordinarily draw so large a check; presumably Jesus meant such fasting when he explained to his disciples who had failed to heal an epileptic: This kind of thing comes out only by prayer and fasting.

Because fasting is so arbitrary, devoid of the glamors of taking exotic drugs, and out of phase with so much of each day's coddling, nesting, feeding, garbing, arousing, and diverting of the body, fasting easily becomes somber, and may slip into masochism. The Buddha warned explicitly of such extremes when he counseled instead the Middle Path; and Jesus insisted that those who fast for altered consciousness do so with a warm spirit and countenance, saying nothing to advertise their hardship or add to the force of stress. Setting can aid in avoiding extremes in fasting when it includes the felicity of fasting with a like-minded group. Members of such a group find times when they do not want to talk, while under the spell of far-inward stirrings. But they also find times when it is refreshing for them to talk, or to hike, or to listen to music, or to read aloud as monastics have done, or to keep times of intercession for others. A spirit of teasing, some of it about food and not a little about any tendencies to drawn faces, may contribute the signaling and sharing which keeps altered minds moving towards their best levels, especially if there be times of improvised fun and clowning, and improvised group celebration—like that of the Kansas City young people who ended their group fast by communion in no impiety with coke and potato chips, as the blood and body of their Lord. A group which meets for a seminar or workshop lasting through a weekend or week offers a promising vehicle for a shared fast, made even more valuable when not every group in the same seminar or workshop chooses to fast with them. Later, groups and families which have covenanted for high play with the Creative Forces can fast effectively by keeping the same time, even when apart.

During a fast, there are individual instruments and vehicles of setting which may help to keep consciousness moving towards its optimums. Photographs of those well-loved and respected (such photos as those the psychologist used in his LSD session with the housewife, and those Cayce kept on the wall above the place where he prayed and spoke in trance); cherished paintings; music which lifts and unfolds in form; flowers or leaves or a hillside view which reveals Nature's unruffled becoming; poetry; and passages of scripture from East and West—each can offer resources for setting and inward signaling, as well

156

as for sharing with others, among which thoughtful seekers may find their way. And if the fasting person makes his own imaginative forms by devising music or by sketching, by writing out thoughts which seem to unravel themselves, by working out interpretations of his dreams or of puzzling periods in his life, he can give his fasting the best of creative direction without that forcing which too easily brings on black moods. Indeed, fasting offers a unique laboratory where an individual may test out what is productive for him, whenever he needs the inward peace and ultimate grounding which Ishmael touched in the center of the herd of whales, and which Jesus counseled in prayer to accompany fasting. Later, in whatever nonfasting activity the person seeks to let high play find its way, he may turn again to the songs and signs, the sights and insights, the memories and hopes, the reading and gardening, the puzzling and praying, which he found gave illumination and bursts of joy to his fasting. These will be found to be the same resources for him to use to prepare to meditate, or to aid his dream study, or to work on an invention, or to set out to love the unlovely. Fasting, with its chemically altered states which do not drastically disrupt the self-regulating shutoffs of the psyche, offers the small voyage where one may try out the harpoons, oars, flags, chanties, and even the crews, which may turn any of his whaling towards high play.

To set the body using its own means for shutting off normal consciousness, and starting up altered consciousness, it is necessary to fast long enough, usually more than twenty-four hours. Such a time span allows the body metabolism to reverse its handling of blood sugar, contributing new contents to the bloodstream which meet those endocrine secretions stimulated by the direction given to the fasting. A minimum period might begin after the evening meal and continue until the eating of breakfast, or break fast, two mornings later. Not a great deal longer seems necessary to get started, though individuals need to explore their own rhythms and lengths of fasting. Crash programs and dramatic excesses do not appear to enhance fasting, since they produce unwelcome stresses which hamper the easy movement of high play through its cycles; setting out to fast for a week at the start accomplishes little. And fasting for the secondary gain of losing weight only confuses the mental set by calling fresh attention to the ever-demanding body. That fasting which seems to offer choicest fruit of altered consciousness, apart from the more limited fast periods and practices in Ramadan and Lent (which may be as significant symbolically as chemically), is fasting repeated often enough so that the body gets used to the process. In time, the body itself may signal a readiness for fasting, whether seasonally or more often—perhaps under the impetus of those times of truth and transition when the mind seeks to be psychedelic on its own initiative.

How nervously most moderns tend their bodies may be noted in the question, often asked, of whether the body needs to be given water or juices or snacks, as assurance it will not expire. Since the physiological gain in fasting is partly that of diverting energies from the lengthy alimentary canal, with its busywork of shipping-processing-packaging-delivering, complete fasting from food and drink offers maximum rewards, except in those rare cases when a physician would order otherwise, or in very long fasts. And since part of the exhilaration and release of consciousness in fasting comes from the set which clarifies who or what is in charge of an individual life—whether the body or some other center of being—there is merit in taking the body into quiet partnership for this adventure, by refraining from signaling anxiety to it in little sips and snacks. Many a body, like a pampered pet, seems after a time delighted to be set free to roam far fields, dropping the tight routines of feeding. And when the time comes for risking altered consciousness without the aid of fasting, as when one must enter without reservations into a grave marital struggle, or must fashion for community action a program so original as to get results without polarizing opponents, or must enter into morning meditation in a noisy household, that body which has moved about freely

158

in the unfed state may find its way more surely, because of its previous workouts in special body chemistries of fasting for high play.

Waxy mobility appears early in a time of fasting, signaling new ways of thinking which may follow. The usually restless and stirring physical frame may be put somewhere and left there. During a fast directed toward high play with one's fellows and the rest of the Creative Forces, one may cup his chin in his hand and find it there an hour later—not through cramp but through quiet absorption, as every vital energy normally pledged to digestion is released to work out the chemistry of altered consciousness (which may be the same unknown chemistry that LSD so abruptly triggers). At the same time, the mind can also be placed on a thought and left there. The tempo of mental life changes, offering less rattling around among sensations and perceptions, so that deeper inward grooves of meaning may be cut. Further, the logic of reflection begins to change. Where normal waking consciousness reports events which stream past like boxcars on a freight train, reading off signals to alert the psyche for action, the typical process in fasting is one of contemplation. Consciousness operates in depth, as when a strong microscope is slowly turned to focus upon successive layers in one small slide. The special identity of a loved one, the force of an heroic life, the absurd mysteries of forgiveness, the happy chatter of a child, the balanced weight of justice, the beauty of the divine which is sung in a psalm—whatever the mind is placed upon which is congruent with an individual's true inner set and concerns, this the fasting consciousness seems able to hold and unfold.

Above all, the tensions of values which need reconciling in one's life, and the creative ground for such reconciling, offer themselves for thought during a fast. Many a quarrel is worked out towards peace, or the outline for a difficult paper sketched, or company hiring policy reshaped, when those who fast put their minds to concerns where tense low play has signaled that some form of valued high play awaits release. Such problem solving, during and after

159

fasting, is not dissociative trickery done with the mind. The effort to be creative, to gain insight, to stand quietly before the reality of a situation, must be made in a set which allows for the Surpriser, for the One who was shaping all games before the players were called forth. Otherwise the deep contemplation in fasting becomes graceless fixation, as the force of having startled the body with a new regime is met and directed by the force of trying to have one's own way, and only that, in a problem taken up while fasting.

Fasting without celebration is a meal without wine, a greeting without an embrace, an interrupted song. A group which has fasted needs to tell tales of its people and its tradition, to recall group memories, to savor the identity of members; this is its work of sharing, to advance the reorientation of consciousness. An individual who has fasted alone needs, during his fast, to let go and be himself, glad for whatever life has called forth in him; he needs to enact his gladness in dance or speech aloud, if he can manage these without unduly startling his neighbors. There seems to be a cramp of soul to be freed in fasting through a mighty stretch of the goodwill muscles of mind and heart. The one who is fasting may also want to venture service, so valuable in any altering of consciousness, even by such simple tasks as writing a letter, or sewing at the place of another's holey heels, or repairing an electric socket to bring more light into a shadowed world. Or he may transact business at last with the One who is reputed to have eyes too pure to behold evil; he may find that holding his evil fearlessly before the Face, in confession, acts to disclose at once how he may begin to draw strength and judgment from the compost of that evil.

As most historic cultures have indicated by traditions and exercises, there are other kinds of meaningful fasting than abstention from food and drink. Whenever a basic routine is broken, a long-standing style changed, firmly but without violence or anxiety, a shock to the nervous system follows which may be used to produce endocrine

160

Club Cocktails. They go where you go.

Club Cocktails are ready to drink
real cocktails.
Hardstuff.
The Whiskey Sours are delicious. Ditto
the Daiquiris, Martinis and all of the 8
other Club Cocktails.
3 fresh drinks per pop-top, quick-chill can.
Don't forget the straws.

Now that you have a book for the weekend, we can give you a weekend for the book.

Bermuda, Puerto Rico, Jamaica, the Caribbean, Miami, Mexico at weekend-sized prices. Call us or your travel agent.

 EASTERN The Wings of Man.

and other chemistries which unlock and relock the mind for high play.

Fasting from speech, whether through a meal or overnight or on an entire weekend, offers its own adventures, if it is undertaken not in denial but in discovery; the goal should not be glum silence, but searching for those clarities of thought, those nuances of concern, those felicities of phrase, which ordinary speech often clouds rather than expresses. Fasting even from thought, that internal speech, is the method of meditation, to be examined below. Fasting from particular speech usages, such as the constant half-conscious use of I-me-mine for attention, may offer its own aid to focusing attentively and imaginatively on other people in true play. Fasting from the jargon of a faith, or from psychoanalytic or hippie or establishment jargon, may offer its own nudges to clearer and truer thought, by demanding considered meanings, and attention to what others understand or can use, in place of uttering reflex quotes. And even more useful and disorienting for high play is the effort to fast from negative talk and negative thoughts about other people, for a period of self-directed or group-directed discipline. To be effective, however, such fasting in co-creating high play must be undertaken in order to say and to think, instead, those things which are constructive and helpful, though sensibly discriminating. For the constant peril in seeking to alter consciousness by altering an activity is focusing on the undesirable rather than on the practice of the desirable. To make this mistake is to assure the unwanted result that consciousness will anxiously fill with the very contents it is told to avoid. Only high play drives out low play.

Vacations may allow mind-altering fasting from routines, when undertaken as playful adventure, rather than as more crisis and craving. So, too, sexual fasting, or fasting from work or study or money or the social whirl, may contribute to prized altering of consciousness, if undertaken to achieve alert, co-creating originality in other periods of exactly the same activities. Self-denial is not the point in fasting, though self-denial may be highly relevant to carrying out the chosen ideals of one's life. The only self which needs to be denied in fasting is—as has already been suggested in the discussion of stress—the self-denying, self-belittling, self-contradicting, self-doubting self. The person taking such stances of selfhood creates dangerous compensatory currents below the surface of his consciousness. But even negative selfhood is best denied in the accident of filling consciousness with the delighted sense of the disporting soul which is the hallmark of all effective fasting—as Ishmael found when suddenly he must fast from fishing, in the center of the whale armada.

Not a few modern encounter groups have reinvented old practices of fasting from particular senses by simulating blindness or deafness, thereby discovering from touch and the orchestration of kinetic senses how the universe seems to play itself forth unendingly into consciousness when allowed to do so. Extended sessions of group nudity may have their own impact to unlock consciousness from its usual tight moorings, when these sessions are handled as fasting from the stereotyped trappings and defenses signaled by clothes and their associated roles, rather than given over to the heightened sexual stimulus which almost inevitably takes over nudity in a culture which features autointoxication. In such fasting, well prepared by the development of a group covenant in long hours of sharing, the woman who has thought her beauty hopelessly marred by breast removal may find that others still rejoice in her lovely grace. And the man who has felt himself awed by men of imposing physiques may find he has been struggling symbolically with his own father, and thus with his own overbearing conscience, when he takes his place among the naked and harmless men and women of the venture in purposeful high play. In a sharply contrasting activity, fasting from usual taboos about the dead, when a group spends several quiet hours with a corpse, allows the loosing of yet other habitual controls on consciousness, so that the mind may alter itself under the weight of the presence of the body lying on the line between here and hereafter. This was the fasting counseled in the small but penetrating book of the Israelites called Ecclesiastes, as it was of Buddhism elsewhere.

When attempted not in violence but in wonder, and sought in the effort to come alive, to come awake for the next full-sensed encounter with a person or a tune or a pup, all such selective fasting may bring its own rewards. Like drug taking, which fasting greatly resembles except that it relies on the body's own self-regulating chemistry and shutoffs, fasting says a quiet no to all autointoxication. For those who have wondered whether all labor is belaboring, whether all playing is panting, whether all true existing is emoting, whether covetous crisis and craving are the whole story of cross and crown, of bo tree and Buddhahood, the quiet and sly delight of the human spirit set free in fasting may come as a refreshing breeze. For them, both during and after fasting, colors may dance in new hues, children's faces become the Unseeable Face, a good story tell as much as any scripture, and the next phone call offer a conversation with an Ishmael.

Queequeg, the appealing South Sea cannibal of *Moby Dick,* sits motionless as he fasts for a day and a night in a cold room of a Nantucket inn. Atop his head he balances his little god figurine, placed precisely where another faith prescribes the action of tongues of fire and stipulates that hands be laid on for baptism, ordination, and healing. Ishmael, the ecumenical Presbyterian, has been considerate of Queequeg's previous rites, but this unearthly quiet rite, giving up all steaming chowders of clam and cod, upsets him a bit. He lectures his harpooning cannibal friend on the extravagances of what he calls his Ramadan, borrowing the term from Muslim fasting. But Queequeg is not the only one who fasts in this tale of whales. Ahab drives himself through not one but many sleepless and foodless days and nights, staring moodily across the waters for some glimpse of his adversary beast. His mind spins, his thoughts roam so far as even to bring him what seem memories of having lived on earth before. But always he circles back to his primal set of revenge. Upon his head there is no figurine, and he has no thought of braided thorns upon the head of Another. His thought is on the outrage of his whale-severed leg and his whale-insulted manhood. When his consciousness alters from his fasting, it turns upon itself, and drives to eerie depths equaled only by the deeps of the impersonal sea, and by the alien immensity of the white whale, both of which Ahab meets for his final undoing.

Meditation

A mother of four goes up a hillside to an outdoor chapel of stone ledges. She is at a lakeside retreat on an extended weekend where more than a dozen couples are gathered to study, to work in small groups, to try their hands at ventures in the arts, to share their nightly dreams, and to do the judo of high play in discussions together on the subject of "Manhood and Womanhood." Now it is time for the corporate morning meditation on this third day of their weekend. As she climbs the path up the hill, she is joined by an old friend, Hugh Lynn Cayce—a man seasoned in meditation. "When are you going to start speaking up?" he teases her. He knows that she is shy, and often overshadowed by her doctor husband. He knows, too, that the years of homemaking have taught her more than she realizes, some of which he has seen in her paintings. "I think it's time now," he adds. "Come sit by me."

The meditation begins simply, with verses from the Psalms made into an affirmation of high intent with the Coming One, which the group repeats before it falls silent. Then an hour passes, while nothing is said. The spring sun beats down on those quiet ones, some with heads bowed and some with faces up. As the time draws to a close, the shy mother weeps softly. She is not sad but undone by joy. Something inside her has melted and moved. Something like the very sun has shone into every corner of her awareness, stopping all of her thought except wordless thankfulness. She is smiling in embarrassment as she rises to leave, for she cannot stop her weeping, now coming with little gasps of joy. "It's all right," she says to her companion, and she slips off into the woods. She knows what has happened to her. Did not Psalm 46, which they had used in their affirmation, say that there was ever a river, the streams of which would gladden the citylike realms of consciousness?

She is never the same again. Beginning that very day, she enters fully into the remaining discussion sessions of the weekend and quietly takes a leadership role in the period for modern dance. Before long, she is guiding discussion groups which accompany an adult class back in her home community, and next she trains to become an adult educator. Soon she is leading adult classes in three cities at once. Like Hannah of old, who had her womb unstopped for a manchild in midlife by going on a pilgrimage and a retreat, this mother found herself quickened to a new birth. But her birth was to the masculine skills with words and ideas and leadership roles which she had always feared, yet which came in their season to grace and complete her womanhood, starting with that meditation on the hill.

Wherever meditation has been regularly practiced, in India's caves or Europe's cloisters, on China's mountains or in Japan's gardens, in Israel's synagogues or on Islam's sands, it has required a whole-souled turning of the being Godward. That the concept of the God so approached varies sharply from culture to culture, as well as from individual to individual, makes it evident that meditation is not chiefly conceptual. Thought is used to still thought by the Sufi and the Hassid, the yogin and the monk, the sage and the housewife. Symbol is used to exclude symbol, and feeling to step beyond feeling. The medieval Hebrew term for meditation was *devekuth,* clinging—which aptly suggests how in meditation thought may be used to hold in focus, but not to process, the Reality which is sought.

The outward manner of the meditating man so resembles that of the man at prayer that meditation and prayer are widely misunderstood as variants of the same process. But they are markedly different, as the trance-

165

speaking Edgar Cayce insisted—though he also reminded that they required each other for the fullest action of altered consciousness. In prayer, he said, the mind is filled with consciously willed intent and imagery, whether of praise or supplication or some other act. The screen of consciousness seems strewn with words, decorated with ikons, lit by colors of meaning from within. In prayer the human spirit mobilizes itself for willing partnership with the One in the play at hand, using prayer forms old and new, rehearsed and spontaneous. Consciousness builds an altar fire, lights candles. But in meditation the fire comes somehow from outside consciousness, as Pascal noted in the treasured scrap of paper sewn into his coat, telling of the time of tearful joy in holiness which had blazed one night for him. In meditation an action is recognized and welcomed by consciousness, but not thought up or intended into shape. Even when there is no fire, but only the glowing of the unseen spark of the divine within the one meditating, in response to the wind of the spirit which passes over it, consciousness only heeds, accepts, clings— but makes nothing happen. As Cayce so often suggested in his quiet discourses, meditation is getting out of the way of the divine action in man's body and being.

Many busy moderns find it passing comprehension that something important could transpire in their consciousness which was not initiated by their will and concentration. Yet those who have taken strong drugs may know the quality of being overtaken by meaning, rather than thinking it. So may others who have stood transfixed by the sea, or met a crisis through strength which seemed beyond their own.

Because the first contents which spill into consciousness, when discursive reflection is slowed, tend to be imagery from various layers of the unconscious, many mistakenly suppose—by analogy with experiences of drugs or other ecstasies—that meditation is flooding the mind with one or more symbols. Certainly one of the sweetest fruits after meditation may be the spontaneous emergence of a symbol which illuminates one's whole life, often by

166

coalescence of inner image with outer event or object. A memory of a perky bird may slip into phase with the dove of peace, and touch the life-giving, sky-wheeling dove of the spirit, as a symbol which follows meditation at greater or lesser length. But meditation is not birds. Insofar as symbols are present at all in the specific act of meditation—whether in the fabled and chanted Om symbol of the Hindu, or the "Yah" of the dervish who seeks to whirl his body and mind into ecstasy not of his own making, or the loved prayer of psalm or affirmation which joins the believer to his people and tradition in older Egypt or China or the modern West—the symbols are there to hold and still the mind, not to fill it. Attempts to aid meditation by visualizing or by feeling-arousal only slow the process, for they mix in flows from other levels of the unconscious, together with a flow whose origin is never fully fathomed by the consciousness bowed in meditation.

Perhaps the apt image of meditation is conception, as the trance-heightened Cayce suggested. Something very small is quickened to life, in its own way, with the aid of meditation. As the mind is stilled, a conception, an impregnation, an awakening occurs in the far recesses of the fire-ringed circle of individuality in the psyche. A growth is begun and nurtured which will come to its own term. If not aided by outward action and principled risk-taking, the total happening of meditation may be little more than a glow of goodwill occurring at a later encounter where the person finds himself able, for example, to drop his aggressiveness more easily than before. But if the new life secretly begun in meditation is supported by what the Buddha called right mindfulness, deed, speech, and vocation, through the graceful spirals of high-play creativity, then the consequence may be permanently changed consciousness.

Few are those who have not felt an inner tug to stand tall, to reach out in love, to speak the truth, at some moment of crisis or of lip-biting silence, whether in glancing at a newborn baby, in hearing a report of a political schism healed by inventive compromise, in reading a solid

167

biography, in noting a lilting musical performance, or in embracing someone after forgiveness of real hurts has just transpired. Meditation as conception is a sustained effort to allow such tugs a good term of pregnancy and timely birth, by preparing the person to be more than he ever was before.

To be sure, pregnancies develop unseen, and not every meditation has an outward sign or consequence at the time. But there is a term, a ripening, which follows from meditation as surely as any in Nature, though it may reserve itself for those who will submit to the slow, patient discipline of stilled, quenched, and focused thought which is no thought, but only holding ajar the door where the Unconditioned may enter. Those who have known bitterness, and found it slowly and permanently melted away through meditation, could speak of the process, as could those who have had a life style of manipulation which they found slowly and irrepressibly turned toward high play, through meditation which lets the human being become human, through an impregnation by the Other.

But the slow coming to term, through meditation, of some new richness and integrity of personhood, some new diversity which yet has unity, is not without encouragement along the way. The persistent effort to get out of the way for the Unseeable Light, the Noiseless Sound, the Unfashioned Seed, offers moments of awareness that something important is happening. Often, as with other modes of heightened creativity for which meditation prepares the way, there is an initial spinning, and restructuring of perspectives, as if a magnet were startling the needle of the mind into a new direction after pulling it loose from the old. Then there may follow the lift stage, the filling up, as if compressed laughter or bottled dance or distilled praise were being pumped into the body, straightening the spine and firming the frame for the next high play. If focusing comes, it is not at this point on a deed or a thought or a person (any of which may come later), but upon the Present One, the impossible White Whale which offers the soul glory, suddenly swimming very near and stopping all chatter or plans or memories. The "on" stage which may follow in meditation is typically the grace to let be, to let the One be the One, doing with the meditating person as it will, not by overwhelming him in gripping force as does unconscious imagery, but by undergirding him where he needs it, often to his surprise.

And the kickover effect in meditation, if it comes, slips past all analogies. It is silver shot into flesh and blood, light piercing light, delight disporting within delight. Something Not-self seems to answer and to leap ahead of the self. This full crowning moment has often been written about and sung in many tongues. At the meeting of person with Ground, of player and Third, of co-creator and Creator, there comes a flooding of consciousness with stillness so gentle and poised that the universe seems to stop on the point for its own soundless reckonings. And with the stillness, which brands the human spirit more surely than any word spoken or direction given, there comes a melting field of light, spreading itself easily over the entire field of awareness, sensed as the secret behind every cherished memory of good sunlight on the face. This is a light which cannot be inspected or directed, and in a way not even visually experienced, but only entered into. For at such times, when the person is in his Homeland and knows it, there is no weighing or measuring, but only taking up relationship with that which has given itself as the Light. When shortly the inward radiance seems to melt and flow like nectar across the mind and into the entire body, the words of the psalmist about such meditation seem appropriate: "Sweeter than honey, yea, than much fine honey." The quality encountered transcends senses, yielding only trembling nonsensual meaning. Purity, goodness, kindness, firmness, adventure, patience, run their brave colors into one white, and there is no craving; yet this primal happening has a joy which no other experience can quite reach, except as it reminds of this one, or contains a touch of it. Once having known the wonder of full meditation is always to want to return to it. But the desire is not to possess it so much as to be

169

graced by it, quickened without haste into more being, and more being-for-others.

As the inner flow recedes, tears and smiles may be found on the face, as in the thoughts behind it, but what can words offer? One is slow to leave the place of meditating, yet is not a prisoner of the time; for the gift received is felt as a gift of becoming which is now ready to happen, of treasure not to be held but released in action. The sharing and service which seem right, when meditation moves through its entire lighted path, are less words which may squeeze and lessen the event than action which may round it out into high play with the One who is always near. Especially does that action seem fitting which in any way takes the chains off a fellow human, so that he may step forth for right good whaling.

Work comes easily for some time after the mind-stopping be-in of full meditation, as do study and love, and also prayer. In all of these may be noted a remarkable boost to playfulness, to engaged co-creating with others, as though one had somewhere been baptized in the primal lava from which all worlds are made, and initiated into that becoming which calls all things into their best forms. Defenses are lowered and made serviceable: the veil of rationalization becomes a sturdy web of reasoning, and the retreat of regression becomes a sensitizing to the troubled withdrawals of others. One's familiar and bristling spears become pruning hooks, not by magic, but with ease which is greater than usual. There is a poise and general adventuresomeness which lead to asking for the next sailing date of a *Pequod*.

Are there dangers in meditation? If it is undertaken by a person split against himself, acting against his own good counsel and the counsel of those who love him, and if he is unwilling to risk closing that split, then this altered consciousness, like any other, may fling the person to levels and energies he does not want and cannot use, with the force of his stress. But bringing wounds, cracks, and flaws of personhood to be healed is appropriate business for wordless meditation with the One who makes all things

170

new, provided that the meditating person makes no advance stipulation of where he will block the new-making. There is danger if meditation be diverted into mere symbol mongering and visualization; such processes may draw upon powerful unconscious energies to lock in the mind on either chosen or unwanted symbols, until consciousness must make a mighty effort to free itself of fantasies through its own Caesarian section, as the stimulated psyche swells with images. If, further, the conception process of meditation be distorted by relishing of the meditation experience as experience, rather than marked by peaceful clinging to the Third which is the One in order to become a channel of blessings, then the consequence may be a dangerous intensity in some activity of the life. For, as many an ascetic textbook of older times will verify, immensely strong energies seem released by regular meditation. Not channeled into productive, taxing, and loving effort with others, these energies run loose. The resultant power drives, sex drives, or other monomanias only confirm the truth of Ahab's lot, when he opened his consciousness by wordless slow pacing of the decks of his ship, with intense concentration. He came to the doors of meditation before the awesome Visage. But he reduced the confrontation to one he could manage, with a whale, instead of clinging, clinging to the One—as finally Ishmael clings to the empty coffin which saves him.

If fasting surprises body and mind into fresh becomings, regular meditation cleanses and directs them for the helpful action of the high-play cycle in any activity of the daily round. To give some time in the morning, when energies are fresh, and in the night, when the concerns of the day drop away, to the strange old art of meditating is to keep emptying the inner conduits of the psyche of all blocks to the creativity which is next needed. Cayce urged such regular meditating for everyone, not as a pious exercise nor a leisure-time luxury, but as a necessity for the best of daily high play. The next act after meditating which requires high play may be offering a drink to a nondrinking friend who needs it this one time. It may be deciding to sell all and follow the sun with a rock band, or with a rocky band of investors in a chain of motels. It may be sensing the good thrust of a crowd at last ready to march for peace or justice without becoming inflamed or weary, and standing up to tell the crowd. It may be finding that the time to speak to a troubled friend is not yet, except in the whole-souled goodwill of a silent blessing. It may be in discovering the right tempo for a poem or a painting, a psalm or a pirouette, a palaver or a pounding. Whatever the next need for a quickening, a lift, a focus, a heightened and steady skill, a ridiculously useful inspiration, a dogged hanging in there, the work of meditation seems to be making the way ready. As an activity, meditation is not complete until the discharge into insight and action occurs.

What Queequeg thought while he meditated without moving for a day and a night, he does not tell, and Ishmael cannot guess. But Ishmael has his own intuitions of the nature of meditation when he reflects on the head of a whale. Coming directly up to that vast, wrinkled forehead, whose eyes are set at the sides and whose mouth is out of sight below, he confronts the stupefying in flesh, a mind-stopping incomprehensible bulk of becoming. Yet he notes that meeting a whale head-on in the sea is no time for mere musing or dissociating; too much is at hand in the all-excluding reality which here presents itself to the whaler. Consciousness must now be focused and knit and heightened as never before; the mind must be so collected that it can shortly step into its true greatness for the business which will follow. Ishmael finds a moment of truth in the sea which is not unlike the moment of truth for the undrugged mind, when it is lifted on a wave of grace in meditation to discover Who is there, with featureless lighted Face.

CHAPTER SIX

DREAM, REVERIE, AND LIFE FORM

Using Dreams

The school counselor's dream is absurdly simple. Yet as he tells it now to the other students in his graduate psychology class, he must stop to get hold of himself, so strongly does it affect him still. He did not intend recounting it to the class when he came that night, for there was so little of the dream to report. But during the evening other students have remarked on how peaceful and alert he looks. Finally, one student asks, during a discussion period, "John, what's got into you? You look like the Buddha, sitting there as though you had just awakened to the world. What's happening to you?" So he tells his dream.

The sun came up. That was all.

The dream affected him like no other he could recall. Slowly the sun came up, filling all horizons with light. As it moved, something moved within him, so that he was transfixed at the sight. He seemed to know, even in the dream, why primitives turned their faces to the sun in worship, and why the gospel with the same name as his spoke of the true Light that lights every man. The dream did not make him a sun worshiper, or a worshiper of anything new. He is not surprised, however, to learn from the class that devout Hindus have for centuries offered a morning prayer, the Gayatri, toward the sun. For since the dream his inner landscape will not grow dark. He feels infected with light, delighted with light. On the day after the dream, when his work at the school was as rushed and harassed as usual, he found himself working with unaccustomed ease, as though he were saying inside, "On all this the sun shines, too."

He finishes what he can say about his dream and the classroom falls silent. Finally a woman says softly, "My God, I would like a dream like that."

In the modern West, dreams are seen chiefly as containing symptoms of mental illness for a specialist to diagnose. But in other ages and places their work has been more highly valued. Chuang-tse of China used his dream of being a butterfly to give him a metaphor of waking life, and to suggest how close to normal consciousness are those altered states which flutter near to it. Greeks of the first century who needed healing of body went to the temple of Asclepius, where they sought a transformative dream encounter with the divine, while over the sleeping Persians and Egyptians of the same age hung a night sky full of dream portents. It was a dream vision before battle which led to the Christianizing of the Roman Empire, for better or for worse, just as a dream had several centuries earlier led the parents of the founder of the faith to flee unbridled state power in retreat to Egypt. As in Israel's history, including the dreams of the legendary patriarchs of Genesis and the able dream interpreters named Joseph and Daniel, so in the prehistory of preliterate tribes was dream guidance often highly valued. Among primitives a dream might serve as a signal to do battle or to stay home, as a sign of where the spirit of a departed ancestor had lighted or as an indicator of vocation or totem. Unlike dreams in the modern consulting room, the dreams of primitives often had more than individual standing; weighty and startling dreams might require ceremonial telling to the entire tribe in the middle of the night. As echoes of the adventures of the fathers of the tribe, celebrated in tale and song, dreams were prized as instruments for altering consciousness. To watch the sun rise in a dream, as the impersonal and unfailing life force given to all living things, was a more-than-personal happening.

From the perspective of the trance-counseling Cayce, dreams were an indispensable means for every man's self-knowledge and self-transformation, as well as for guidance in his daily affairs. As early as 1924, when Freud's claim that dreams were the royal road to the unconscious was not widely granted, Cayce was insisting that the person who ignored his dreams was a person without his full weight; to him, dreams were central business for modern Western man, who needed to complement his knowledge of the outer world with new knowledge of the inner world of mind and soul. Interpreting more than sixteen hundred dreams of seventy individuals over a period of twenty years, the trance-quickened Cayce showed exceptional skill and balance as a dream analyst, which has been reported in Sechrist's *Dreams, Your Magic Mirror* and in the present writer's two works, *Edgar Cayce on Dreams* and *Dreams in the Life of Prayer*. Indeed, there were some features of Cayce's dream counsel which were as incredible as his medical counsel or historical reporting; he showed that he could recall for dreamers all or parts of dreams which they had forgotten, could place the exact time of night when specific dreams occurred, could predict the content and time of night of certain dreams, and could correlate dream symbols with a fantastic array of information about the dreamer—including his physical health, his childhood, his present relationships, his business problems, his personality structure, his sex life, and even the events of his near future. Again and again, the trance-speaking Cayce showed why he could make the claim that no event of importance occurred to anyone which was not in some measure first previewed in a dream.

As Cayce worked with dreams, he traced their origin in the dreamer to three levels. Some dreams were, he said, somatic dreams, arising out of body needs in diet, exercise, balanced activities, or medical disabilities; a small proportion of these dreams were meaningless, reflecting disturbed blood chemistry, but most dreams which originated in the body deserved attention and interpretation as guides to better health. (In making this claim Cayce was tracing a direction of dream study in which modern dream research has only begun to move.) Many more dreams, Cayce reported from the vantage of his altered vision, were produced from the "subconscious" as it responded to conscious concerns of daily life, along lines of habit and life style and temperament which were the substructure of the personality. Some of these dreams were focused on solving problems of daily affairs, and many more were focused on building or balancing the person as a human being; the two functions at work in all dreaming were problem-solving and person-growing. To Cayce, a third source of dreams could also be traced, not only by him but by the careful student of dreams; this was the work of the "superconscious," which included both the individual's soul and the "universal" realms of the impersonal and the divine. Such dreams, which focused chiefly on growth of the individual, but also upon the essential processes of his co-creating with others, had a special character and force, and were often poetic or mythological in content. To do the work of such complex dreaming, in Cayce's view, the psyche used three meaningful kinds of contents which might be interpreted by any layman who studied his own dreams, not alone by specialists. There were literal representations of circumstances and events (what psychologists call "signs"); these were commonest in health dreams and dreams of daily affairs and problems, though they rarely occurred without some mixture of other kinds of dream contents. Then there were "emblems" or meta-phoric contents in dreams, where some human experience or object or activity stood in whole or part for another; in the Cayce view, most dreams were comprised of such practical and effective figures of dream speech. Finally, there were "symbols" (what psychologists call "true symbols"), whose meaning was rich and evocative, rather than precise; these were the substance of visionary dreams from the superconscious, and were what biblical dream interpreters had employed in the divination-by-dreams called Urim.

To the trance-sleeping Cayce, anyone who set out to do so could learn to recall his dreams, unless he were hiding something from his surface consciousness which he was unwilling to face. And anyone could learn to make useful sense of the trends and thrusts of his dreams, by study-ing them in series, and correlating them with events in his daily life, with structures and forces which he could dis-cover at work in his own personality and body, and with theories of human nature and growth before the One. By patiently coaching scores of individuals, some working to-gether in groups, Cayce showed in two decades of work on dreams that his claims were not extravagant, however unusual in his times.

The modern urbanite, whose knowledge of his dreams is limited to a few troublesome nightmares plus some be-wildering night dramas of illogical acts and unstable faces, finds it strange to imagine that dreams might work to alter the degree and direction of his consciousness in the direc-tion of high play. Yet the person with first hand experi-ence of drug-loosed imagery may recognize for himself that dream material works upon the mind much as does material of psychedelic trips with drugs; if he looks closely, he will often find the same themes, the same plots, the same people, the same objects, in his nightly dream productions as in his more extravagant drug-triggered productions. And he may observe for himself why dream researchers such as the present writer report that every useful state achieved in drug experiences may be found occurring to dreamers in spontaneous forms, paced and timed for the dreamer's needs by the self-regulating shut-offs of the sleeping psyche. However, he will need to remember that working with dreams is not free of all danger, simply because the mind and spirit of man are dangerous. Dream analysis may be used for escape from reality, for inflation with self-importance, and for manipulating others with supposed night messages about them. Especially for the young there is need for firm anchoring in the worlds of vocation and love and belonging, before intensive and prolonged attention is given to the underworld of dreams.

Each stage of the high-play cycle may be introduced, strengthened, and enriched by dreams, which leave their subtle effects on waking consciousness. The refreshingly disorienting action of the first level of high play comes so regularly in dreams that it may be predicted for anyone who works responsibly with his dreams. He may have a road map dream, laying out the terrain of his life and suggesting to him with force and clarity where he tends to go and where he might be better advised to go. Such a dream often comes to a man choosing between staying a salesman and risking further high play as a manager of salesmen; or it often comes to a woman who must choose between husband and lover. Commonly, at this level, the dreamer finds himself in a new wing or floor of a dwelling, feeling to his surprise that he has living space, qualities of personhood, which he has not even used. Or he may confront a dream demand for a rescue, a bold military feat, a steering of an auto or some celestial or nautical craft, and gain from the dream some clarity and confidence about the direction and quality of his life. He may see at this level of high play in dreams the face of someone whom he loves and respects, standing as an unexpected challenge to honor a value which he has forgotten in waking life. Often, in dreams, the disorienting action appears in making the low high and the high low, as the dreamer confronts a minority person and discovers what he has ignored or repressed within himself. The Buddha is reputed to have

178

seen in waking life, despite his father's anxious protective-ness, the famous four sights or Four Appearances which quickened him to journey after final Reality: a beggar, a sick man, a dead man, and a yogin. So each dreamer at this level may find his own four appearances to rouse him to new life, just as the image of a voyage led Ishmael to the whaling docks.

At the second level of the unintoxicated lift, the surpris-ing boldness and joy which wells up into a readiness for anything, dreams again offer typical contents. Of course, many such dreams are erotic, where the exciting union of man with maid quickens the pulse and potency of the dreamer; not to dream in these terms, and often and ad-venturously, would be strange indeed in the human ven-ture. But other buoyant dreams come as readily in the ways of knowledge or action as in the way of love and devotion, depending upon the dreamer's temperament, values, and development. One who has doubted his mental capacity may find himself in his dream speaking to a crowd on a difficult subject, and making rattling good sense. One who questions his own courage for action may find his dream self in the thick of battle, bouncing from blow to blow with magnificent unconcern as he carries the fray. In dreams of this level, waters may rise, plants break free of the staggering heaviness of earth, animals gallop or stalk playfully, and even unseen presences move like angels in and out of dream scenes, as the tug to be, the vital and building surge, arouses in the sleeper and carries over into his waking life.

As the focus level of high play emerges in dreams, it may draw sharp attention to the dreamer's evil, or to his smallness of spirit. Low play may be highlighted, from which new becomings must be set free. Out of Oedipus ties painfully revealed in dreams must be found the dreamer's choice for stalwart independence which gives others freedom to be themselves, rather than bound to him in office or school or church, as readily as in the family circle. Out of violence, tempered courage must be won, as dreams may show in slashing struggles which yield to

179

ceremonies of induction to manhood or womanhood, in long ago or modern scenes. Whales may be pitted against crews, automobiles against drivers, schools against students, as the goods and trophies of life are reset into proper perspective by dream challenges, rather than kept for autointoxicated coveting which violates the Mosaic Tenth Commandment. Or the dreamer at the focus level may find himself running from train to train, plane to plane, street to street, until he must make his stand and risk his neck—exactly as he needs to quit running and playing with possibilities in his daily life. Whisking the dreamer to far lands, dreams may beckon the dreamer, Moses-like, to try the untried in Egypt. Flinging him impossible tasks which he does with dispatch, they encourage him to trust his growing potency. Joining him to the warm flesh of another's body, they invite him to risk the demanding intimacy of real love, where all games must be played without external sanctions or destructive weapons, but only with needed bat and glove (each fully sexual images, and fully appropriate for high play).

The "on" stage of high play in dreams is woven freely into the focus stage, wherever dream challenges are met with potency to carry them off. Singing, digging, performing rites, developing theories, fasting, meditating, leading pickets—whatever the needed skill or sensitivity, the dreamer seems taught in his dreams by the best of tutors. Especially in dreams at this stage can he find the flash of spontaneous and accurate ESP about the hidden, or the distant, or the future, or the complex, which Cayce insisted was a potential for every "subconscious," and not reserved for specially gifted figures such as Cayce. The sex of unborn children, the face of a stranger not yet met, the price at which a product would sell effectively, the cause of a puzzling lover's quarrel, the dynamics of a coming accident, the ways of distant peoples, the nature of dying, the ineffable Holy Presence—whatever the dreamer could not find with his senses, yet truly needed for his growth in co-creating with others, might be found in dreams. But to reach such aid, the dreamer had to be living, said

Cayce, a productive life which could use the discoveries, and had to stretch every conscious resource in the direction of the answers which he sought in dreams; a busy and skilled consciousness was the best keeper of the wide-ranging subconscious and superconscious. At the "on" level, not only skill and information to meet daily challenges emerge, but life stances are affected—as when kosher Peter is shown in a dream that he may eat any meat and still glorify the God whom he has perceived. Patience, abounding goodwill, sobbing forgiveness, racy hijinks, the altered state of life beyond death, dramatic presentations of layers of the psyche as living tissue—with all such contents the dreams of the "on" level beckon the dreamer to high play.

But it is especially the kickover effect which makes some dreams remembered for years. In such dreams the dreamer is twice himself, as he seems met by that which aids him, changes him. The kickover may come in the stab of a pure shaft of color, it may be a melody, it may be a wind that rises, it may be the tall stone shaft of a cathedral in a city, it may be the lined face of someone dearly loved, it may be the steady gait of pounding down a path to reach what had seemed a hopeless goal. Somehow that thing happens which is second wind to the human spirit, the inexplicable gift which is only to be received, not coerced. The fearful woman is suddenly pregnant in the dream, and knows upon awakening that her selfhood will come to its full term; the work-frustrated man has a brilliant dream-spun idea of how to co-author his colleagues into their best selves. In these becomings more than "on" adventure is at hand. For in such dreams life shapes itself into its ultimate doubleness, into that bipolarity of soul and Creative Forces which is too often misread as player overwhelming player, or player possessing trophy, or man revenging himself on a whale. In dreams of the kickover stage the dreamer finds the very cosmos playing with him, answering him, calling him by name (indeed, as Cayce noted, it is just such calling by name which often marks these dreams). The night dramas of this level, rare as they

181

are, leave an invisible birthmark upon the selfhood of the dreamer. Those who have never taken fortunate drug trips to the far reaches of the mind and the not-mind, nor found themselves in an inner Homeland through suffering or through self-transcending labor with those loved, may suppose that the kickover effect, in dreams or in waking, is just business as usual, but a little better. It is not, as the melting and incredible dreams of this level can show when they unfold what Job found when struck dumb and wise by a vision and a voice, or what the walkers to Emmaus found when they stopped to break bread. To say that at the kickover level of high play God meets man while the dizzying Word becomes dancing flesh is already to say too much; for this God has already been man, and this man has always been God's. Life but touches life, spirit answers spirit, and the warm sun rises on the naked and lovely soul. If such must be told as man meeting woman, parent discovering child, Sinai journeyer receiving tablet, Gautama awakening to full-sensed bliss, or the cross pointing beyond itself to an empty tomb, then dreams of this level will use these symbols freely. But the business transacted in such dreams eludes final trapping, and no two of these dreams will be alike—except in convincing dreamers that they have slumbered through many of their days as well as their nights.

The final stage of the high-play cycle, the unfrightened readiness to try what must next be tried, may be found in the lingering afterglow of the best adventure dreams, which are the essence of co-creating play. Even as seeing a movie of a swashbuckling hero sets the young lad walking fences all the way home, and enables him to bear the dubious burden of doing dishes when he gets there; or seeing the movie of a sweeping heroine so fills the young girl with saucy, radiant confidence that she flirts all day with young and old, and can endure the trials of her homework—so those who dream at this level may find a steady and glad flow of being. Who needs defenses or revenge when dreams show that he can outduel pirates? And who needs sarcasm or ploys when dreams show that she can charm not only lovers but enemies? Such dream aid does not come, nor does it stay, apart from the struggles for insight, the hard choices, the risks, which other levels of dreaming foster. But the aid is never far in the wings of the dream stage for those who trust the high-play cycle and seek to live it out.

Stubb has a dream after a threat from Ahab. At the time of the threat and slur, Stubb is incensed and fires back testily, though Ahab glowers him down to his quarters. But in the dream Stubb encounters his own bristling tendencies when he sees his bared behind as though it were studded with marlin spikes. At the same time, he has a dream sense of being honored even by the threatened kick of such a man as Ahab. When he awakens and tells his dream to a shipmate, Stubb finds himself mellowed and less defensive toward tormented Ahab, and feeling better about himself. For like most dreams, this one offers a corrective aid to consciousness, stretching Stubb's responses to Ahab, and enriching Stubb's self-image with a sketch of his own evil and goodness seen together.

The Reverie Method

The group of a dozen men and women has just listened to a recording of a stately and key-climbing instrumental work by Wagner. As usual in their times of seeking autonomous inward visions by a reverie method, the group members have prepared themselves by study and discussion, and by a time of quiet attunement. Then they have imagined a starting scene suggested to them by their instructor-coach, and allowed the music to prompt upon the screens of their minds whatever spontaneously developed for each of them. These are active mid-life adults, leaders in the business, political, and arts life of their community; they are representatives of Catholic, Jewish, and Protestant traditions. Some have pioneered in sponsoring low-cost housing projects in their community of Virginia Beach, Virginia, and some have been active in black-white dialogue groups. Each Tuesday they have taken time out from demanding routines of office and home, to study together in a small house lent for the purpose by one of the group. In the mornings they have studied a series of texts in medical psychology, as well as concepts from the Cayce materials, paralleled by selections from novels, plays, and the Bible. They have told each other their dreams of the past week, while eating sandwiches for lunch, and then have worked at laboratory projects such as the reverie which now engages them, before hurrying off to cram what they could of the day's work into a few hours before suppertime.

This day they are studying Laurens Van der Post's true-life account of his two successive explorations in Africa, *Venture to the Interior*. It is a story where he lets his native Africa stand for the dark continent of the unconscious in Western urban men, which must be joined with the bright but sometimes dangerously shallow Europe of consciousness, if such men are to be whole in their humanity. To accompany the Wagnerian recording, the group members were asked to envision a rugged African mountain, such as the locale of a tragic climb on Van der Post's expedition; after the mountain they were asked to see a city. All saw these two scenes, each in his own timing and details, during the music. As they finished their reverie, they took some quiet time to reflect on what they had seen. Then the instructor explained that he hoped they might use their quickened sense of Africa's wildness, found in their reading and in the day's discussions, to catapult them into a meaningful vision of its direct opposite: the busy life of a modern city.

A musician, the busy mother of five, speaks. She saw first, she says, in that peculiarly clear vision which such reverie sometimes affords, a group of blacks and whites struggling up an impossible cliff near the top of the mountain. They almost reach the top, when it becomes clear that they cannot make it, for none are tall enough, and their tossed ropes and hooks will not hold. Yet it seems to her they must make it or fall to their destruction. Then suddenly, she continues, she saw a black man step forward on the ledge and gesture to the white man to climb up and stand on him—not on his shoulders, which would not give enough height—but on his very head. She sees in her reverie-vision the boots on the black hair, and notes the unflinching pain; the sight seizes her strongly. Next, the white man catches hold of a projection on the rock face, gets his footing, and hoists up the black man, to stand in turn on the white man's head as he reaches for the next ledge. Nothing is said, during the scene of strain on the mountain; there are only the struggling bodies, each depending on the tallest which the other has to offer, and each bearing the hurt from the other's weight on his erect and individually formed head.

In this fashion, the housewife reports, the entire group makes it up the mountain. From the top they see below them, on the other side of the mountain, a city whose inward life is somehow visible to them from this height. It is a busy city, perhaps a city of the future, stirring with work and play. People seem to be building, everywhere, and often singing as they build; work goes on in compounds not far from homes. Black and white are there, enjoying each other as distinctive equals. She has never seen such a city, she adds, nor even imagined that city life could be so buoyant. Yet the imagery is so strong, the sense of active shared life so vivid, that she finds her personal feeling for city life filling with hope, even as she speaks of what she has seen. "It could be like that, it could be like that," she stammers. But to get to such city life, she perceives, people will have to lift each other, to carry each other—as the black man has often done for the white man in the past, with the weary labor of his body, and must now do with the judgments and demands of his head. The white man will have to understand the gift which has so long been made to him by blacks, in order to match the gift with action as totally relevant and original as he can devise, out of his own flesh and feeling and head.

The woman who tells this reverie experience moves with her husband and family, within a few months after

185

the incident, to a large and often riot-torn city. There she takes up a program of graduate studies in which black and white are joined, and helps to build an experimental grade and high school which cuts across all racial and economic segments of city life. She is determined to be working at her full stature, as it comes time for more and more people to stand atop each other's heads.

Carl Jung has called a similar reverie method, done without music, one of "active imagination," which he warned against undertaking lightly. What is unleashed, when the mind is encouraged to turn into its depths in deep reverie states, may be so strong as to unbalance sanity. To be sure, the risks in such altering of consciousness towards high play are fewer than the risks offered by strong drugs, hypnosis, or methods of dissociation by concentration and deep breathing, because the procedure is wholly conscious, and may usually be shut off or reduced in force by the light touch of thought. Further, when the reverie experiences are productively handled, they are weighed and talked through and acted upon, rather than left as dazzling or bewildering vistas of the inner landscape which may return to trouble or upset the viewer. But the reverie method of altering the mind is still dangerous, because it reaches so deeply into the psyche as to enter the fire-ringed circle of inward individuality, and to penetrate with its aid the farthest impersonal reaches of the mind.

Many who have taken drugs for memorable and transformative inward journeys report that by such reverie times with others, carefully prepared for and followed up, they have equaled and even surpassed the most prized of their drug-induced experiences. For as in the best of any altered state, this procedure touches more than fantasy, more than imagery; the true springs of a life may be found, and all motivation shifted towards optimums. Even that which seems beyond personhood, as its Ground, may brush against consciousness and bring a gasp of recognition in tears or joy, though it may only lamely be described in words.

What is the altered state reached in such reverie? Many a therapist has found, as has the present writer, that at times those who are thinking deeply about a particular dream of theirs can "dream it on" while awake, following up in autonomous imagery the last remembered dream scene, until a helpful denouement is reached. And therapists who use projective methods report that at times when a patient lingers over a thematic apperception picture, or over a photograph of a loved one, or over a drawing he has made to suggest the best currents of his life, the patient seems to reach a point of suspension over some "well of his being." In this state, whatever he speaks has the ring of truth about it, while he makes admissions which he could not previously endure, or accepts his gifts and talents which formerly he brushed off in feigned modesty, or recognizes the worth in others whom he previously rejected or belittled. Just such a state is the one to be built slowly and supportively in the reverie procedure. It is a state which some report they have already entered at a time when their lives were laid open by crisis, or already found when love elevated and united two radically different lives in a difficult joint becoming. It is a state which some have guessed when what began as a discussion turned into a speaking of ultimates in a group, with such peace and goodness that none wished to leave the room, though no more remained to be said. It is the state which the entranced Cayce described in his terms as one of "strong and high vibrations," when surface consciousness might be directly attuned to the "superconscious" gifts from the soul and the One.

Drawing a distinction between "automatic" and "inspirational" writing, as two kinds of altered states showing surprising autonomy for any writer who cultivated them, the trance-counseling Cayce never failed to urge the "inspirational" writing as preferable in its effects on the psyche; this type of effort allowed holding consciously to a high set or ideal, and fostered inward promptings by attunement to the Creative Forces, rather than leaving the dissociated psyche vulnerable to unwanted forces from

187

within or without. In similar vein, the trance-altered Cayce encouraged artists and musicians and inventors to seek their inspirations through prayer-surrounded inward "openings," just as he encouraged many to seek in similar absorbed states the emblems of the best in their individual soul's journey, which they might draw or paint as a "life seal."

Some version of vision-producing methods appears to have had a place in many religious traditions of altered states. The best known is certainly the method in Ignatius Loyola's Spiritual Exercise, used for centuries by devout Jesuits. Sybils and seers and oracles had their procedures in Greece, while initiates in the mystery religions of Hellenism and Egypt reported that they were taken through successive vision experiences on their journey to wholeness and holiness. Parallels may be found in primitive rites as well: The Plains Indians made visions the central endeavor of their entry into manhood, and African efforts to incarnate archetypal visions in ritual possession have been well documented in rites from its peoples, as well as in Africa-derived rites of the West Indies. Mohammed's visions set the pace for many an earnest group in the history of Islam, while visions of Bodhisattvas lit the way for founders of sects in Northern Buddhism. How far the people of Israel taught vision-producing methods is unclear to scholars (though Cayce referred to such work in the little-known schools of the prophets); certainly David knew how to use music to elicit healing material from the unconscious of troubled Saul. Traditions of powerful inward symbols may have contributed to the vision experiences of Ezekiel and Daniel, and to later use of similar visionary material by John of Patmos, in the ecstatic Revelation which closes the New Testament. And Paul assumed that those who read his letters would know what he meant when he described being caught up into what seemed the "third heaven." Yet in all of these traditions there is little to suggest that those who sought or welcomed autonomous visions did so in the quest for merely colorful experiences; for not novelty or intensity, but closure with the One in order to be a channel, marks the way of high play.

All of the warnings previously noted against springing the lock of the mind when undue stress is present, or when there is an unexamined set of narcissism or negativism, must be repeated again regarding the reverie procedure. Indeed, the guided reverie might better be left out of discussion of altered states, because toying with it leads the wrong way from sanity. Yet if the method is used in a spirit which is tested and retested, within the circle of an honest and loving group, to make certain that the intent is high-play co-creating with the Creative Forces, then its use may disclose to the seeker such creative energies at work within his own deep mind as may stagger him, and bless him, with their force and content.

Several preconditions need to be met if the reverie venture is to have an opportunity to reach its optimums. The best setting appears to be a group which has covenanted for high play, where love and humor and good judgment can protect the balance of those who seek inward treasures. Further, the reverie method requires group experience in sharing and interpreting dreams of members, for the vision symbols are of the same order as those in strong dreams, and reflect the same individual concerns. Further, the capacity of a group to build up what Cayce called "high vibrations," by shared meditation and prayer for one another, grounded in experiences of vigorous work together, often makes all the difference between reverie effects which are merely colorful and those which are so deep and rich as permanently to mark the lives of participants. But perhaps most critical is the group's set, its agreed and serious purpose to put into the lives of others whatever individuals find of value in their reverie experiences—as the musician-mother turned from her reverie city to a real city where she might build for a better day. A set for thrills, or a set for private enjoyment (both of which seem innocuous enough, yet may embody exactly what Cayce called "sin"), will usually vitiate the reverie process, allowing perhaps a few novel fan-

189

tasies, but leaving the depths of the psyche untouched. By such shutoff the mind appears to protect itself from material which can as readily traumatize as transform the seeker after altered consciousness.

An enduring and taxing group bond seems required for the most promising reverie efforts. Only those who know each other at several levels, and trust each other's intentions, can open up enough to allow decisive inward visions to occur and be shared. A serious class, a work team, a family, an arts group, a social action cadre, a commune—each has its potential and its limitations, depending in part upon the quality of past joint sharing, and depending also upon the relative freedom from dependence upon a parent-like leader in the group. Even strangers on the same kind of quest for optimums with the Creative Forces may be brought together for an intensive weekend, and helped to covenant together at sufficient depth for the reverie experience to take its place among the shared events of the weekend.

Whatever the group, its members will require some freeing of their habitual defenses and poses; without this freeing in advance, the reverie material which emerges will concern itself chiefly with opening the gates of encounter within the group. Going off to some lovely and refreshing setting can make it easier for all participants to leave worries and façades behind. Nature, which allows her many species to follow their own ground plans and seasons of development, offers her special encouragement to discarding phoniness, as she does to recalling primal realities which operate without committees and contrivances. Within the chosen setting, time must be allowed for sharing before the reverie period. Defenses exist for good reasons in the economy of the psyche; they are not to be dropped except as firm bonds of understanding and regard, and even of affection, may be put in their place.

Those who are preparing for a reverie journey together need to talk of their real lives, however obliquely they do so at first, in discussions focused on literature, on theories of human nature and society, on their children or parents, their peers or their enemies. The seekers need to eat together, to tease, to use their bodies with some abandon, to do some things on the spur of the moment, and to engage in strenuous and meaningful tasks together—such as fashioning a form in one of the arts, but not excluding chopping wood or washing dishes at full speed. They need to give each other nicknames, and to remark on each other's clothing and ways of working, as they also need to get past the first awkward moments of worshiping together. They need to celebrate the distinctive manhood and womanhood which they see in their small company, and to build up a common stock of phrases and stories, as well as of shared nighttime dreams, so that later they may pass around their reverie reflections in some awareness of the spears and pruning hooks which project from each life.

Finally, the company which seeks the best of reverie adventures needs a time of demanding and disciplined reflection on a book which all have read, or on a systematic presentation by one or more members. Such firm use of rational consciousness does not hinder the unconscious but frees it for its imaging work. Preparation by wide-awake and orderly thought sets the reverie method apart from many a drugging and damping of consciousness (though it was the preparation by concentrated thought in weeks of advance therapy which helped to give depth to the LSD healing of the neurotic housewife).

At the appointed time for the reverie venture, quiet surroundings are essential. To be interrupted by noise or intruders while turning the mind loose for its Grails is to experience a shattering which may discourage not a few from any further ventures along these lines; a discomfort which is more than physical occurs when the mind snaps shut to protect itself from disorientation. In the quiet setting, participants need to sit or sprawl comfortably where they can see each other in later times of sharing; but at the time of the reverie they will want minimal light, so that the visual sense may retreat in favor of the inner eye of imagination.

191

Participants in a reverie will need to be assured that what they are about to do is not difficult or strange for them, but only a carrying further of processes which constantly orchestrate thought—as dreams show, as daydreams show, and as may be seen in the little flicks of recognition and comparison in the back of the mind at the entry of each new event or person in the day's happenings. They will also need to be assured that they will not be pushed into any reporting which they do not choose, nor made the objects of psychological gamesmanship when they share their experiences. And they will need to be asked to hear music without listening to it; that is, they need to let the music serve them merely as a signaler, a scene changer, a prompter or promoter. Those who love music and listen to it with care will need to make a conscious effort not to hear it musically; for this reason using music which is relatively unfamiliar or at least not trite offers the most useful potential for the entire group. (Because vocal music calls attention to mind-binding words, and to the personalities of performers, it is often more difficult to use for reverie than instrumental music; and because popular music is more limited in tempo and melody and harmony, and above all in form, it is often more difficult to use than serious music.) Whatever their musical backgrounds, all need to be encouraged not to force the mind, but only to invite it to the small plots and settings of the reverie experience, so that the mind may then roam on its own, with the music. Actually, the skill of holding the mind to a limited range of symbols, and yet giving it freedom, is no small attainment, and some may need a number of runs without hurry or pressure to accomplish it.

The music chosen needs to be loosely matched to each plot situation, and needs to contain significant turns of changes in tempo and orchestration and development—exactly what is meant by "movements" in larger works. Just a few minutes of music are needed for the first ventures, since running too long may snap the thread of an unfolding inward plot, and will hamper the process of reporting experiences around the group. Later, experienced participants can handle as much as an entire side of an LP record, still keeping the form and focus of their original assignment.

It has been the writer's experience in using reverie procedures with hundreds of subjects for fifteen years that the first few situations offered for reverie on any one occasion need to touch some of the major bases of personhood, so that the healing compensatory work of the psyche may proceed, and after that the way be opened within the unconscious of each participant for deeper levels to respond. Four such bases are those which might suggest themselves to any thoughtful person; of these, the first two may be required to give the reverie method its best momentum and freedom on a given occasion.

One base is biological. Situations offered to touch this dimension of personhood are those which stir physical, animal spirits, in such scenes as a waterhole in Africa at night, with appropriately varied and somewhere stealthy music (to suggest the threat in the passions, which reverie imagery may handle in spontaneously creative ways), or fish in coral reefs, or wild horses, or even cells in the blood stream. Any setting which is wholly animal will suffice, and only the initial situation, tension, or sequence needs to be suggested, not the details of development which are the individual's adventure of the reverie. For those who are unable at first to enter freely into the animal kingdom in their mind's eye, imagery of primitive dances or peasant rituals may allow them an approach to basic organic drives which will not upset their equilibrium. But the possibilities in sheer animal imagery should not be lightly passed over. Many an overcontrolled and sedentary urbanite finds strong and refreshing energies quickened for his high play by such reverie, so that his cheeks color in telling what he experienced, and his walk shows a new spring at once. These reverie efforts with the forces in protoplasm may prompt appreciation for Freud's helpful work on sex and aggression, as two resources needed for all of man's journeying to optimums.

The second base of personhood to be touched in reverie is of course that of controls. It is the realm of conscience, self-image, and authority which Freud called the superego. Any kind of regal setting, or court scene, will do nicely for this purpose, as will scenes of military or village authority. In creating such scenes, as in the animal scenes above (and in using projective pictures which may be made the basis for spoken reverie without music), keeping the action removed from daily life frees the fantasy, as fairy tales do. For this second base of personality dynamics, musical fanfares and processionals are easy resources, but the best musical development will suggest the press of a heavy or authoritative musical figure against another musical figure not unlike an individual who is finding his ground. Ominous or heavy passages, and a few uncertain musical shifts or pauses, will provide the kind of prodding which may loosen the tight controls systems of the seeker, even during the reverie, offering him new ways to face and tame his pressures of shame and punishment and guilt, as well as to accept and handle guilt or fear or greatness of heart, which in a particular case should not be further ignored.

A third base to be touched is that of unique individuality. This level of meaning is more difficult to reach than those above, because it is so often a charged personal concern for participants. The scene of a teen-ager walking alone, and beginning to understand and rejoice in himself, offers its promises. So do the situations of an old man or woman with a child, or an individual with his pet or horse, or the predicament of landing in a strange country where one must fall back on his own resources to get out. Not strident heroism, but honest and appreciative self-awareness seems the most useful focus.

Fourth, there is the base of corporate life and action. Touching this base allows the mind to open up from its own inner resources the manner in which the seeker might more deeply relate to others, as co-creator with them in shared tasks and celebrations before the One. A scene of strong potential is that of an exodus of a whole people to a land of their new beginning. But sailors bringing a ship to port will do, also, as will villagers on a day of great ceremony, or even a Robinson Crusoe family.

Once these bases have been touched (or at least the first two), it is possible to move into situations which bear upon particular life issues of participants in the reverie time. Clues for designing reverie situations for this stage ought to be drawn from preceding group discussions, from what has been read, from the contents of shared dreams and role plays, and from the real-life experiences of participants who have opened up with each other. However, the actual situations chosen ought still to be those which are set away from the present company, in other lands or times, or out of doors, or at other age levels—just far enough from real life to let the psyche of each participant spin its plots without fear of personal exposure, and just close enough to catch the riddles in each life. Man and woman together are often useful primary characters for this deeper level of reverie, whether they are set as working in the fields, as entering into ceremonies of initiation, as handling a death, as caring for their children, or as journeying to the Far West. What is needed for results of maximum value is some event where prized human values are pitted against each other—as in the contrasts of wilderness and city, of working and playing, of race with race, of old with young, or of loving with principled quarreling. When this level of adventure in reconciling daily-life opposites has been negotiated, then it may be possible to reach still deeper into what Cayce called "superconscious" levels of the psyche. However, arbitrary depth of level ought not to be the criterion of worth in the reverie venture, but rather relevance of imagery to the real existence and service to others of the visioning person. What is needful for any individual may pop out at the first release of his guided imagination or at any stage thereafter; beyond that point, his fundamental plots and tensions of values will only repeat, in varied imagery.

In time, however, and often at later sessions when the reverie experience has become familiar and trusted, scenes that may seem impossible to visualize, because of their depth and complexity, may be set before the mind and find themselves welcome imagery. The set for reverie at this level must still be towards productiveness in high-play co-creating, or the material will be blocked for the seeking mind. Examples of situations which may now be tried include the unfolding of evolution, the history of an entire people, the journey of the soul through earthly experience, the human riddle of war and its overcoming, and the healing of bodily illness. To be sure, each such challenge to the imagination needs some specific and representative content to get the mind started; but once launched, the psyche may move through visions so rich and sweeping and meaningful that only those who have tried the reverie or a similar process can quite believe what develops. Perhaps the ultimate themes of faith are the most difficult to elicit in forms which are not contrived. Partly this is so because such themes of faith—trust, love, grace, hope, truth, play—are most valuable to participants in the settings where they have occurred in previous reveries, anchored in the same kind of concreteness which they require in daily life. Yet when individuals have worked together at the reverie method, as well as worked together at demanding tasks, they may find it possible to highlight the themes of fullest spirituality, or high-play, co-creating, by gently nudging the mind towards scenes which have spontaneous overtones of the holy. The scene chosen may be as simple as that of a man and a woman dealing with water and the wind; it is surprising how many will find in these ingredients, without being told to do so, the elements for being born anew—as Jesus suggested in using these symbols. Or reverie participants may be invited to sit at the base of the Bo tree long after the Buddha, or to happen on the scene where a biblical prophet worked a healing after all have

196

left. Or they may follow the underground stream of hope which surfaces at a Woodstock and watch it flow back into city life for a generation. To attempt literal entry by reverie into the changed scenes of man's encounter with the One is to ask the mind to toy with idolatry. But to wander near those times and places in reverie is another matter, and one of no small consequences in unsanity for high play.

How one man responded to reverie situations, over a period of months, may suggest something of how the process works. He was a man reared by a dominating and at times psychotic mother, who infuriated his wife throughout their marriage by refusing to struggle creatively with his spouse; instead, he alternated between aloofness from her problems and explosive demands that all family problems be settled at once. Then, in a reverie of a man and wife quarreling to racy saber-dance music, he saw a couple fighting with swords, and watched the man cut off the woman's head. The severed head sailed up into the air and then settled back on the woman's shoulders, while the couple went right on fighting with no harm done to either person. Obviously, the reverie contained an invitation from his own psyche for him to undertake that fighting which does not destroy another, yet takes the other seriously. The same man, struggling over how to use the force of his manhood, yet contain it in productive ways, saw in a subsequent reverie a column of marching soldiers, while a powerful male dancer moved in and out of the column in freedom and grace, never interrupting their march or his dance. Clearly, the reverie offered him a symbol of the force in contained freedom which he sought as a personal ideal. And the same man, unused to sharing his innermost feelings with his difficult but gifted children, saw in a later reverie an old man and a boy riding off on horses to meet an old Indian and an Indian boy, where the four of them ceremonially and silently cut their hands and joined palms, to let the blood flow in each other's veins. The experience set him to looking for ways and times of sharing with his children which were deeper than

197

the tricks of manuals on parenthood. Once again, the same man, often despairing of loving his volatile wife, whose extravagances reminded him of his troubled and driven mother, saw in deep autonomous reverie a very old man and a very old woman climbing a tortuous mountain path in a storm of wind and rain. At one point on the high slope the skies cleared, and he saw them turn to embrace each other in the full and loving closeness given by their years together. As might be expected, he found in this un-expected but welcome vision something deeply compelling for him, to which he could often return in the months and years which followed, as he began to find at last the spon-taneous high play of loving his spirited wife.

Not everyone who shares in a reverie process will move into episodes of such force and decisiveness. Often it is only about ten percent of a group which is deeply struck by what transpires, though at times it may be a third. The rest are likely to find the visioning journey refreshing and intriguing, and may long afterwards glean meanings from what they experienced and from what others shared with them. But not everyone needs to be psychedelic, or mind-manifesting and self-transforming, at the same time; those who do quicken to the most decisive moments of personal meaning will be those whose minds are already stirred toward some definitive change, as their dreams and waking choices at the time would show. The reverie only affords them a vehicle in which consciousness can be met part way in daylight by the unconscious, beginning the unpredictable dance of becoming in high play which reaches out to others. Times of life transition, and times of Jonah-like growth in new qualities, are those in which the reverie may often make its best gifts to an individual. But reverie may contribute to a group, a family, or a people as well, by working to handle the invisible weight of either suffering or celebration.

After each reverie situation has been allowed to follow out the music to completion, there is need for a brief pe-riod without talking, to avoid jarring the altered mind as it returns to normal consciousness, and to allow time for notes to be made or events to be rehearsed again in memory. Then lights may be added, and those who are ready may be invited to speak. Sometimes those who are ready are those who volunteer, and sometimes it is those whose smile or tears, or grave or bemused expression, invites an inquiry which carries no pressure. There is gain in telling the tales, for often the maximum force and sense of the reverie come in putting the scenes into words for others, when the gift of the unconscious meets the marshaled forces of consciousness for sharing; even a small experience may prove unaccountably gripping in the act of quietly telling it. Yet not everyone needs to recount his inward journey at the time; some in the group may have had an experience to be inwardly treasured or measured, or faced alone in its puzzling threat, and then told later to a chosen few, if at all. Each who speaks needs to understand that he must take the responsibility of unraveling for himself the meaning of the reverie which he tells, but that he may find aid from others for this purpose. The best group commitment will prompt members to help one person, or a few, to reach to true optimums, even though all may not have their chance to speak of their vision, but must let their inward energies build within, toward the next reverie effort. Such group effort is taxing effort. It requires giving alert attention to each teller, whose widening eyes or broadening grin or choice of charged words suggest to his peers that he may be touching upon something in his reverie which is more important to him than he yet may realize. Together, the sensitive group members can help a member to pull forth the bittersweet fruit of his vision, often asking him to repeat again the scenes where he seems most involved, until he harvests from them his own true meanings. If his vision has gone deep at all, it will be found to contain fresh definition of his present human choices that engage his deepest ideals; and it will be found to suggest forward-moving reconciliation of his conflicting opposites. Yet the group can only offer him possible interpretations under the constraint of their alert attention to the one who speaks. For obviously there are no right answers to the questions raised by reverie symbols, just as there are no right dream interpretations. There are only meanings which answer in greater or lesser degree to the person who has seen what he has seen, felt what he has felt, in his inner world. But when the set and the setting, the shutoff and the sharing, allow individuals to experience the strongest autonomous materials in their reveries, they repeatedly observe that they discover new qualities within themselves. Until they felt it so keenly, they did not know that they might so love, so risk, so belong, so play, so fight, so endure; yet once the experience was given, they knew it to be theirs, and could build upon it in daily life.

The danger in the reverie procedure is the danger of neglecting to support the ego, which must endure and interpret and act upon what comes before it. Because of this danger, the reverie method does not combine well with drugs or with psychological methods which may back the ego out of the action, instead of lifting it to maximum strength and awareness. When the reverie is handled with requisite care, the ego can protect itself in each venture; in scenes which are too charged to handle, it will help to shift the flow of imagery to material which is merely colorful or picturesque, often reported as more like a movie or painting than felt as an immediate experience. The time of telling and interpreting also offers its special dangers to the ego: the psyche is immensely vulnerable when defensive coverings are let down at the same time that strong inner energies are loosed. For this reason, no belittling interpretations ought to be offered in the reverie group, even when they seem obvious. Low play requires lifting into high play, not mere rebuke. The gain sought is not only new behavior, or new labels for old behavior, but new personhood—a more enduring gain. Part of the force of the best reverie experiences of altered consciousness is their direct handling of individual evil, which may not be ignored as easily as when the same evil is presented in conveniently forgotten dreams. The challenge to both the individual and the group which sees the outlines of such low play or no-play is to place it against the tales, legends, scriptures, theories, literature, biographies, and group memories, where such evil has been seen and transmuted before, under the grace of the One which can make all games into high play.

Because mind and body can carry only so much concentration at one sitting, sixty to ninety minutes appears a maximum for most reverie and sharing periods, and often much less is better. Beyond the limits when body restlessness begins, the danger of disorientation in uncontrolled panic or weeping grows greater. Quitting while ahead is counsel just as valid for the reverie method as for any other approach to altered consciousness. So is the counsel of moderation. Prying the mind loose too often merely throws its healing and compensatory currents into reaffirming neglected tasks of daily life—as may be seen in imagery of practical matters, or in imagery whose triviality cries out that the psyche be left alone.

As Melville tells his whaling tale, it is Ishmael, Melville's spokesman, who has the most to share of reverie-like visions. Whatever Ishmael touches seems to remind him of something like it, yet more classic or richly human. He draws on memories of travels, on Greek and Oriental and primitive faiths, on love and on business, on church and on courts, on myths and on pure playful fantasy, while all the time walking the boards of a whaling ship. As he handles the oars, the whale jaws, the breakfast steaks, the letters from home, the fights in the forecastle, the strips of cooking whale blubber, he keeps on that playful-purposeful journeying where anything that consciousness encounters may echo its musical way into the recesses of the unconscious, reaching at times to the very center of selfhood. As Ishmael stumbles onto a painting in a hallway, or hears a prophecy, or has Ahab staring at a whale's head to ponder all that the head has seen which men would fear or like to see in the ocean, Ishmael does not so much invent images or draw likenesses as note how he keeps happening to himself—with a richness which makes programmed reverie experiences unneces-

201

sary for anyone with such an ample soul. He leaps from describing a huge white whale to describing the ultimate purity and majesty of whiteness alongside the ultimate ghastliness and emptiness of white. And in so doing he lays bare what the best of reverie images hint: the uncertainty of all games with the unpredictable but loving One, which will do what it will do with all players, to get them to their unseen and destined optimums.

Finding the Life Form

The biology professor has taken to studying his dreams. He knows he should be studying technical journals to keep informed as an expert on South American reptiles. He knows he should be writing up his latest expedition. Yet for months he has found that nothing in his work holds his interest. He stares at his papers and shuffles his card files as if to work, but then for hours at a time he looks out of his office window. When a student or his assistant comes in, he rouses himself, but nothing has taste for him and he does not know why. To be sure, his marriage ended in divorce not many months ago; but he had known the breakup was coming. Besides, since the divorce he has filled his leisure hours with a procession of attractive women such as most men his age would find only in fantasy. Still he cannot get to work. In desperation, he has turned to his dreams for a lead, on the counsel of a friend. He keeps them recorded neatly in a notebook, with parallel columns for associations and interpretations, much as he has always studied specimens.

Now there has come to him, in the night, a dream which has startled him with its strange turns. It began with a tree outside his bedroom window on which he saw climbing a large iguana—one of a species whose arms have always reminded him, because of their smooth and alluring strength, of the women who fascinate him. The creature in the dream climbed deliberately to the top of the tree, where it turned to face him and was suddenly transformed into a small shrine, a templelike structure such as he had seen on biological expeditions to India. The shrine was empty at first, and then there stepped from it a man. The man was perfectly proportioned, whole and strong and gracious of appearance, but very small. His face was grave and thoughtful. He walked easily down the trunk of the tree toward the dreamer—who awakened at that point feeling that the man was somehow himself, yet a stranger.

Weeks go by while the professor works out the dream. He sets beside each dream symbol the associations which it evokes for him. And he compares the dream with his other dreams having similar themes, though he finds none with the abrupt transitions of the tree dream. One day he recognizes in the face of the small but perfectly whole dream man a hint of the good manhood which he had treasured in an associate of years ago; this man had believed in him more than had his own father, and more than the professor believed in himself. And the man knew much of iguanas.

Slowly, the professor gropes his way further into the dream, feeling out the progression there from sexual energy to the lift of the vaulted temple, and then pressing on to the force of the whole-formed man—a figure with wholeness and balance which he has not felt about himself for years. Painfully, the professor weighs the meanings of his fascination with Nature (both in his profession and in his busy love life), against the meaning to him of such cultural enterprises as temples and arts and history, which he has always regarded indulgently as mere diversions to the true scientist. In time he decides that his manhood, his full manhood, may be blocked for him until he begins to wrestle with the ultimates suggested to him by the strange little shrine atop the dream tree. He begins to read philosophy and mythology; he takes a course which probes the recurring ethical questions in the human life-span. And he seriously considers committing suicide, raising a gun in his hand, and weighing for hours the questions which imminent death offers.

Then there comes a time when he chooses to offer to an

associate some of the helpful, fatherlike training in skills which he has never received from his own busy father, and whose absence he has resented from his boyhood on. Next, he decides to discover whether women can be more for him than lovely iguana bodies to be sexually enshrined; he limits himself to a relationship with one woman who is a fellow scientist, and finds that their sharing deepens toward love in long hours of talk while on professional trips together. Then he finds his energies showing bursts of unaccustomed activity. And one spring day he is surprised to find himself cataloguing specimens in great spirits, preparatory to writing a technical paper. A discovery hits him: the whole manhood of him has appeared, and is growing to full stature at last. The man from the tree has walked right into him, to stay.

Describing the function of dreams in adult psychotherapy, Carl Jung once wrote, "Each of us carries his own life form—an indeterminable form which cannot be superseded by any other." Going on to develop the idea, Jung pointed to a pattern-giving center of activity in the psyche, well outside of surface consciousness, and never fully inspectable by that consciousness. He referred to a structure not far from what Cayce called the "individuality" of a person—his inner identity which must be squared with his outer "personality" (which Jung tagged the "persona"). In the view of the Cayce trance source, all souls were created at the same time in the original Creation. But each soul was given its own snowflakelike uniqueness, whose unfolding would be its glory as it became a conscious companion with God, man, mind, and matter in eons to come. Life after life on earth would be required to develop a soul's precious uniqueness (for those souls which chose earthly existence), as would interim stays in realms of altered consciousness between earth lives. And beyond the regions of earth were yet other existences eluding the full grasp of earthly consciousness, which were those "many mansions" where the soul could grow and serve until it had become as truly "one with the Father" as had the Christ soul. In this view, when each soul entered a given lifetime, it chose some constellation of values, some heraldic crest of its own true themes, to which it dedicated the particular lifetime. This inward, purposeful pattern became its life form for one existence; all true growth and service in that lifetime would develop along the invisible force lines of the life form—a form which did not specify how far the individual would grow, but only the directions of his best growth. To find the life form was serious and important business for any soul, and often the content of his unconscious as it fed him dreams and fantastic and sturdy waking promptings; finding the life form was part of discovering a person's true "individuality" with God, upon which he could ground his vocation, service, and relationships with others, and with which he could bear the pain of suffering in the time of history and the company of people where he had chosen to live. Clarifying the life form for others was the essential business of Cayce's life readings, in which he traced a number of past lives for an individual as well as his present temperament, style, emotions, talents, weaknesses, and commitments, in order to call to his remembrance his own far-inward uniqueness and promise as a soul.

If there is in fact such a seed design in each person, as both Jung and Cayce suggested, then finding it may be a critical task for growth toward optimums. Otherwise such a form will surely be projected outward by the individual (as all unconscious contents tend to be projected when they are stirred) until they are consciously recognized and made a part of the person in his apt deeds and speech —by "application," as the entranced Cayce described the antidote to such projection. In being projected, the life form—felt as the lovely, beckoning, tormenting inner shape, the very form and face of personal worth—would take on many awesome faces. It may be seen as the potent job to be landed, as the nation which must be defended, as the divinity whom others must be pressed to adore, as the leader who must be followed at all costs, or even as a massive white whale to be intimately known only in mortal combat. Where there is no final "I" which is glimpsed as the true life form, then some "you" becomes "You," or some "it" becomes "It." Play becomes a deadly two-handed game to which the Third is not invited, or in which the Third is squeezed into a goal at hand.

The concept of the individual life form is not a prominent one in modern Western thought. Indeed, beneath the surface of Western reflection move considerable currents against the suggestion that each man bears an individual destiny which is not his fate but his call—his *vocatio* from God, which makes his vocation into living, rather than just a living. The burden of Neoplatonism, with its inhuman archetypal concepts of church and God and soul, appears to have rested so heavily upon the medieval spirit that when nominalism finally won the day against such realism in the birth of modern science, nominalism carried the play clear off the field. As a consequence, modern man tends to think of himself as a product of extrapersonal accidents of genes, circumstances, education, technology, and means, so that he is a child of his somatotype, traumas, and subculture. Looking nervously over his shoulder at the Darwinian landscape of blind struggle for survival, glancing at his lapel badge to see where he is in the Marxist class struggle, and hoping that his Freudian slips do not betray his personal weaknesses, he finds it singularly unappealing to speculate on his final uniqueness as a person. Besides, would not such uniqueness tend to be undemocratic, if it did in fact exist?

But other cultures in other ages have seen the life form differently. India and her child Buddhism peered down the ages at what seemed a succession of lives for each person, and found it useful to contemplate the particular form and potential of any one life—although Hinduism and Buddhism differed on how far that might be contained and signaled in the circumstances of caste birth. China and Japan tried noble birth and ancestral lineage as vehicles to carry and awaken the life form, with results as problematic as results of the same effort in Babylonia and Egypt. In some contrast, individual gods and goddesses for devotees who chose them were offered as bearers of the form-quickening process in sectarian Hinduism and in Northern Buddhism; similar redeemer figures for individual choice were offered in the mystery cults of Greece, Asia Minor, and Egypt, all of which set up shop in cosmopolitan Rome. The long-standing Catholic practice of encouraging individuals to identify with patron saints may have offered psychologically similar vehicles. And the Protestant practice, on the American frontier, of giving each child a Bible verse thought to contain the riddle of his life was not so far from handing him his own Zen koan as might at first appear. In some contrast, Judaism drew upon the biblical concept of the "heart" of a man to suggest his life form, which could be evoked through the play of Rabbinic contrasts, rehearsed for individual *bar mitzvah* occasions. Not only Calvin but such Western giants of introspection as Paul and Augustine and Kierkegaard each sought to discern some form, however complex and ultimately indescribable, in which an individual's life might be found anchored in a kind of predestiny with the divine, though the unfolding of that form might take the individual so far as to cancel any shallow sense of predeterminism. Freud tackled a similar question as he puzzled over the "choice of the neurosis" among children of the same family, and over the "repetition compulsion" which seemed to make individual lives circle around a few compelling questions and traumas. In the modern scene, it may be the quest for the defined life form which keeps alive weary old astrology and adds magic to the stage roles of little theater ventures, just as it does to the analyst's hour or to the heroic risks of a protest campaign.

To be sure, living as if unfolding one's individual uniqueness were all that matters can be deadly narcissism, whether in the boring prattle of the intoxicated or in the cruel flailings of a neo-Ahab who has not yet seen a white whale. For this reason, inward approaches to finding the life form through dream and reverie and meditation (or through more risky drug experiences) must be matched by outward approaches in the ways of knowledge, action, and love. But when the cycle of high play unfolds to its farthest reaches, it is often the guiding sense of an inward life form which seems to free an individual's efforts to reach true optimums, rather than letting them sour into posturing or craving. Moses at the burning bush, far from his people and with his life seemingly wrecked by the murder he has wrought, can still think himself in the life-outlines of an offspring of Isaac and Jacob, spirited wanderers with Yahweh, though Moses bears an Egyptian name and has an Egyptian education and foster parents. In such a life form he is able to walk before Pharaoh with the careless grace of the God-paced nomad.

How is the busy modern to think himself down to his core, where his uniqueness may also lie cradled in the heritage of traditions of his people? Dream and reverie may contribute much to disclosing and clarifying an individual's life form. They require study in sets or series, to disclose which figures of weight most often appear in them and which decisions seem most often set forth; the resultant imagery may be linked together to make an individual Pilgrim's Progress. For one way in which to probe the life form is to see it as a journey, a saga, a fairy tale, or a life myth. The form which emerges is always richer than vocation, though vocation is a decisive ingredient. It may be useful to start the sketch of the life journey by thinking of oneself as a lover or lawyer, as a whaler or wholesaler. But the full call of one's life tends to ring out beyond one's occupation, though resonating with it— as Jesus told the rich young ruler to seek a new kind of riches for the next stage in his life, and told some fishermen to fish further but for a different catch.

Carl Jung set forth his autobiography as a life myth, by using his dreams to show his wandering between the two conflicting poles of science and religion which loomed over his journey. In so doing, he highlighted the tension of values which characterizes the life form read as journey. There is the pilgrimage of the woman who seeks beauty with wisdom, or the charming youth who must grow up but stay young, or the fighter who does not wish to kill, or the priestly ritualist as businessman, or the nunlike

208

idealist who must love or die. No such formula by itself catches the thrust of the life form, but a formula which embodies tensions may suggest a structure which dream and reverie can amplify. Until such a personal structure is guessed by an individual, his dreams are likely to point to its absence from his serious reflections. A vivacious and talented housewife, for example, who had too long sunk herself in her husband and children, dreamed of watching in envy as defined public figures rode past her in a parade of floats. In the dream she then retreated to move her bowels, where she noted with rueful satisfaction that at least these basic products received their form from her. In such imagery, dreams put the question of the life form: Who are you, after all? Sometimes dream suggestions of where to look for the missing life form are offered in actual shapes, rather than in symbols of a journey; dreams may show hollows left by absent bodies, may present beautiful abstract designs and shapes, may offer embryos or animals which seem human, or may call attention to others who wear their vocation and station as easy garments which do not swathe them into formlessness. Especially useful hints of the life form may be found in dreams which return the dreamer to the place of his birth to make their point, or take him back to a classic childhood setting where he and his parents once stood at the exit of his Eden.

Dreams and reverie material, however, can offer only seminal contributions to delineating the life myth, the life form. Sooner or later the person bent on finding and responding to the form of what Cayce sometimes called "the higher self" must search out the meanings of his life so far: his failures and successes, his beings and becomings, his belongings and loosings. If in the process he can find in dreams or in deep introspection (whether initiated by reverie or meditation or creative struggle or pain), the hints of gripping themes which seem to come to him, as the entranced Cayce suggested, from his own past lives, then he may find the adventure of seeking his life form heightened for him by this added mystery. In any case, he must make lists, inventories, sketches of this trait and that in his makeup, drawings of layers upon layers within him, notes on what others say of him who love him or doubt or fear him. Alongside such materials he must lay his most cherished memories (and those distinctive indicators of basic themes in personhood which Alfred Adler noted, the earliest memories), as well as his personal columns of "spiritual, mental, and physical ideals," whose study Cayce so earnestly enjoined upon everyone who sought to grow to his optimums. And he may profit by making his own roster of live saints: those figures in his biography who have most stirred his finest deeps.

Misunderstanding his own life form, Ahab refuses the plea of his first mate to turn the *Pequod* around; Ahab insists that the decision to continue after the white whale was made billions of years ago. For the captain, destiny and fate have—fatefully and fatally—slipped together into one concept. But the individual seeking his own true life form need not, like Ahab, confuse his own destined form with fate-laden archetypal patterns from the far impersonal layers of the psyche, when the seeker begins to recognize that each life journey leads out from its particular beginning towards a fulfillment which was in some measure foreshadowed at the start. To begin life with brains is to be stuck with the question of power. To begin with position and influence is to be stuck with the question of justice. To start with a beautiful face and form is to be stuck with the question of truth in relationships, since people will persist in falling in love with the image and ignoring its wearer. Likewise, to be born a woman who loves easily and thinks with difficulty is to begin a different journey from that of a woman who thinks easily and loves with difficulty. And to be born a man who weeps easily and fights painfully has very different consequences from being born a man who fights easily and weeps painfully little. Pressures experienced in similar childhoods leave one child responding to subsequent pressures with belligerence, while another child responds by placating;

210

both must enlarge their life styles into fuller life forms if they are to avoid lingering in low play. Further, the child who grows up listening to and trusting his brisk consciousness must stoop very low when at last the journey to the underground of the unconscious must be made in some crisis. And the child who grows up listening to and trusting the piping and strumming of his unconscious must stretch very high when finally he must carry a conscious banner for a noble cause. Besides such inner themes of transformation, the life form of each individual carries his version of the crucial pact, storied alike in fairy tale and *Faust*. For a woman, the initial bond of purity with the father and the fathers must be both honored and broken, as she takes on, in the name of her father, a covenant or pact with a male Beast—and loves Beast until at last he is man and she is Beauty, but more. For a man, the initial bond with the mother and the mothers must be both honored and broken, as he learns from the feminine not only love but his love-transgressing creative imagination —which he must compact with God or the devil to use in created forms, for a particular people whom he knows to be his own. All of these elements and more are in the life form, to be searched out in sharpest conscious reflection as well as in the dimmer light of dreams and reverie.

How can such complexity of form be held before the mind, in some signaling device which can channel and free an individual's energies from the fire-ringed circle far within? Jung experimented with having his patients draw or paint their most charged dream images; examples of such productions may be seen in the plates of Frances Wickes' volume *The Inner World of Man*. Taking an approach not greatly different, though it placed more emphasis on symbols drawn from seeming memories of past lives, the trance-counseling Cayce guided scores of individuals to draw or paint their uniquely individual "life seals" out of material he suggested they could find spontaneously occurring to them during prayerful and stilled attunement to the One. Examples of the results may be

211

seen in the Violet Shelley booklet on Cayce's materials entitled *Symbols and the Self*.

A modest beginning at signifying one's life form may be made by drawing a personal coat of arms, or a shield, or a scroll. For this imaginative task the seeker after his optimums may turn to whatever symbols mean the most to him, not forgetting those suggested in dreams of iguanas and temples. Artistic skill is not the needed ingredient. Even geometric designs or simple stick figures may convey strong meanings to the one who draws in earnest. Balancing off the necessary and conflicting opposites which he finds within him will stir his imagination, even as he draws. And focusing on his central values will require both his honesty and his judgment. Is he, for example, to think himself as starting on his life journey a confidant to beauty, or to truth, or to goodness, or to that mysterious unifer and breeder of values called holiness? What will signify the treelike character of his life, by which he is seen to put forth branches, yet ever to keep the same trunk and roots?

Far from being psychological toying, such a self-defining and self-welcoming effort at heraldry may be a catalyst to lift the games of daily life toward high play, where every player is seen flying his own unique colors, worthy of salute even when soiled or torn. Many kinds of symbols may be explored in the effort of creating such an emblem, or series of emblems, from which the best contents may be shared with an intimate search group. There is medieval symbolism, and there is mythology. There are the familiar and classical implements of work, of study, of love and the home, of religion, and of battle. There are pairings and groupings, and there are occult and cabalistic figures. There are creatures and scenes of nature and the parts of the body. There are the people and times of history and the pillars of biography from the East and the West. Under the tutoring of dreams and reverie, paced by steady self-analysis answering to the observations and demands of others, designs may be worked out to mark the peculiar promise and peril of one unique life, and to guide the unfolding cycle of high-play stages.

But not all signaling and celebrating of the life form needs to be visual. As old traditions in many faiths require giving new names to novices and initiates, so groups of modern seekers may confer names or nicknames upon one another. Sometimes the name so given is the person's own full name, rescued from its discard in a past conflict with family values. But sometimes it is a name which emerges in a dream, or in a story told, or in the style of the person. (In his "life readings," the strangely attuned Cayce sometimes counseled individuals to adhere to certain names or spellings of names, as best for their present lifetime.) All such name giving must of course be gentle and tentative, and the name offered must answer to the bearer of it, for name calling is as regrettable when artificially flattering as when artificially belittling. Similar in its effects on waking an individual's sense of his life form is addressing the person as son or daughter of a particular parent (an ancient practice, seen for example in "Simon bar Jonah"), or as son or daughter of a certain region or people. Rightly used, these designations can help to frame the individual's uniqueness, not obliterate it. Further, race is the rock from which one is hewn, and not to be overlooked as a footing for personhood. Black is beautiful if one chooses it to be. So, even, is colorless white—as Melville noted in a chapter on the demanding contradictions of whiteness.

A different kind of signaling to reinforce the sense of the life form may be offered by an individual's handling of possessions. Even while they serve consciousness, hand-me-downs often tend to cripple unconscious individuality unless the objects are somehow structurally or functionally modified by the receiver; the unconscious seems rarely to forget (as anyone may test for himself) where the things at hand originated, and in what spirit. Many a young couple have thought they were doing well with used clothing and furniture from relatives—until they came to the realization that they would be better off sitting on the floor in their underwear, or in one self-chosen outfit apiece, than dwelling in the trappings of others. Poverty is not the question here (although poverty and riches offer their own challenges to be probed in seeking out the life form, as do the meanings of force, sex, one's word, and death—the five questions of the Sphinx). For the purpose of reinforcing the life form, it is valuable to select a few fine things which reflect the identity of the user, as his own gold and silver qualities, the unmarred carvings on his soul, or his polished tools of skill and discrimination. Not only art works but even bathroom fixtures need to reflect the considered choice of the person bent on cleaving to his own life form. He may work through many styles of belongings in one lifetime and return to great simplicity of possessions as his life closes, but his chances of being himself along the way run higher if he can signal his true identity to his consciousness, whenever and wherever it begins to alter. He may be best off if he can also signal in some form what the Israelitic patriarchs signaled to themselves when they put up a pile of rocks where they thought God had spoken to them. A tune, a sketch, a book, a ball, a ring, a snapshot, or any souvenir of true high play is more potent for the lift of the undrugged cycle than any trophy of low play, however impressive the house or car or wife or membership which one has acquired in current status markets.

And if, further, one can signify to himself how his strengths rose out of his failures, then he may be allowed to walk with Ahab at Ahab's best, on the whalebone leg of the very species that bit him. For the secret of the life form does not seem to be perfection, which belongs only to the inhuman realm of what Plato called archetypes and Cayce occasionally called "the gods." Instead, the potency of the life form appears to lie in its fostering of the scrolled and hidden design which was the One's first business with each, and each man's best business in co-creating which brings forth the life form in his brother. The stark challenge in many a Cayce trance counsel was this: "Until ye can see in each person that ye meet, though in error he may be, his special worth that ye would worship in thy Lord, ye have not even begun to find the meaning of brotherhood."

Part III

FIVE OUTWARD APPROACHES
TO HIGH PLAY

CHAPTER SEVEN

COVENANTING GROUP AND OPUS

The Covenanting Group

More than a hundred people interested in the ideas of Edgar Cayce are gathered from points across the nation for one of a number of weeklong seminars at Virginia Beach, Virginia, where they will undertake drugless ventures in altered consciousness while they study together. Under the guidance of Cayce's son, Hugh Lynn Cayce, a man in his sixties who is an inventive genius in group work and unexcelled in his knowledge of meditation (as may be seen in his book *Venture Inward*), the seekers are placed in intensive small "project groups." There they will be confronted by the same six to ten group faces for an entire week, in a program of the Cayce-oriented Association for Research and Enlightenment.

Always in the same group, they go to lectures, they talk, they eat, they meditate, they work on assignments, they argue, and they get on each other's nerves. They despise having to do everything as a group when they must all go to the laundromat so that one or two of their number may wash clothes, or when none of them can eat until the last straggler of their group arrives at a meal. Yet as they swim in the ocean together, or do dishes together, or get up together for a 2 A.M. period of meditation, or talk over one another's dreams in group sessions, they find themselves secretly beginning to like one another as well—despite individual peculiarities which still are irritating. They grumble that they will never again enter such a project group. But they observe the crucial group-chosen disciplines in which they pray for each other; in time they find that they are often laughing together, even when they voluntarily fast while other groups stuff themselves. They tell each other their biographies, each with its sadness and its hope and final uniqueness. And they continue in their classes and discussions on the theme of the week: how to live a balanced life of growth.

As the days and the nights go on, they find that they no longer only abide one another but actively choose one another. The time comes when they do not want to work at any task, or discuss any serious question, unless their whole group is present, for they have come to savor each member's special contributions. Out of their dreams of one another they begin to speak aloud the truth which they see about one group member after another, and to build mightily upon what they want to bring out in each person of their little company. There are tears, there are howls of laughter, and around the group faces young and old shine in the sharing, which is now so searching and quick that the original group "enabler" or leader is no longer needed, but has become one more member of their crew. In quiet times, and in speaking times, they find that they can shift together to ways of high play, as real when grave as when gay, in which they seem unaccountably close to what Cayce called the Creative Forces of their lives.

What goes on in groups where a kind of people-field is

generated with such force that the consciousness of members may alter to permanent changes?

Two processes in all groups must be considered. On the one hand, there is the group function of completing a task, whether winning a battle or getting the supper dishes done, whether studying Cayce or robbing a bank. On the other hand, there is the function of building up the personhood of group members and enhancing the process which fulfills their life forms, whether this is done through therapy or through earning, through training or through thinking, through discipline or through abandon. While it is a convenience of thought to think of task-oriented groups (such as committees or firms or armies) and of person-oriented groups (such as lovers or families or project groups), both kinds of groups must perform both functions. There must be enough task orientation in any group to accomplish a minimum of housekeeping, or order, or specifying agenda. And there must be enough person orientation in any group to sustain a minimum of morale, as well as to generate leadership and fellowship.

This bipolarity in all group life is carried on by each group's combining of a corporate set, to accomplish appointed or chosen tasks, and a covenantal set, to build members and improve their ways of growing together. Each group or institution puts together the two sets in its own unique way. The corporate set, which predominates in large institutions but may also be primary in the smallest shop or platoon or family task force, involves only as much of the lives or interests of members as is needed for the task at hand. This set tends to structure itself in handy offices, rites, duties, privileges, titles, ideologies, and similar apparatus familiar in collective life —whether of the arts or of arsenals, of child rearing or of consumer polls, of picketing or of professional football. By contrast, the covenantal set, which predominates in a small encounter or project group of peers, but may also be expressed in the life of a nation or a people (as well as in a campus or a commune or a Woodstock celebration), engages the deep values and full personhood of

221

group members. This set tends to foster decentralized or shared and spontaneous leadership, as well as fostering informality in slogans and places and rites.

How these two sets are put together profoundly affects the life of any group or institution, whether a pair of lovers or an organized revolution. For the two sets require each other, to keep shared life in that vital balance which produces optimum co-creating in high play all around. The corporate set maximizes the development of ego strength and productive consciousness, while freely drawing on the problem-solving and compensatory levels of the unconscious which are ever ready to serve consciousness. But the covenantal set gives freedom and stimulus to the life-form level of the psyche, together with the deeper levels of the unconscious which offer the greatest force and richness for all permanent growth towards optimums.

Whenever one set begins to overbalance the other, in one or many institutions, then a surge of spontaneous corrective efforts may be expected. When, for example, the shared life of China or India had been too long locked into narrow structures of village and region and class, there came in modern times thrusts toward new corporate sets, which might in time clear the way in each land for freer and richer covenanting. The thrusts have been breathtaking in their force in both countries, though different in each. And when, by contrast, large numbers in busy Western societies have found their lives too fragmented into special roles of work and recreation, of consumer and voter, until all existence has seemed corporate, involving but limited and shallow parts of personhood at any one time, then a stirring began to find new ways of covenanting, new religious ventures and new politics, new sexuality and family groups, which have seemed to rock the established forms of the culture with their force. It is against such a background of cultural changes that the peculiar potency of contemporary small encounter groups must be understood. They work to reactivate the cov-

222

enantal set, and therein lies their strength for members—though of course also their limitation.

Such groups often handle traditions and doctrines so lightly as to infuriate those who think that all groupings must serve particular tasks in the established institutions and programs of therapy or religion, of social reform or moneymaking or family togetherness. As their members work at building their unique people-fields in their own ways, they may meet for a weekend or a week, or weekly or—in some groups of campus or church or clinic or command—they may meet daily. Whatever their schedules, and however they are named, such covenantal groups set about "letting the life process be the content" of their shared sessions. Where task-oriented groups concentrate on mastering concepts, or on getting someone elected, or on drilling for oil, or on performing Bach or rock, these people-oriented groups concentrate on such questions as "Where are you headed?", "What did you really mean?", "What would you like to be doing here instead?", and "How do you feel about her?" They pay special attention to the hidden and surface exchanges in the group by asking "Have you noticed how Jerry has gotten into the action in specific stages?", and "What is the effect on our group when we try a period of meditation together, as compared with focusing on Phyllis' marital problems—or is there any basic difference?" The strength in all such questions is their intense concentration on the real values, real commitments, real ideals, real styles and defenses of participants, whether the focusing is done chiefly by talk, or is given added force by role playing, drug taking, non-verbal exercises, reverie procedures, and the demands of planning a program for others. Life after life within the group comes under scrutiny for what it is, with its puniness and greatness combined. When the exchanges are open and rich, small covenanted groups find that they are rarely misled for long about individual members; accordingly, they can offer sensitive and accurate evaluations for each individual, so essential to any whole-souled growth toward optimums. They can in effect give "readings" which are so helpful and penetrating that even Cayce would have little to add—as Cayce himself pointed out. At the same time, such groups at their best can offer more than evaluation to their members. They can aid the forward-moving energies and choices of each member, and foster spontaneous psychedelic changes, often with greater impact than the services of a professional social worker, priest, or psychiatrist.

For the jury of the peers is as potent in the living room, or on the sands at Virginia Beach, as it is in the courtroom. The group which grows to be truly loving comes to stand to its members for the human family. Not surprisingly, such a group often develops, however unselfconsciously, its own procedures for initiating members into larger life, for confirmation of maturity and ordination in specific work choices, as well as for blessing adventurous marital choices. Especially does the covenanted group exhibit the capacity to hear confessions and offer collective forgiveness to its members, in its own forms and nonforms. The impact of this forgiving is stronger than might be guessed by those who have not experienced its riotous grace. Out of the talk and the yelling, the laughter and the tears, the embraces and the promises, the insights and the touch phrases, there can emerge a group state of "speaking the truth in love"—amplified by spontaneous reference to tale, legend, myth, art, theory, and scripture—which peels away low play from whatever it touches. And there may emerge from the pleading and the teasing, the remembering and the saluting, especially when reinforced by appointed times of intercession, a group field of force in prayer and meditation which would delight a contemplative monk. As the members speak of the primary games of their lives, in the open and often frightening group sharing, they may find such hope, and such determination upon optimums, that they turn completely around in spontaneous altered states.

But the participant in such a group not only begins his own high play at last, he activates chain reactions of high play among his relatives, fellow employees, and even strangers and enemies—all of whose surprised and sometimes hostile responses may serve to prod him along his path of growth. It is small wonder that Alcoholics Anonymous, with its potent people-fields, has been able to stop the flow of alcohol and lost lifeblood among its drunks, where prisons and pills and ostracism have often failed. Nor is it surprising that similar processes have had large effect for drug abusers (in ventures at which Synanon pioneered), for gamblers, and for other victims of compulsions, while it is often asked whether churches and synagogues ought to be Sinners Anonymous, using similar processes in convenantal small-group life. The impersonal Cayce source, whatever it was, valued small study-growth groups so highly as to lead Cayce to invest the best energies of the last two decades of his life in developing the methods, materials, theories, and trainers for such groups. Many of these groups used two anonymous and biblically oriented little manuals for growth entitled *A Search for God,* and developed around Cayce's concepts.

But the effort to maximize the people-field by covenantal set has its perils. The group may lose track of the corporate set, concerned with what Cayce called "service" in worthwhile tasks, while concentrating on "attunement" in sensitivity to each other and to the One. Members may so stifle constructive study—or art or social action or other sustained tasks which build conscious ego strength —that their sessions end in trivializing exchanges, seeking vast meanings in essentially small offerings which are not screened by the demands of man-sized labors. When this happens, a further peril usually appears. The process of people building is itself turned into a task to be mastered, into special skills and prowess, rather than kept a full and meaty engagement with the Third who has bet on each, and fires the life form of each in unique ways. In the name of good group process and building persons, the task-set so familiar in surrounding institutional life may be imported into the group doings, producing requirements of specified orgies of disclosure, or of stylized breakthroughs,

225

or of rituals of "How I have been helped," or of references to doctrines psychiatric, religious, political, psychic, or hippie. In time, such a set grinds the faces of group members as can a poor marriage or a tyrannical office hierarchy, even though it is offered in the name of building people.

Preventing such an outcome requires an everlasting clarifying and deepening and renewing of the covenant within which the group meets and works. As the Cayce source insisted, the ideal which brought the group together and held it together, the ultimate set, would determine most of what followed. Such an ideal ought not to be conceived as a constitution, nor as a set of meeting procedures, nor some pious hopes. It would have to be thought out to the point where it was found so rich and deep as to be covenant with a living Person—in the Cayce terminology, with "the Christ." The point was similar to that made by the Jewish philosopher Martin Buber when he observed that there was no lasting way to bind people together for mutual growth and transformation except where the center of the group was "transpicuous to the divine."

By working on the covenant, group members may put into perspective the task-oriented or corporate function of their venture. They may soon discover that if their people-field is to avoid paralyzing narcissism, it must be joined to ventures where daily work and growing is done, in more conventional routines. To join their intimate circulation to larger social musculature, members may strive to make their jobs and homes and interest centers freer for high play. Or they may try projects which the encounter group sponsors for those outside its charmed fellowship. Or they may try both methods. However they set about it, if they are to give their alterings of consciousness the fixing action of sharing and service, they must take up tasks for outsiders which are as rich and difficult as the often painful but sometimes glorious sharings within the group life. As strong as the people-field itself, so strong and demanding must be these tasks undertaken for the non-

group—yet always undertaken in that cool, swinging indifference while fully engaged and loving which marks
the life fresh-minted in the best encounter groups. Where
each hour of talk or meditation is so matched with an hour
of original effort away from ingroup snugness, in conscious search of high play—at the workbench, at the world
peace meeting, at the worship venture, or in the whirl of
lovemaking—then the encounter group may bear its rich-
est fruits, and bless even old and hoary corporate structures with new life.

As keepers of the traditions of altered consciousness,
religious movements have had their historic versions of
covenantal groupings and fields, within which consciousness might safely fluidize towards highest play. India has
had its traditions of gurus with disciples alongside more
conventional structures of family and village life—structures which Gandhi sought to infuse with new covenantal
force by inspiring them with shared tasks of productive
high play symbolized by the spinning wheel. The Buddha
altered Indian tradition by introducing its first church,
the missionizing Sangha or company of monks. China,
where Buddhism traveled as India's great cultural export,
developed the covenant of the ancestral family across several generations, creating a groundwork for modern Communist cells and communes which commit themselves to
sacrificing present comforts for the welfare of future generations. Japanese Zen, drawing on Chinese Taoist traditions, developed groupings for altered consciousness
which interspersed periods of retreat with active life in
family and government and business. As Islam experimented with its own sects and schools and traditions, it
produced the leveling *hajj* pilgrimage (so like the gather-
ing at Virginia Beach of a weeklong seminar and project
grouping), which made Islam the one religious tradition
least tainted by racial and class discrimination. Israel,
drawing upon the same biblical legacy, developed its traditions of covenanting in families and tribes, in which the
stranger and the orphan had to be accounted a true place.
There was also the covenant of the whole people of Israel,

brought by Yahweh from Egyptian bondage and taught by judges, kings, prophets and reformers, as well as by suffering, in the work of a chosen people who beckoned others to ultimate homeland with God, even during the centuries of no Jewish nation. Christianity early chose the polycultural covenanting route of the Hellenistic mystery religions, discarding the ethnic identifications of its parent Judaism and setting for itself the unending problem of the nature and ground of the bonds which it espoused "in Christ." Through the centuries of its development, Christianity developed new covenantal forms for monastic ingroups, as did Buddhism, and later produced two poles of Christian group life: the church and the sect. The church sought to be the established vehicle for all true believers in a nation or a people, while the sect sought greater depth and purity in its covenant, often at the expense of traditional forms and comradeship. The tension between church and sect was in part the tension between corporate and covenantal sets, continuing today in the strains between conventional church life and the reforming-renewal movements—each of the latter on its own pilgrimage in some marriage or courtship with psychiatry or Eastern faiths.

But religious groupings do not necessarily hold center stage in the search for covenants for altered consciousness in today's world. The mutual pledges of civil rights and peace workers, who seek not only to alter behaviors but at times the minds and hearts of their members and others, and the new covenants of guerrilla theater groups, or of house communes, may cut deeper into the selfhood of participants than any covenants which members have yet known. Psychiatric know-how, augmented by accumulated lore of group life from such efforts as A.A. and the National Training Laboratory, and by social psychology research, has produced a stream of programs, respected and suspected, in every major city and major campus area: encounter groups, growth groups, sensitivity-training groups, marathons, meditation groups—all bent on optimums.

Wherever the covenanting group, whatever its origins, quickens the cycle of high play in its members, it finds specific effects with which to work. Group members learn to watch for that initial disorienting or fresh remark, whether of sly humor or sober insight, which reveals that someone in the company has begun to move, to make connections, to get himself and others into fresh perspective. If not in a remark, the first level of co-creating high play may show itself in an act, a gesture, a spontaneous dance, a willingness for fisticuffs, or the crinkling around someone's thoughtful eyes. Next may come a contagious lift in group spirits, again either in levity or sobriety. There is a mounting sense of things to say, lives to live, impossible dreams to dream. Ideas may come fast, from all around the group, so that the field of sharing fairly crackles. To keep the growing lift at this stage, a group soon learns to avoid undue negativism or undue cuteness—just as research on brainstorming recommends. At this stage energies from the unconscious realms of members are being mustered and directed which will in time work their own critical refining, under the pressure of a solid group set towards productive high play.

Now the focus stage may begin, often but not always introduced by the one who started the initial burst of exchanges. What before has been interesting and stimulating group interaction may now step up into intense reflection, calling for individual action, and decision, upon whatever is before the group. It becomes apparent that in the general hubbub of the previous stage a shaft has lodged in someone; he has caught the full force of the meanings so far shared in the session. Whoever he is, when he speaks it is time to listen, for the life-arousing, life-cleansing focus stage is coming about. That group which has worked at the high-play cycle will have learned to mark in each member the timbre of voice, the vocabulary, the lean of the body, which accompany focused co-creating. If, however, the group now falls to chattering and sparking back and forth, as do many groups at this stage, then the chances of moving on with the high-play cycle are less-ened. But when the group can fully and doggedly attend to one or two of its members who are coming into focus, staying with them and tugging and listening as though rowing for a great whale, then each member can find himself approaching that high seriousness and clarity which marks the sharply focused ones.

In the "on" stage, exchanges come with greater care than before, since people are not simply reacting to one another's stimulus but responding to each other with their very lives. Periods of silence may be as rich as speaking, while thought builds on thought, act on act, decision on decision, around the room. What must be kept alive and moving in the group at this time is so like a living creature that no rules for its care will suffice. Part of the venture is making sure that one or two members stay "on," even when this limits the number who can speak in turn of their problems, their concerns, their discoveries. Better to climb up with one who can pull up the rest (partly by what Cayce called "raising the vibrations of all"), than to pull him down and the rest with him. In the "on" stage, the most valued contributions will sometimes come from someone who has heretofore held back, or has been so glib as to hold back his deeper self; his true sharing is assurance that the covenant for growth to optimums with the One is working.

Whether the kickover effect of the undrugged cycle now follows does not seem susceptible to group control or planning (though experience my teach the wisdom of what the entranced Cayce observed, that group meditation and prayer, both at meetings and daily while apart, could do much to open the way for meetings between that which was man and Not-man). When the kickover makes its rare appearance, it may, however, be recognized and welcomed. Even in a general "on" time, when people speak slowly and truly, when person meets person rather than person meeting social object, when demons and angels are brought from deep chambers and gently admitted into the room, when spontaneous touching and holding joins walking and weeping in flows not interrupted by happy silence—there and then may still be noted that extra shiver, that special joy, that whole-selfed alertness for loving, which tells the visitation of the kickover effect. As this stage arrives, those whom it reaches do not require as much aid as before to keep focused and honest and open. One of the marks of the kickover effect is the individual's capacity and desire fully to attend to others without losing his own depth and clarity. In speech at this level, which Quakers historically prize, form and content meet in easy grace of expression which is never forced rhetoric; even the entranced Cayce shifted to spontaneous poetry when he entered this stage. If the group is fortunate, and knows how to receive gifts of grace, then the kickover effect may spread gently around the room, offering a trembling vitality which cannot be pretended or pushed but only accepted for its aid in refashioning and unfolding the lives of those gathered. The effect may not stay for long, but it is not needed for long. It will leave its permanent mark on the lore and tradition of the group, so that members will speak of that time when "you said" and "she was sure," and "he remembered" and "we agreed"—and will give thanks to the One as they do. Like all lovely gifts, the kickover does not require much handling at the time. Rather does it require, when it reaches its fullness and begins to ebb, assurances from those who know what they say, that action will follow from the visitation to the group. Then those members of a group are blessed who can offer spontaneous forms, for there is often need of some celebration or thanksgiving, in dance or in silence in eating or in embrace, in prayer or in foolishness. No formulas alone may supply this need, and lucky are those who know how to use new forms so that they enhance the old, or old forms so that right then they are new.

As the high-play quickening makes its departure, amid shared doings as simple as happy grunts and stretches, or as complex as any libations to the divine, it will leave in its wake peace and incredible goodwill, not merely as a suggestion or a hope but as an active force that will roll right on into the members' daily lives. The cycle will be found to have deposited its own golden silt of inventiveness, of imagination, of easy confidence that problems may be tackled—in such jaunty buoyancy as may alarm associates outside the group until they see that this is no pose nor swagger, but a way of high play in all games.

Whether the high-play quickening moves down a quiet channel of group study, or down a boisterous route of role playing and imaginative exercises (such as those developed in that radioactive center of high play, the Esalen Institute in California), it will bring dangers as well as rewards. For since the group so easily becomes microcosm for the human venture—family and tribe, state and history, church and hospital, job and crusade—the ancient human patterns tend to be rehearsed in it, often compulsively and unconsciously. Parent-child transferences occur among members with gripping intensity which astonishes those not familiar with the ways of the parent game; such transferences may prompt efforts symbolically to destroy or emasculate leaders in the group, as well as lead to symbolic pairings and polarizings. Romance games will appear in a variety of subtle or unsubtle advances or repulsions, not all of them pleasant or useful or easily controlled. And the work game may be as cruel as battle when some in the group seek their long-betrayed heroism in its activities. Religion games are easily played in the sharing of compelling images and quotes and rites, or in the upsetting of these in the name of some new ultimate. Whatever is authentically human tends to be re-created in group transactions under the force of stress and set, modulated by setting and shutoff and freed by sharing and service. Accordingly, the development of trouble and conflict between group members may be the best of signs that the group is getting ready to do important business where consciousness needs to alter and can alter. Yet low play is not high play. The effort must always be made to draw from the pains, the strivings, the longings, those seeds of goodness in every fixation, those talents locked up in the armor of every defense, those true hopes hidden in every extravagant demand. Such a process is so taxing as to require of members no less than real love to carry the process past the point of novelty.

The love may come. The path on which it comes, with greater freedom and purity in successive sessions, is likely to be a path made by what members do between meetings —as the Cayce source never wearied of pointing out. For there are no skills or exercises of group process, no sensitivity trainings, which can take the place of resolutely following out daily assignment and tasks of becoming, upon which the group has agreed that its members will act and report back at the next meeting. Representative of such between-meetings focuses is that remarkable set of twenty-four which the trance-speaking Cayce suggested to a study group, who later wrote up seven years of experiences with these tasks in two little volumes called *A Search for God* (described in detail in the present writer's *Edgar Cayce on Religion and Psychic Experience*). But even these graded focuses for growth, like all such training sequences for high play, need the concreteness of group-invented assignments to be carried out between meetings. And surely part of the group disciplines, as the Cayce source patiently urged, will be unhurried clinging to the One in meditation, both at group meetings and between them, as well as daily intercession for group members by name—often in alternative time slots which members may try to reach together at least once each day. To pray for another in some honest and regular way, with whatever language or unvoiced thought, is to forestall using him within the group, and to foster cherishing his true life form, even if one must later fight him to bring forth that life form.

Ahab has no covenanting group, though at the end he moves toward one when he takes to his cabin to live with him the demented yet clear little Pip, whose strained spirit seems so much like his own, and whose love almost turns him back from vengeance on the white whale. His crew have some measure of covenantal ties on a journey which sees friendships formed and ripened, men risking their lives for one another, and weaknesses faced and overcome while they eat, dance, kill whales, tell stories, stare at the distance, do housekeeping, fall ill, and briefly pray, in the spell-cast circle of their ship. Yet their covenantal bonds are not articulated or cultivated, but ever subordinated to the task of whaling, and even more to Ahab's personal task of revenge and prowess, until there hangs like a dark cloud over the *Pequod* the question of whether men in their busy ventures afloat and ashore can ever belong to one another in any fuller way. At the last, the gaunt New England captain seeks in the ecstasy of skills at which he is a master to find that touch of life on life, flesh on flesh, being on being which he can neither find nor make in covenant with God or man, but must instead try to force from the body and blood of the whale, broken and shed for him.

Making and Marketing an Opus

Two college girls carrying heavy suitcases struggle to push through a crowd on a train platform. They are obviously returning to campus after their midyear vacation. Because it is time for the sleek, stainless-steel train to depart for Colorado, they are anxious to get aboard. Yet they are a car's length from the nearest entrance to the train, and the crowd gathered tightly around a celebrity will not part for them. Nobody moves.

The celebrity is a large graying man in a rumpled suit and an ample mustache. He hardly seems the world's foremost interpreter of Bach's organ music, which he is. Nor does he seem one of the greatest living philosopher-theologians, which he also is. And there is nothing in his shaggy and untidy appearance to suggest that he is the physician-head of an African jungle hospital, whose financial needs have brought him to the U.S. to lecture and to play organ recitals. But it is clearly this man and his wife upon whom the reporters and photographers, and the dignitaries of the academic, art, and philanthropic life of a city, are turning their every attention, striving to catch phrases in French and German with which he answers questions. Nobody wants to be interrupted by college girls while hearing Albert Schweitzer speak—not even those few, including the present writer, who have just spent two hours in a leisurely luncheon with him.

The last call to board the train is given, and Schweitzer and his wife move toward the steps where they must enter. Then Schweitzer catches sight of the girls on the far edge of the crowd, still calling out to be allowed to pass. Without stopping his exchanges with reporters and admirers, he ambles through the crowd to the girls and casually picks up their heavy suitcases, shouldering a way for them to the entrance of the train. It all happens quickly and cheerily, and it is not until the train has pulled out that an awkward silence falls over the lingering admirers. They have come to pay honor to a man whose way is to make things happen, to produce at the top of his ability in music, in scholarship, and in medicine used to redress the flow of services between white man and black. But the honor which they offer seems hollow before the obvious thought: he who is a creator in large tasks is creative in small things, while those who only stand and appreciate may be creative in neither.

To the modern Westerner it seems unlikely that he could transform his consciousness towards optimums by making and marketing an opus—whether an organ work, a treatise on reverence for life, a medical center, or a spring housecleaning, a computer, or a shopping center. He finds it easier to conceive mind-altering moments in the task-oriented groupings of other times, when he might have fashioned a warrior's sword, or set down god-inspired Homeric prose, or even marshaled a frontier wagon train. But his imagination does not readily seize on the mind-altering potentials of installing an elevator, writing a PTA report, organizing an appliance sale, or holding a cocktail party.

Yet, as T. S. Eliot has suggested in his bright and brittle drawing-room play *The Cocktail Party*, all the elements of heroic initiation and sacrifice are in principle as present

235

in giving a party as in dramatic martyrdom in Africa—where one of Eliot's characters is crucified alive on a mound of ants. For what is required for the creation, development, and final marketing for consumption of a man-sized opus, whether it be a concert or a crusade, a love affair or an insurance company, a manual or a machine, a political party or a cocktail party, is wedding the best of consciousness with the best of the unconscious—in its transpersonal vestments from far inward realms. Making this point, the New Testament of Hinduism, the *Bhagavad Gita,* sets its definitive and soaringly poetic encounter between one man and God at the edge of a battlefield. In that activistic setting, so unlikely for Hindu nonviolent asceticism, the counsel of the divine Krishna is for Arjuna to step forward and complete the opus of the battle at hand, while keeping the spirit of high play which does not mistake the temporary trophies of war for the fullest becomings of the warriors. In an authentic psychedelic vision which emerges just before the battle begins (precisely as Eliot climaxes his play in a scene just before a party begins), the divine Krishna shows himself to Arjuna with such appalling richness of form that, like Job, Arjuna cries he has had enough. The scene is one of the most stunning and devout in all of religious literature. Yet the mind-altering vision is not given to Arjuna for the glory of a colorful experience as such, but that the man who thus sees the divine may act, may love, may gain understanding, by creating the opus at hand.

Such an emphasis on finding divine companionship in altered states, created by strenuous co-creating with others, parallels the frequently used quotation in the Cayce readings: "Study to show thyself approved, a workman not ashamed." In the view expressed by these Cayce materials, man was at his best when he struggled to bring forth a work, a creation, household, a pilgrimage, which was consonant with his life form and which so taxed his inner energies as to place him in touch with the transpersonal or "universal" helping energies of the divine.

To create an opus, some noble form which uses all of

the creator's resources, requires using consciousness, under the direction of the ego. Concentrated thought must define a need, set forth a problem to be solved, identify opposites to be reconciled in the opus. The long hours of conscious work in the garret which prepare the artist, the long hours with sales reports which prepare the businessman, the long hours with retorts and journals which prepare the scientist, the long hours of phone calls and serving meals which prepare the gracious party hostess, the long hours of talking with people which prepare the political leader—these are often overlooked in speculation on the marvel of an inspiration which one day leaps to life in a transformed person. But it is the disciplined surface consciousness, with its tools and languages and array of instructive failures as well as successes, which is able to code the unconscious for a precious discharge at last. There are, of course, those times when the vision of a man seems to emerge without his effort, to coalesce with the currents of a time which make it relevant (and of course much of the Orient, like Cayce, would argue that past-life karma gave the visionary his needed preparation and opportunity). But inspiration even in the gifted is more dependent on conscious "study" (as Cayce so often emphasized) than many might imagine who expect to tickle the unconscious into greatness, whether by devotions or drugs or daimons, or by covetous crisis and craving.

However, even the most trained and talented consciousness must be met by the unconscious to accomplish the making and marketing of an opus which totally engages its creator or co-creators. Maya, that dancing girl of the imagination, must step forward from problem solving and compensatory levels of the unconscious, as she draws over the problem her iridescent veil. For her aid, no ego-mastered skill will substitute; the creator of an opus waits for her, and waits. But whether he knows her haunts makes a difference. The man who has met his own good imagination in fashioning an art or business opus recognizes the gift of that imagination for the opus of solving a civil-rights crisis. And the woman who has met her imagination in developing the opus of a better school for her children recognizes its aid when she must try the opus of real-estate saleswork to support her growing family. Those who have not done large business with the inner spinner of patterns may stumble over Maya's compensatory imagery, masquerading as true solutions of the problem at hand in order to trap them into postponed personal growth. Then they may fall in love with someone who bears at that moment the visage of their own creative unconscious, and must interrupt their work on an opus while they sort out shadow from substance in their relationships.

It is in the charmed light within the fire-ringed circle of the life form where Maya best dances, whether for an opus in athletics, in religion, or in manufacture of mousetraps. Mere brainstorming from the unconscious does not often produce the enduring form, though the art of brainstorming (where conscious criticism and evaluation are withheld while suggestions pour forth for recording and later selective action) is a valuable tool for the makers of an opus—and not too different from the reverie method, except that it does not go as deep into the unconscious, and focuses on an outward task instead of on an inward becoming. Maya dances too freely, too long, in brainstorming alone. The person who is able to develop and offer a worthy opus for dollars, votes, attendance, coworkers, theoretical confirmation, or revolutionary action, is typically the one who learns that his best creations are those which fit within his life form. A man bullied and threatened by his father develops a chain of men's clothing shops where others can celebrate the manhood not originally shared with him. A woman betrayed by poor guidance from her rationality-dodging drunken father manages to work out, amid the press of her later life with her own family, the canons of theological insight which she shares with suburban couples who have almost forgotten how to think, until assembled with her in a study group. A musician son of a master composer of Modern Romantic music creates his own works in a spare modern mode which makes its occasional Romanticism shine all the brighter. A woman reared by a martinet of a mother rears her own children in great permissiveness, which is so infused with her identity and her children's identities that the resultant controls are more compelling than family rules or punishment schedules. A man of great curiosity about Nature and sex has been unable to share his wondering boyhood discoveries with his parents, and becomes as an adult the able curator of a university museum. From out of the deep questions, the journeying riddle of each one's life myth (questions which Cayce called each one's karma), springs the opus which really works, and which wholly engages and in time transforms the creator.

Yet even as Maya answers the seeking consciousness with her helpful dance, in the confines of the life form she must be met by an ego-captained consciousness which is ready to go to work. For even the most original of inventions requires manufacturing, projects require scheduling and staffing, visual designs require executing in oils and watercolors. Conscious skills count, as do conscious canons of criticism, guided by conscious pledges of will. The task of the opus maker, once he is inwardly inspired, is to hold fast to the tools of his trade. He must hammer out his new image in the media of meetings, people, signs, slogans, systems, songs, or mahogany. Once more the unconscious and conscious currents meet in that embrace so essential to the most turned-on states. Out of such person-integrating and demanding work on the opus, in the office, the laboratory, the kitchen, the mine, the strategy tent, there comes the inner circuitry which can carry full force when next high play is needed—whether for silent meditation or for the awkward discourse of youth with parent, whether for clarifying a dream or for risking extinction by a worthy opponent. Out of work comes free and pertinent fancy. Out of the opus comes opening. Out of labor comes lightning.

When the opus must be marketed, the gifts of the unconscious are needed once again. There is a special interplay of consciousness and the deeper levels of the psyche which occurs in the pricing and sale of a product, whether for dollars or some other value or approval. This interplay comes about through having to decide which public the creation is to reach, whether one's family or strangers, the wealthy or the privatized, the taste makers or the tasters. Part of making and marketing any opus is answering the question which burst open Schweitzer the organist and Schweitzer the philosopher: Who are your people? While in some societies the answer to this question is supplied by caste and other social devices, in modern mobile and expanding Western culture the question is often more difficult—and more rewarding—to ask and to answer. In part the answer may be found in the fire-ringed circle of the creator's life form, for his people are likely to be those who can suffer or have suffered in ways like his own pain and pent-up longing for wholeness (as Cayce insisted in tracing such currents from many lives), though not necessarily in the same tasks or towns as his. But there is a further source of the answer to the question of who are the fitting people, or the fitting market, for a science fair, a neighborhood cleanup, the uses of atomic power, a new method of food processing, a biography. This is that deep region of the unconscious where lie the hidden forms of a generation, in what Jung called "the collective unconscious" and Cayce called "group karma."

Among those who struggle to make an opus which shall prove to endure are always some who push their converse with unknown jinns of a people and a time, until they design and market a creation which seems to act upon everyone who will let it. Gandhi and King design crusades for truth-force toward freedom. The founders of A.A. design a vehicle for drunks. Van der Rohe and colleagues design spare structures of architecture for overstimulated modern city dwellers, while Pete Seeger and others design songs for the flagging modern spirit. And it is not only the famed who do this crucial work of touching the deep unconscious—or karma—of their times and people. Perhaps the same work is done in some measure by the designers of each contemplative Japanese garden, each solid college term paper, each humming factory work team, and each doorbell drill for the polls. In the view of the entranced Cayce, each such task completed might add to the weight of constructive "thought forms" which had more than personal stature, and could channel the aid of the Creative Forces in a given age; indeed, such work could offer authentic participation in the redemptive action of "the Christ."

To construct and deliver a man-sized opus, then, leaves the creators thrice blessed; in the excellence of their products, in their own mind-altering becomings while under creative demands, and in the helpful currents which they stir in their fellows. But the perils of making an opus, alone or with others, are as great as the rewards. Setting out to produce a product or program tempts its creators to autointoxication. As a consequence, the question of how to make something noble, or how to make something happen, without coveting a particular goal, is the focus of the *Gita's* principle of nonattachment to the fruits of one's labors, as it is of the Buddha's doctrine of *anatta* or nonself, offered as a guard against the notion of private becoming at the expense of fostering the whole field of high play. Similarly, Jesus encourages his followers to seek the kingdom of God and His righteousness in delighted indifference, yet confidence, regarding "all these things" so necessary to the games of life. The question is how to disport in eternal mildness of joy, not apart from chasing whales, but in the midst of whale slaying as an opus which stretches to every horizon.

The historic religious traditions have differed on how to make the opus serve self-transformation. Finding Hindu tradition too steeped in lush imagery, some of it fertility imagery, the Buddha set off towards simplicity of opus both in his discourses and in such daily-life symbols as the saffron robes of his monk-followers; in this respect he was the Mohammed of the East, refusing to let his followers become trapped by projections on graven images of the deity, or by conceptual images of the divine spark which they thought was encapsulated within themselves. But the Buddha's piety produced a faith which often merely paralleled the forms of government in the societies where his teachings flowered, not always entering as readily into the opus making of political power as into the search for beauty and truth. Why Greece chose to exalt natural forms, including the human form, for its high play in opus making, while Israel turned away from Nature towards history and law, remains one of the puzzles of the developments of peoples. The differences between these two cultures endowed Christianity—child of both Israel and Greece, yet reared in the arms of Rome —with conflicts through its long history, as men of this faith have struggled to make serviceable and mind-springing forms without becoming captives of these forms. Monks took on selected forms, not including the forms of woman, while emperors created kingdoms on vast political canvases, and popes commissioned artists to do murals of Christ as royalty. The Reformation brought the Calvinist marriage of forms of faith with the forms of nascent capitalism, as so often noted by historians, while Lutheranism tried piety cast in its own forms but erected directly adjoining the cultural forms of work and politics. In all of these versions and others, the central Western thrust had been to trust the making of an opus as a vehicle for the transformation of the mind Godward—whether that opus be a political or business structure which dominated monuments or newspapers, or the mechanical structure of a spinning wheel or a universal school system or a Ford. In the process of dreaming greatness through know-how, the questions of know-why and know-where for far transformings have often been shoved aside. In a people so surfeited with the making and marketing of things and causes, can fashioning the opus still aid consciousness to alter?

Certainly the high play cycle appears in the making of a high-purposed opus, especially when that making is joined with activities which discard form and deed—as do meditation and in some sense each night's dreaming, where forms are wildly arrayed and dispatched, and no labor done or products sold or votes gathered, except symbolically. The flash of possibility which inaugurates the undrugged cycle of high play has been well-reported in chronicles of science, industry, the arts, and politics. "It could be done" is the gasp of delight and sometimes awe which starts the process of quickened creativity, when someone guesses a way to solve a problem which seems right to him in his very bones—which is to say in his life form. The flash becomes a steady lift, of one creator or several, as more and more possibilities are seen in a process which brainstorming well represents. Connections are perceived, resources called to mind, analogies used, distant happy prospects envisaged, workers and specialists recruited. Even the dreams of the creators take account of the lift, sometimes by using the opus as an emblem for the solution of other problems of the dreamers, and sometimes by improving the inspiration or invention under way. What the focus stage next accomplishes, in the making of an opus, is sorting out who will be involved in the doing, and in what way. If not distorted by forced crisis and craving, the undrugged cycle will do its own work of quickening some to continue with the opus, or suggesting to them a better and more timely focus yet, while separating others for whom the task might prove harmful or irrelevant. But no mere decision by impulse will suffice for the focus stage; concentrated discrimination and evaluation are required—and even these will not always sort out the Judases of great intent, whose efforts must apparently fall into fixated low play in order to achieve their anxious growth.

If the makers of an opus follow through with decisions to try this task, take this journey, plant this apple seed, then there may follow the "on" stage, lasting for hours or recurring in some form for months or even years. How far the "on" productivity may be sustained seems dependent in part on the pact of set with the One which the co-creator has made in the deep recesses of his mind, whatever he has said to others. This pact, which is in fact a covenant, specifies what he will try to do, and for whom, if the gift is given him to fashion the form which he has

243

seen and sought. If he does not break the pact by selfishness or indifference, nor vitiate its power by too much talk, he may find himself not only with a heroic opus, or the groundwork for such an opus to come in the next generation, but with a completely altered life—as Schweitzer found for himself. And at times the opus creator may even encounter the rare but precious kickover effect, when he is met by that which he is sure is not his own force alone. At this stage others may catch and share the vision which he can offer to them, for they grasp it as somehow their own, and as a making which goes with the grain of the universe. In such sharing, revolutions are born at the cost of the lives of willing marchers, and arena lions are faced with the same easy indifference and directness that others bring to whales or emperors, art critics or employers, children or wayward spouses. The full test of whether the creators can sustain high play is now upon them, for they are potent and they know it. In their heightened strength and originality they may destroy and grab, or they may forgive and release and build; the history of the Caesars illustrates both choices, as do biographies of saints or of social lions.

If fidelity is kept to the One, whether in success or failure of the planned opus, then there follows that cleansed readiness which leaves its mark of confidence for the next venture: "The difficult we do at once, while the impossible takes a little longer." Powder is left so that the next flame of co-creating may ignite from a small spark. And there is also a gift of meaning given for old forms. He who has led a revolution at the office or the factory can find the issues which made his ancestors revolutionaries, and can glimpse the true questions behind the pat answers of stereotyped political slogans. He who has taken his place in a little-theater opus can walk in step with the buskined stride of the olden Greeks, and can laugh to the challenge that Shakespeare knew in competing with bear fights, held on alternate nights in the same theater which offered his plays. He who has labored to shape a clump of peers into a working encounter group can find himself in the halls and groves of ancient prophets and priests and founders, belittling none when he asks himself what Freud or Moreno would say of their group processes.

Ahab is faced with the choice of opus which sooner or later faces every person who seeks to live to his optimums. Ahab can make a carcass, or he can make whale oil. The forms of the acts are similar, for either way he goes after Moby Dick. But the meanings in each opus are different. He can choose to force upon the white-humped beast the directed destiny which his own depths have failed to yield to him, when his life form is mocked by his outward dismembering. He can cry out the old human threat to make others conform, if he himself cannot transform. Or he can take up the instruments of whale play, sharp as death though they are, and move himself and his co-creating men into that fierce but rolling encounter of high play with all the elements of sea and air, mammal life and manhood, which lured them onto the *Pequod* in the first place. In the end, Ahab chooses to seek by force the form which has not yet found its flowering within him. And the trackless, formless set survives him.

CHAPTER EIGHT

IDEA AND PSI

Studying an Idea

The burly architect who is also an engineer runs his own firm, which occupies an entire floor of a Chicago Loop office building. Each day he orders, cajoles, salutes, swears at, and inspires his crew to turn out a heroic flow of work; together they design sewage plants and churches, schools and jails, office buildings and retreat centers. When he is not hovering over an employee's drawing board for a lightning conference in which he may pencil a few strokes of his own, he is on the phone checking out the strength of building materials, or the specifications of a site. Or, after a time in the office, he jumps off to a construction location, puts on a hard hat, and makes certain that contractor and crew are following the plans for a job. With the men on location his language is even more salty than at the office, and his ferocious impatience is bearable only because everyone grants that he is a master at his business.

At an all-day adult education conference in his home suburb, the architect is introduced to Martin Buber's idea of I-thou and I-it relations in all interpersonal exchanges, as well as in relationships between men and Nature, and between men and forms—such as buildings. His agile mind is stirred, and some thought which he has been trying to think for himself is moved nearer to his conscious grasp. Still, he is dubious of the claim that I-thou relations are necessary to keep I-it relations from becoming frozen and destructive in the day's work and loving. With slowly growing impatience, he listens for several hours to talk of "being present," of "dialogue" between lives rather than "dialectic" of arguments, of "being seized with the power of exclusiveness" in the I-thou encounter, where the "Eternal Thou" is always also addressed as Third. Finally, his blue eyes snapping, he speaks up. He describes an "encounter" between himself and a hard-nosed foreman on the previous day, and observes how sterile would be an "I-thou" meeting at a construction site with such a man. "Besides," he asks, "what if you don't like the son of a bitch?"

But this is not the end of his grappling with Buber's idea of I-thou relations alternating with I-it relations necessary to do the world's work. He begins to read paperbacks by Buber; he leads an adult discussion group in his church on Buber's ideas; he talks over Buber's concepts with his wife while they drive to and from work each day. He remembers his own distinctions between those who are essentially phony in their relationships and those who get the same work done with the same people, but somehow endorse their doings with their whole selves. He draws on his self-made but rarely discussed code of what he thinks is finally to be trusted in dealings with customers, employees, family. He thinks about the best of his sex life. And he turns over in his mind his own celebration of his faith, which fires up with the art of Chagall, and in a different way with the art of Picasso.

247

He decides to experiment with I-thou relationships, and chooses the encounter which Buber calls the *Blick,* the open glance, in which two people in a moment may so exchange looks that they give to each other the freedom to be each a "Single One," an unfractionated person, totally present right then. One cold afternoon he walks down Michigan Avenue and finds a shoeshine boy approaching him, carrying his little stand and kit. He does not need a shine from the lad, so would consider it phony to ask for one. Instead, he looks at the boy in the direct, unposed glance of "meeting," about which he has been reading and thinking. The boy draws close and pauses for a moment before hurrying on in the cold. He says just one thing, tells just one secret, with a spontaneous grin. But what he volunteers is stamped with his right to be, his final credentials as a whole and unique person in the midst of impersonal buildings and traffic which at the moment offer him no shoeshine trade. "It's my birthday," he says, and that is all.

The idea of I-thou "meeting" becomes reality for the architect. But many months are required for the force of the idea to soak through the very woodwork and paperwork of his busy office. In time there is mischief and delight in the air on his floor of the downtown building. There is the same rough language, the same headlong hurry. Yet people evidently like each other, even in the act of exposing one another's appalling stupidities. The architect builds his people, and they do more of the same, confirming what they see in each other that is able and durable, even in those whom they do not choose for intimacy. Hierarchy of command is still strong in the firm, but so is a hierarchy of patience for any who will stay with a given assignment until his wits threaten to unravel, past all bunglings to the time when a shiny new building is dedicated. The forms of the buildings designed begin to be more original and daring, even though the experimentation costs the firm some clients; the architect has begun fresh dialogue with forms as well as with persons. Even out on construction sites his anger is more spicy and less personal, just the bite of hard work which grips him and everyone else. In these ways the idea of a philosopher in Israel changes a man, his firm, his buildings, and his relations with strangers, in Chicago.

Hindu tradition has reserved for *jnana,* the way of knowledge, a place of distinction in the effort to alter consciousness towards high play; the place is equal in honor with that of *karma,* the way of action in creating and marketing an opus, and that of *bhakti,* the way of devotion to man and God which can so readily be found in the love within a balanced encounter group or family. But for many in India, as in the West, the effort to alter consciousness to its optimums by systematic thought has seemed a game for scholars or gurus, set apart from the bustling mainstream activities of the human family. Is there a way so to train and focus any good mind on an organizing concept, carrying the idea forward from a first intuition to final stages of application in daily life, that something authentically psychedelic occurs? Can the way of knowledge serve dentists and hardware dealers, students and show-business people, lovers and diplomatic leaders, as truly as it does sages?

Most people know the satisfying stillness which falls over a room where serious exchange has gone on for some time, when those present have been grappling for the truths of their lives, rather than for the truths of propositions and positions alone. At such moments a strange potency and peace, which Cayce called "high vibrations," seems to be in the air. College students linger in a classroom when this occurs; mourners linger after a funeral to tell stories of the dead person whom they loved; lovers who have weighed their life forms and agreed to part still pause and touch, when truth has been spoken between them, and the ground where they stand is holy ground; a scientist alone in his lab sees under his microscope a connection which confirms his surmise about the growth of embryos and he paces the floor in wordless wonder at his idea.

No mere name dropping of authors, no gossiping with technical jargon, no toying with sweeping categories, can qualify as working with an idea at the depth needed to spring consciousness loose towards its optimums. The idea studied must be an organizing idea, one capable of application or use as analogy in several settings. Evolution is such an idea. So is cosmic order, celebrated as *Rta* in the old Hindu Vedas, and in Kant's disclosure of two things which stunned him into altered consciouness: the starry heavens, and the moral imperative in man. So is the dialectical process in history (Hegel's idea, with which Marx has won a third of the world). So is the tension of the ego with structures on opposite sides of it: the id and the superego pressing the ego into uneasy compromises called culture. So is Plato's concept of archetypes, and the Greek-originated dream of democracy. And so is the idea of reincarnation in Eastern and Western traditions, as well as the yet more strange idea of divine incarnation in human flesh—both of which were in Cayce's thought and part of its impact on many.

Still other ideas whose study may spring the mind are to be found in tracing the central themes of a people, whether an historic people or some people of prehistory examined by Margaret Mead or analyzed through their myths by Levi-Strauss. There is the study which both stuns and frees the mind as it digs out the underneath logic of thought in entire culture regions, as Haas has suggestively done in *The Destiny of the Mind,* and Buber has done with Hebraic and Greek thought modes, and Otto has done by using the Roman term *numen* to illuminate the sense of the holy in many cultures. Similar mind-bending challenges may be found in pressing thought to grasp a given century of history or the forces in one man's biography. And to make models from one discipline and try them in another has its own exhilarations, whether the concepts be those of electrical polarity or chemical valence, of biological tropism or social specialization or psychological individuation. Especially rewarding, though not always spiced with the novelty of fresh data, is the effort to formulate canons of method in finding truth, both for science and the humanities; to weigh the claims of correspondence, consequences, and coherence as truth-finding models is to prime the mind to discharge not only insight but new ways of being a mind.

Simply to tag such notions is not to handle them as psychedelic ideas. As organizing ideas, they must each be studied until they reveal their components, subideas which must be thought together in some yang-and-yin constellation until the mind boggles and finally grows in the effort to follow them out, calling upon patterns from the far impersonal levels of the unconscious. Such organizing ideas must be sat with until they offer their hints of the self-transforming in all Creative Forces, and signify not only themselves but many structures—as the physicist Pauli has shown how careful thinking about angels led Kepler to true ideas about the stars, which Kepler could then empirically verify. Perhaps the organizing ideas are the substance of a college education; the senior is lucky who can count enough such ideas, which he can use with grace, that he fills the fingers of both hands. And luckier still is the person who has used such organizing ideas to think so deeply and truly that he has learned to arouse within him the coiled snake of all creativity that both India and Cayce called *kundalini*, which can bring new selfhood with its uprising.

Just as making an opus demands that refined and skilled consciousness be joined to productive levels of the unconscious, so does finding and working out an organizing idea. Ultimately, it takes all of a man to think a big thought to the end where he can use it in new ways; he is not the same man, structurally or dynamically, after he has worked the idea into his daily affairs and soberest reflections, that he was when he began. Making certain that the weight of this process was recognized, the entranced Cayce sometimes emphasized his saying in life readings: "*Study* to show thyself approved." And he always completed the quotation with the words "rightly dividing the word of truth." In his view, not only the opus but the idea could transform a man Godward, if one let it do so and kept his high play "unspotted from the world."

Because a thought can be formulated and offered to others more quickly than can a relationship or an invention, studying an idea easily tempts to autointoxication the one who grasps it, whether in scorn of those who do not see it or in seduction of those who are offered a magic theorem. Study of an organizing idea places under stress those who think easily, for they may present each new major concept as validation of their claim to an intellectual throne. It also places under stress those who find thinking difficult, for they are enchanted when an idea finally breaks upon them. The corrective in each case is partly the work of a covenanting group with a high set, since ideas bent to the work of a community spring to their tallest, while ideas kept as private shoots harden and decay. Inspiration from an idea may come to an individual, but revelation, in the sense of that truth which transforms him and his fellows towards their optimums, comes out of covenant, where the demands of set meet the opportunities of sharing and serving.

The healing and destructive force of organizing ideas has been a major concern in the religious traditions so long charged with altering consciousness towards optimums. The Buddha built upon Hindu speculation and analysis by presuming it and then rebuking its overclaims, when he asserted the concepts of no-self and of nothingness-Nirvana (the process of such rebuke is not equally successful when the prior stage of systematic reflection is omitted, either by an individual or by the people of a faith). By contrast, other Indo-Aryan traditions and peoples walked closer to the edge of that intoxication which is believing that propositions are reality—as did some of the wise Greeks and yet more of the earnest Persians. China offered in Confucius its own Plato, holding out idealized concepts of true manhood and just government, yet it also nurtured Lao-tse, who used his Logos-like concept of the Tao to drive men out of the

252

world of concepts into real life, where together they might be and do. On the other side of the world from China, in the inhospitable desert country of the Middle East, Israel and its stepchild Islam carried conceptual luggage as light and functional as would befit nomad peoples, quite in contrast with the heavy speculative doctrines of their neighbors in Egypt and Asia Minor. But the concepts of the Torah and the One, of covenant and righteous holiness, of Allah and his will, were not simple concepts, however spare; they required carrying in tale and commandment and saying, so that their complex sharpness would not be dulled into dogmatism. Christianity early claimed its Greek and Roman inheritance of analytic thought, while treasuring its Hebraic inheritance of historic and poetic imagery, with results which have made the Christian work with ideas ambiguous down the ages. How to think out to the end the concept of Christ or of the City of God, of Grace or of sacrament, while keeping supple to the mind-opening imagery of "Him who brought us from exile" (the entranced Cayce used both kinds of thought, in all of his serious discourses), has been the baffling task of Christian efforts to use ideas to alter consciousness. Not surprisingly, when Marxism and psychoanalysis sprang up in the shadow of Christianity, they struggled with similar tensions between doctrine and tale, concept and myth, demythologizing and remythologizing. But both these movements offered, in the Communist cell and in the intimate therapy grouping, that primary covenant which corporate religiousness often has lost, as the vehicle in which an idea may be tested and clarified and worked into individual lives, in the bonds from which lasting revelation always comes.

What the people-field of a covenant offers to the psychedelic work with ideas is grounding the ideas in the life forms of individuals in the covenant. Each person may know *about* many ideas; he may *have* only a few. For each individual, a few final constructs coalesce and continuously rearrange and open up in what he knows for sure, the gospel according to him. His few fundamental conceptions are too rich to be reduced to formulas, and continuously put forth new branches and complexities, but they are there, giving his life its grandeur and its fears. One man is gripped by the notion of forgiveness; he was branded by it in a pitiless childhood (and the Cayce source would add that karma sensitized him to undertake and to respond in a particular way to that childhood). If such a man works through the demands for both severity and mercy that lie in forgiveness, he will discover that through his gospel of wise forgiveness pour many convictions: no capital punishment, healing between races, the reconciling power of loving sexuality. Another may be held from within by the idea of thanksgiving; he was marked by it in a thankless childhood. As he works through the relations between true dependence and true independence in thanksgiving, he will come out with fresh and compelling ideas of worship, with appreciation of the stupefying bounties of Nature, with ideas about national pride. Another is bound to the stake of loneliness; his shyness and fears have tied him there. As he gropes his way towards full belonging with others, he will mark a trail down which angels may gladly tumble, while his speech is of communes, of man and woman as equals, and of government programs to stabilize the economy. The few final ideas at the core of a man are his greatest confusion and in time his greatest achievement, his curse and his blessing, his despair and his good news. Consequently, the mind-altering work with ideas is not solely a search for a great scheme, a universal theory; it is also the search for that scheme, that theory, which can echo back signals from the individual's life form. From growing into one's own ideas comes not narcissism, but the Word made flesh, in ideas of man and Nature, God and history, which make the mind peaceful and playful, even as they illuminate it for co-creating with others.

When the light surmise brushes the mind, in the first trembling wonder of an idea that starts the undrugged cycle of *jnana,* of high play through knowledge, the need is for time to reflect. The student must look up from his book, take a walk, eat something, ponder. Too often this first stage is aborted by the pressure to cover some subject, master some theory, expose the mind to some material, instead of letting an idea stand forth. Better to fail a course in the struggle with a real idea, however, than to pass the course with honors and pass by one's own becoming, as well. The lift stage allows garnering all sorts of associations, illustrations, and implications, which sometimes come faster than they can be written down, and usually faster than the mind can link them in decent order. But this stage is the time, as Nietzsche said, in which to receive and not ask who is giving; order comes later. The exhilaration of insight at the lift stage, such happy echo and pattern of thought, often occupies a seeker for some time; indeed he can become a dilettante having flirtations with ideas as others do with lovers, but never risking congress which might produce demanding offspring, as implications for action. Yet when high play is his hope, and he has a covenanting sangha to help him, he may keep the lift going until it moves to the focus stage.

At the focus level of high play with ideas it may become apparent to a man that because of his idea he must go to Egypt to free his people, or like Hosea take back his widely sleeping wife, or leave the halls of his fathers for a no-budget pilgrimage with the Buddha, or try to put his idea onto film, or organize a committee, or give a certain book to a friend. To each the outcomes of an idea are his own, and sometimes wrong; but the truly mind-altering idea has consequences, not just corollaries. Mercifully, the same censoring processes which keep dreams from the dreamer not ready to digest them also appear to keep ideas from dawning on the consciousness of one not prepared to handle them—though it is possible to have an idea of an idea, and to love loving rather than love a person, or to build for builders rather than to build a structure. In just such ways the human spirit sometimes shields itself from the full force of the focus stage, and the individual may turn back to collecting more half-ideas, as a substitute for having to do and be something definite with one idea—

255

one system, one theory, one method, one author, one vision.

But if the focus is answered as the Buddha answered with his journey the shock of the ideas in the Four Appearances, then there may follow the "on" stage which so delights the one who has taken the risk of systematic and patient thought. Now he not only guesses things, he can predict reliably from his idea. He not only sees connections, he can act effectively upon his understanding. He not only grasps Buber, he can glance at a stranger. Whether the kickover stage also follows depends in part on how he has used the "on" stage; in the Cayce view, only "application" of an idea in many activities of daily life would bring full "understanding," out of which might come a visitation by the Wisdom of the One Force. In the kickover stage a man may see pattern in war and peace, and run for office, without running from his defeat. Or figuring out the nature of power may make students knock on voters' doors, instead of knocking dormitory food, and may help them to find in doorstep encounters the inexplicable kickover of power with others which is not power over anyone. But the kickover in a humanity-sized idea, which Cayce ascribed to the "universal realm," eludes words. Many think they have known it when they have not, and are dumbfounded to discover what high delight they have been missing in their normal, useful, agreeable sexy lives, before they stepped into that softly ringing circle where ultimate meaning rang all through them. To enter the Lincoln Memorial in Washington is to guess how one man may have walked with his few great ideas; the highest of high play is hinted in the figure of any man, black or white, who thinks it not unreasonable to follow an idea through the door of death, so that fuller games may go on for all players.

As always, the high-play cycle leaves its sense of readiness and release. Even the man who later betrays his calling to his final truth, and to action on that truth, keeps what he has known for sure (through all later lives, in the Cayce view). Samson, who took the abstinence and fasting

256

vows of the Nazirites to enable his consciousness to alter, knew the flash of truth from the One, as he rendered judgments among his people. When he let himself be symbolically castrated, as his hair was cut, he joined the ranks of those who betray the truth which they have known. But like the castaway doctor on the tramp steamer who still knows excellent surgery, Samson knows where he has found truth, as well as strength, and can turn to that relationship for a final mighty judgment which incorporated execution with the idea. To be there once with an idea, in full play with the One, is to know where one can return. Students who helped each other through the mud at Woodstock knew that they could help their people through a morass at Washington, and in every wayside and suburb as well, so long as they could move free of bitterness or scorn, in co-creating high play.

Ahab is gripped with the idea of killing the whale which hurt him—an idea with dimensions of patricide and deicide, as well as of human sacrifice and even of crucifixion. But Ahab thinks his idea alone, apart from those bonds of commitment and sharing which can transform raw image into revelation. He has not always stood so alone, for his body carries scars from the lightning which struck him when once he shared in Parsi rites and sought converse with the divine flame in the heavens. That time of pain had not harmed him, but only taught him to look up again when lightning troubled his ship. But when a greater disfigurement comes, in the loss of his leg to Moby Dick, he speaks of his pain to no man. This time he does not look up to formulate or signal to himself an ultimate reality. Instead, he looks down, into the whaling waters, and follows the idea of a game where he alone is master and can prove it. The idea is not big enough; in brief moments of weary truthfulness he knows that it is not. But instead of poising nature against culture, passion against purpose, to arouse the reconciling Third within him in a life-renewing idea, Ahab pits brute against lance, whale against captain, and seeks in driven victory of low play what may not be found without understanding.

257

A Gary, Indiana, housewife wakens at two in the morning. She gets up, and arouses her college-age son and her high-school-age daughter. "Wake up!" she urges them. "Your brother is coming home from Germany tonight." She is excited, but the children groan. "Go back to bed," her sons responds. "You know he can't be coming home tonight. His leave isn't due for two months yet." He and his sister return to their slumbers, not without noting that their mother is rarely mistaken in this sort of perception.

They have grown accustomed to her perceiving when they have car trouble away from home, or when they are coming down with unsuspected illness, or when they have fallings-out with friends. They do not look on her as omniscient, for she is not. But they think of her as more likely than most mothers to be aware of times when her children need her. And while they do not expect her to push her psychic hunches on them, as she does this night, they remember how she has anticipated the return of their older brother from overseas service, after two years in which none of the family has seen him.

On her part, the mother is sure that the premonition which awakened her is correct. From similar experiences since girlhood she has learned to recognize a certain click of assurance, a certain pulse of meaning within her, which weakens as she tries wrong guesses and strengthens as she tries correct guesses, for the content of a felt hunch. Tonight the pulse is strongest for the notion that her son will arrive that very night, two months ahead of schedule, and with no warning. So in the middle of the night she begins roasting a chicken and baking a cake, in their modest apartment; she sets the table, sure that her son will be hungry, as always. When three o'clock comes, the food is ready, but nobody is there.

Then the doorbell rings, and her military son bounds up the stairs and into the apartment. He had his leave moved up, he explains, and at the last minute hitched a ride on an overseas military flight to the United States connecting with another flight which brought him close enough to Gary to allow him to find a ride to his door. The connections have all been made so abruptly that he had not stopped to phone. Besides, he wanted to surprise his family. But who is surprised? There is the chicken and the cake and the table set for him. "I should have known, Mom." He laughs. "I really should have known."

The experience of enlarged perception, sometimes called "sixth sense" or "ESP" or "psychic ability," and more technically called "psi" by modern laboratory researchers, has appeared so often in records of altered consciousness that it requires attention, even in a brief survey of altered states. That primitive shaman figures of Africa or the Arctic, of Australia and the Amerinds, have sometimes been observed using sleight of hand and hypnosis on their gullible followers, has not accounted for all of the instances of unusual perception, and even actions on remote objects, reported by such anthropologists as Elkin and Underhill. Nor has the demonstrable gullibility of peoples of far-off times, who thought that charms and omens gave them daily traffic with gods and spirits, quite removed the possibility that some of the seers and prophets of Israel, the sybils and oracles of Greece, the *magi* of Persia, and the *rishi* and *yogin* figures of India may have had their consciousness alter sufficiently to give them unusual powers of perception and psychokinesis (direct action of the mind on physical objects). Yet all such puzzling phenomena of anthropology and history would remain only colorful mysteries, whodunits for leisure investigation, had not similar phenomena been re-created in lesser degree by modern laboratories using controlled conditions. Especially though not exclusively in altered states, laboratory subjects have shown abilities to know what they were not supposed to know, and to act on targets which they were not supposed to affect. Early experiments on psi in hypnotic states yielded to more rewarding experiments on psi in keyed-up states, and then to recent experiments on the altered states of sleep—where some subjects have proved

259

surprisingly skillful at picking up images sent to them by partners, or even by strangers. In addition, reports on psi as precognition or clairvoyance under LSD have begun to appear in the formal and informal literature on drug-induced states. And at the same time, those who work with small encounter groups, whether A.A. or clinical groups, meditation or sensitivity-training groups, have reported what appear to be spontaneous incidents of group members who participate in larger fields of awareness and action than can yet be explained. As a result, extrasensory perception and its twin of psychokinesis remain on the agenda for optimum psychology, especially in the study of altered states.

Yet no other approach to altering consciousness, except perhaps the taking of strong drugs, appears to hold as many dangers as the systematic cultivation of psi—at least for modern Westerners. What makes the risk of cultivating psi so great is the scarcity of Western lore and practice for its use. In India the claims of psychic experiences have been so frequent and varied, in the history of mind-altering yoga, as to generate traditions which present such experiences as interesting symptoms of growth, useful in the service of others, but dangerous if made a form of power over others. Buddhism, too, has often warned against the cultivation of remarkable psychic powers for their own sake (although Tibet magnified them, as did popular Chinese faith); a typical Buddhist injunction tells of the response given by a teacher to an adept who had spent years learning to walk on the water. Why bother, he was asked, when a ferry would take him across the water for a few pennies? Israel, too, warned against cultivation of magical powers, apart from their development under overshadowing by the One—though Israel's lore of unusual guidance and feats in its early history was matched by reports of exceptional vision and healing powers among Hassidic European rabbis as late as the eighteenth century. Christian traditions of unusual psychic abilities have included centuries of persecution of witches, on the one hand, and veneration of saints, on the other, for the exercise of outwardly similar capacities, all of which could be paralleled in New Testament instances. The same Jesus who rejected the low play of detached powers to coerce others, while tempted in the desert, was reported to have found himself at home in the high play of changing water into good wine for a wedding, daring his disciples to walk on the water, sending for an unseen donkey, healing the ill and the troubled, and reading the thoughts of detractors in order better to engage them in serious exchanges. Not surprisingly, modern Western man looks at psi with uncertain gaze. He sees what may be superstition and magic and fraud, reminding him of the morass of dogma and misinformation from which science has only recently begun to extricate itself. Yet he also sees another part of science fiction which may become reality, as have laser beams, moon trips, and organ transplants. Consequently, when he has a few spontaneous psychic experiences of his own, or learns to cultivate a modest amount of paranormal cognition or kinesis, he wonders how to think of himself. Is he a representative of the next stage of evolution? Is he a god? Is he psychotic? If none of these, is he at least the possessor of a shortcut to success in work, in love, in knowledge? In the event that he answers these questions by concluding that psi differs from all other creativity, in requiring no practice or learning of laws, and no differentiation or integration of the processes within his psyche, then he may abandon himself to his unconscious, waiting upon its every prompting for psychic guidance and powers—and incidentally opening the door for all manner of compensatory material from within himself. The history of those who have become disordered in the pursuit of psychic abilities is a sad one, matched only by the ragged careers and personal lives of the few less-disciplined investigators, when they have been caught in the hope of a new power which might be mastered without coming to terms with the full dynamics of the human psyche. Few psychic investigators have been as conscientious in reporting this darker history of the modern search for psi as has Hugh Lynn Cayce in his book *Venture Inward*.

Yet despite these hazards, psychic ability seemed to the trance-counseling Edgar Cayce to be the birthright of every soul, as natural as breathing when not impeded by poor stress and set. As the present writer has reported in detail in *Edgar Cayce on Religion and Psychic Experience*, the entranced Cayce suggested that psi could be found to work at three levels, by those who sought it with care, and in a purpose of co-creating with their fellows before the One. There was a natural or basic level where psi operated along with the other problem-solving resources of the unconscious, to generate warnings and alertings for the traffic of daily life. Then there was an enhanced or heightened level, where psi operated to foster the creativity chosen and developed by a particular soul in its long journey, by adding psi abilities to other talents in healing, in art, in politics, or some different creative endeavor. Finally, there was psi at an elevated or inspired level, where the individual within his life form drew directly upon the "Universal Forces," through the helping action of his own superconscious and what men called the "Holy Spirit," or the "Christ Spirit." These three were not to be seen as arbitrary levels of psychic abilities, but shaded into each other; however, the limited resources of a man were not the unlimited resources of God, and psi should be seen as extending from humble to dazzlingly complex forms—much as music varies from a shepherd's piping to rich orchestral works which seem to echo the very music of the spheres.

For those not so highly endowed as to have psi forced upon them (from past-life development of it, in the Cayce view), as it was unavoidable for the Gary housewife, the beginning of exploring psi may be study and discussion. Without a grasp of the history and range of paranormal abilities, suggesting how consciousness altered for the famed Swedenborg and Wesley, as well as for the ordinary parents and telephone repairmen and others on whom Louisa Rhine has reported in her research, the clouds of doubt from surrounding modern culture may make sustained exploration difficult, in probing this type of altered consciousness. There are five technical journals in English wholly devoted to parapsychology, the study of psi; but easier to read are surveys by Gardner Murphy (the dean of American psychologists), by the husband and wife team of the Rhines, by Pratt and by Schmeidler, as well as a college textbook by Rhine and Pratt and popular surveys and essays, of which those by Raynor Johnson and by Heywood set a useful standard. Biographies of Cayce, Ford, Dixon, the Worralls, and Garrett present contemporary figures about the reality of whose endowments there has been the least modern controversy (and plenty of controversy about them remains). But reading alone will not produce the necessary mental mural against which to trace the action of psi in altered consciousness. The next step is a journal.

Any notebook will do for a personal record of psychic experiences. All that is required is space to jot down, daily or oftener, one's varied promptings or urgings which might be psychic, along with space to note whether or not investigation corroborates them, and how. The smallest items are often the most useful: a sense of who is calling on the telephone, a glimpse of letters coming in the day's mail, a hint of what is on the mind of an approaching friend, a warning to slow down for a car just over the hill, an alerting that a child has wandered into the street, an assurance that a sales campaign will go off successfully. To begin at once to look for forthcoming deaths, or national catastrophes, or supposed past lives, or details of the affairs of skeptical relatives and friends, is to put the psyche under undue stress; such attempts are usually made in self-justification, compensatory to missing ego strength, rather than as adventures towards an effective, skilled life of high play. Likewise, to tell others what transpires, rather than quietly recording the details, is to strain the psyche, except in the setting of a growth group with a high set; psychic phenomena in Western culture are automatically stamped with a demand for payment of attention, positive or negative.

Other items than cognition may be jotted in the journal, as possible instances of psychokinesis: the time when holding the baby seemed to lower its fever, the lift of mood in an entire group which swiftly followed the lift of one member, the spark which seemed to flash between participants in a play or athletic event or business conference. None of these entries will be coercive proof of anything psychic at work, nor should they be used for any purpose except highlighting where and how one might further develop stable and useful psychic capacities in high play with others. Space in the journal should also be given to dreams. The one who has healing gifts is likely to dream of healing, even if it is only massaging the backs of associates. The one who can see what psychics call "auras" around others, and make some helpful sense of their colors, is likely to dream in meaningful colors, as well. To be sure, dreams may be used to blindfold those already blind; accordingly, some objective testing of psychic ability with Zener cards or other procedures can help to correct pure subjectivity regarding one's own psi potentials. But when dreams are used only to awaken and alert surface consciousness to the possibilities of psychic creativity in daily life, rather than used as mechanical signs or omens, they may offer a relatively safe individual laboratory for psychic investigation. Unlike waking hunches and impressions, dreams cannot be manipulated in the very act of psychic perception, nor squeezed as easily for needless ego juice. And dreams are likely to call attention to needs for personal growth even more quickly than they will signal events which are psychically perceived or affected by the dreamer. As soon as an individual's dreams are populated with the charged figures of his childhood, or with the famous, or when his dreams repeatedly place him in anxious or pompous positions, then the dreamer may beware. For these are common signals that compensatory work is underway in dreams, rather than psychic

264

creativity to meet the needs of waking life, and to lift the dreamer through the cycle of high play.

The first click or twist of surprise in psi, beginning the undrugged cycle of heightened creativity, may be found in extra attention drawn to someone's face just before he speaks, or in an alerting to a boiling pot or a distant boiling temper. Psi of the first stage may come into consciousness as a memory comes, half-idly when the mind is lightly absorbed in a routine task. Or it may come as a stronger assurance; in any case the psi material is likely to amplify normal cognition, adding an extra weight of confidence and a sense of direction, rather than offering a wholly novel image in the mind. Many miss the work of psi in their daily lives because they look for it to be strange and intrusive, rather than more of the same thing which experience and good judgment are already offering. Further, psi at the first level is often more visceral than mental: a feeling, a drawing back, a priming to go, a heaviness of heart, a playfulness, a boldness. By attending to such bodily stirrings, it is possible for the seeker after psi to define a group of feelings which can help him to sort out the possible meanings which run through his mind, as the content of a psychic hunch.

At the lift stage of psi an impression may grow stronger yet—that one may safely continue his journey home, despite a storm, or that a friend elsewhere is in need of prompt aid, or that airline stocks are going up tomorrow, or that prayers for a child in the hospital are having their unseen effect, or that taking the chairmanship of a committee will lead to growth of all its members through their struggles. But even where clear impressions awaken in the mind, they are less likely to be wide-screen panoramas of events than diacritical, as researchers like to say. For the way of psi in its early stages seems to be that of suggesting the fitness in joining two things together: oneself and the person expected for an appointment, or one's car and running out of gas, or one's hopes and the morning mail, or one's fear and a forthcoming repair bill. Learning to check such links is more rewarding than seeking secret mental pictures and ghostly revelations. Similarly, at the lift stage there are hints of the more problematic and less common activity of psychokinesis, when energy seems to be moving in larger-than-normal circuits—sometimes leaving the individual drained, and sometimes only happily weary. Part of cultivating any form of psi at the lift stage is taking what comes and not distorting it, so long as it does not upset the seeker; many block their unfolding awareness and productivity by overinterpreting what occurs to them, rushing into the action with conscious judgments which baffle and frustrate the unconscious in its efforts to be helpful.

At the focus stage, an active response to the psychic happening seems required. Jesus may have found it refreshing to be baptized in a rite common to Covenanters of his time, and he and others may well have seen a manifestation and heard a voice at the time; but the focus stage which followed was a desert struggle which must have threatened his wits, as he fought to find and keep true to his life form and relation to the One, in the grip of what seems to have been raw psychic powers. Equally for those less gifted than he, to receive impressions or to feel potency at the focus stage requires disciplined choice of action. If one wants leadings on the action in wool markets, then one must study and sell woolens; if one feels prompted to aid in the healing of others, then one must not shrink from bandages and loving embraces; if one wants cosmic intuitions, then one must both study the theories of others and work out his own diagrams and propositions (both of which efforts Cayce enjoined on the few philosophers who came to him for counsel). For psi in any walk of life appears to be a fulfillment of creativity, an extra amplitude to the waves of earnest effort in the best one knows, rather than a shortcut to any achievement. Even in the instance of Cayce, who found himself counseling so many people on so many subjects in his trances, it is illuminating to remember that his early life was given to portraying others to themselves in photographs, and that some of his greatest joy in waking life came in counseling young people and married couples in his church groups. A busy and productive consciousness seems to be the keeper of a busy and productive unconscious, provided that the latter is given clear channels by the cleansing and focusing action of meditation, as well as of fasting and such other renewals and celebrations as unclutter the mind and the body.

At the "on" stage of psi a choir may seem to conduct itself, as the singers draw forth greatness out of each other and the conductor, bringing an audience to its feet in cheers. For an individual, process upon process in a task of manufacturing may unfold in his thoughts, or the hand of a surgeon may be unaccountably deft when he cannot see the tissue on which he works. At the best of the "on" times one may take up problem after problem in his daily life, swiftly getting indications on how to help an absent relative, or how much to charge for a service rendered, or what responsibility to place upon an associate, or where to go for the next vacation. Dreams may be opened like ripe fruit. Energies may be summoned to drive a flagging group of workmen or soldiers, or to produce green-thumb effects in a garden, or to cool a fevered head. But to be able to counsel others through psi at the "on" stage is another matter; not a few are misled by their own unquestioned clarity and skill into thinking they can offer equal aid to others. To be sure, when they are "on," those who counsel can counsel, indeed; but legal counsel comes from the attorney, and psychiatric counsel from the therapist, not often the other way around. To adopt the stance of universal counselor or oracle at this stage is to invite compensatory unconscious material at once, which will redress the balance in the psyche by one form of mischief or another. In the "on" times it is possible to discern something at work which is similar to musical attunement. Just as one may alter a note to make it sharp or flat, and thereby fit it properly into a major or minor chord, so one may try altering the content of a psychic leading, and find its force shading off, or growing stronger, depending on how near one is to the unknown facts or processes engaged. Similarly, one may learn to recognize the inner lack of signal which means he is asking the wrong question in relation to his prompting—that a pickup is going on, but the mind is placing it in the wrong bins. The work of a loving and covenanted group can do much to enhance the "on" times of its members, as the Cayce source often suggested. Such a group will not allow members to indulge themselves in pseudo-psychic fantasies which function as escapes from real life, or as ploys for attention. But on the other hand, such a loving and alert group can reflect to the individual those times when the group sees him come alive, poised and coolly awake, and ready to use unpretentious psi in the "on" stage. Further, by a kind of resonation which strongly suggests ESP or PK in itself, when one member begins to enter the "on" stage, others seem to catch the wavelength more readily, and to move to their own quickenings—when the group spirit is one of humorous and delighted helpfulness in high play before the One.

If the kickover stage of psi is entered, then something electric occurs which few will claim as their own agency. Especially at this stage may be noted the prompting to draw forth truth and force and skill from others, rather than presenting it to them; this prompting in any form of high play seems the hallmark of those who are truly inspired, rather than any definitive vision or skill. The inspired become, in the fullest sense, co-creators, rather than leaders, teachers, healers, or wonder workers of whatever degree of talent. Consequently, this stage offers special opportunity for discerning what the New Testament calls the *kairos,* or appointed time for co-creating with God—whether in a protest march, a wedding, an offer of peace, or just keeping silent (in what Hugh Lynn Cayce has called the great spiritual gift of knowing when to shut the mouth). In the kickover stage, also, psi may issue in the long, long view. The goodness of a child being helped may shine into the childlikeness which every mature person must develop, in the journey of his soul. The lift of music may turn into a true vision of the unflagging lift of evolution, unfolding in its speechless patterns not only the destinies of species but of consciousness as well. The end of a day or a task may open into the riddle of the end of life, and presentiments may leap far into the land of death. The confirming of another in his true life form may produce one's own crown from the fire-ringed circle within, as though drawn from another age in history. The touch of love upon the cheek of a sick friend may warm to an invisible fire of healing which seems to flow from one's fingertips, as life greets life in the dance of molecules which did not begin with one's particular birth, and will not end at any particular death. For those who have known the kickover level of psi in their own lives, or seen it at work in a gifted psychic, the effect is to print them for life with a sense of the incredible optimums to which a human being can be lifted, when he uses his "normal forces" to co-create with his fellows in the unraveling or transmuting of chemistry and choreography, love and laughter, power structures and philosophy.

In the stage of readiness and release, it often becomes clear that high play in psychic ability, like other forms of high play, is not man's doing alone. Looking back over each mounting level of heightened creativity in perception and psychokinesis, one may see that at each stage he was tugged, met, struck, encouraged and directed, however gently. There may come to mind the fitness of Jesus' image of yoga with the One (the stem of yoga means "yoke") when he said, "My yoke is easy and my burden is light." For at each stage of high play, what seems to have been at work is those larger forces, larger circuits, which Cayce called the "Universal Forces," having their life-giving, life-freeing way with man, while drawing forth from him the spontaneous force and quality of his God-formed soul. The biblical sentence in which Cayce repeatedly described this process in all high play, psychic and otherwise, was "My Spirit beareth witness with thy spirit, as to whether ye be the children of God"; in the Cayce view, all co-creating engaged the answering "witness" or resonating Force which ever sought to amplify what was

269

best in man. Noting something of this invisible aid in all high play, one may find that old forms and traditions of psi shine with new meaning. That prophets and poets of other times should have spoken to their contemporaries in the Name of the One, with visionary perception, does not seem strange. Nor do healings and wonders seem impossible where people of good intent may have gathered for absurdly blessed high play with the Third who is only One. And whether there are angels that dance unseen in the light that blinds seems no cause for perplexity; if there are not, perhaps there ought to be, and they will be invented in good time.

Ahab takes the way of omen and oracle, when he uses psi. He relies on the prophecies of his Parsi harpooneer that Ahab will not die until he has seen two hearses and the Parsi going before him; too late he recognizes Moby Dick and his own ship as the hearses, and sees the Parsi lashed in death to the whale by tangled ropes. Ahab's striving in his state of fasting, goaded by pain, and carried forward by the momentum of a long and productive life, is like that which woke Job on his ash heap to a psychic vision of the final mysteries of creation, in an altered-state experience which has no parallel in religious literature. Ahab's condition should bring him illumination, firing within him the most prized of psychic experience, which lays bare reality even while it bursts the mind to new becomings. But Ahab does not clear the way for this kind of psi by such speechless meditation as Job undertook after his catastrophes; instead, Ahab relies upon Fedallah's pronouncements, which are accurate but cast in forms of fate, rather than seen in shafts of Light. And Ahab never reaches the transforming vision of riotous creation which came to stubborn but God-pledged Job, when Job saw even the whale—leviathan—as an emblem of the playful immensity of the work of the Creative Forces.

CHAPTER NINE

THE POLITICS OF LOVE

The new academic dean was young, and the faculty had their doubts about him. To be sure, he was a brilliant Whitehead scholar, and his philosophy students loved him. But this was a campus with historic religious ties; while the young dean called himself a Christian philosopher, he had also told his students that he had just read through the entire New Testament for the first time. Further, his administrative background seemed hardly adequate to justify the appointment of the youngest man on the faculty to its leadership. He had been the dean of students for a time, but that was a hand-holding job. Before that he had been a collection man for a finance company, and a football quarterback as an undergraduate. His father was not a scholar but a New England sea captain.

Hardly had the new dean been appointed when he took

action which led the faculty elders to suspect he would show the typical poor judgment of youth, by giving heroic attention to second-rate concerns. He appointed several of the best minds of the faculty to a temporary committee which was charged with designing a course to orient advanced students to graduate study. Further, he scheduled weekly meetings for the Orientation Committee, although its members complained that each meeting was a theft of their research time; and he was an active participant in each committee session. Promptly, he began to urge that in order for the committee members to design a course to introduce students to advanced scholarship, they would need to discover what they, as advanced scholars representing the faculty, were about. He pushed the committee into grudging agreement on a plan in which each of its members, including the young dean, would prepare and read to the rest of the committee an original paper, setting forth his own discipline as he saw it, explaining how he felt his discipline needed to be taught in that school, noting where his special interests lay and why, identifying the methodological hazards of working in his discipline, and finally stating what mattered most to his own individual existence, in his day to day work as a scholar. As each delivered his paper, he would be expected to take significant stands and defend them, or he might find the committee sending back his paper for rewriting and a second presentation—as in fact happened to several on the committee, to their astonishment.

At the first meetings to read these original papers, the faculty discussion was often fencing. But the young dean was ardent in pushing through to real issues, and in supporting each man whenever he took a stand clearly grounded in his own deep personhood, as well as in his scholarship. Slowly, the sessions gained quality and force, until they were no longer chores but highlights of the week for the participants in these exchanges. A second round of papers was prepared and presented by the members, with these statements pointed more sharply towards the specific issues of the work of their school in its contemporary world. Other faculty began to ask to attend the meetings, but were accepted only on condition of their taking full committee membership, which included reading and defending their own papers, in turn.

The young dean pressed harder in each meeting for systematic thoroughness in the papers, for methodological clarity and consistency, for positions which tied each man's work to his real existence and faith, as well as to the life of the school. Others on the committee began to get the feel of his process. Spontaneously, they carried forward the discussions of papers at luncheons and coffee hours, where before the faculty had shared only polite niceties and university gossip. Even more unlikely, in the light of faculty precedents, some of the committee members began to attend each other's classes, and to quote each other to their students, with discriminating appreciation. Broad intellectual positions in education, philosophy, science, the arts, and socio-political policy began to emerge within the faculty, not so much battle lines as they were valuable options in facing the same serious questions. Sometimes faculty feelings were hurt when those who read poorly prepared papers were handled roughly by the committee. But the young dean hammered away at the importance of building the best in each professor, rather than picking on the worst. He led the way in such mutual encouragement by saluting the best contributions of his colleagues, not only in meetings of the committee but at commencements and alumni banquets, at conferences of learned societies and at chapel services.

The spirit of serious exchange on the campus grew infectious. Despite the long campus traditions of splendid departmental isolation, a number of the faculty were now teaching so that, as one student put it, "When you walk into his class, you know the prof has been talking with other profs." Students put together their own departmental and interdepartmental discussion and action groups, adding issues which they felt the faculty did not face with sufficient directness. Some students gave up part-time jobs and took fewer courses, even though this prolonged their

273

education, in order to spend more time preparing for the animated student discussions—to which faculty were sometimes invited for cordial grilling. A spirit of ferment and encounter spread over the campus; several of the faculty noted that the ex-quarterback was making a team.

As the temporary Orientation Committee went on meeting each week, for months which stretched into several years, it polarized the extremes of campus life, as might be expected. Some of the faculty left, in order to avoid such personal and time-consuming exchanges; other faculty were so enthusiastic that it appeared the Orientation Committee and its process was for them the school, with classes incidental. But the main body of the faculty kept its balance, finding the tug of the sharing often so meaningful that several of the big-name professors turned down offers of advancement in positions at other schools. Teaching took on new dimensions: class attendance requirements were abolished, since it was now clear that students would show up for classes which dealt with serious and relevant issues; oral exams were instituted to supplement written exams in every department; both curricula and departmental structures were continuously overhauled. Assignments and research projects, as well as team teaching and team examining, were designed to get students and faculty to the heart of their disciplines, and into forefront questions in each field. Libraries were kept open longer hours, and improvised space provided for the smoking and snacking and talking which seemed to follow so readily where projects were underway around the campus. Students shared in academic decision making at levels never before seen in the history of the school; however, student leaders were pushed towards academic quality as firmly as were any of the faculty, in part by the requirement that students as well as faculty must read and evaluate each set of term papers, in the various courses.

Not togetherness but academic excellence was the spirit of the campus. Twice a year the entire faculty went off together for extended retreats, where they worked on the substance and method of their thought, rather than upon traditional business of grade distributions, faculty leaves, and commencement speakers. The time came when the yeasty process could not be contained on the campus. Some of the alumni formed their own informal professional groups, downtown in the university city, where they read statements to each other and talked and drank late into the night. Nearby campuses invited the dean and other professors to meet with their faculties, in sessions which sometimes ran entire weekends, where the central issue was how to turn a faculty into a "hungry ball club." Off-campus friends of the school began to recruit better students for the campus, and some of the graduates found an unusually warm welcome in their new positions, where word of the campus ferment had spread. A number of the faculty and students took their encounter-process into small political discussion-and-action groups in the community, where they elected aldermen and mayoral candidates on specific issues, but lost not a few contests.

When the young dean himself took his process of taking-one-another-seriously to Washington, there were storm clouds in view. He pleaded before a Senate committee that convicted Russian spies ought not to be executed in peacetime, on the grounds that the nation would betray its deep but often unexamined principles by such vindictive killings. But the times were still shadowed by the McCarthy era and the dean was tagged a Communist. He thought the charge humorous, as did his faculty and student body. But off-campus pressures coalesced and grew ominously strong. Some of the alumni worried whether subjects were covered as thoroughly as in older days at the school, when there were neat departmental lines and no overlapping fields of study, and no classes called off for all-school conferences. Donors worried that graduates might be so intellectual that they would not fit into the institutions for which the school was to prepare them. Some of the parents feared that the school's emphasis on being "existential" might interfere with the picturesque religious life of the campus, where gowned singers had always serenaded guest preachers in the chapel. Finally, although the faculty voted again and again to keep him, the young dean was removed from his post by the top campus officers, and was returned to his teaching of Whitehead.

Yet there were forces set loose which did not seem defeated. Students and faculty found it sad to see Camelot go. They found it sad to see hemlock and thorns never far from institutional life, as of old. But nothing could take away their shared vision of a process which might turn any lumbering old institution into a place of adventure. As the faculty slowly dispersed to other posts, and as students graduated and left, it became apparent to many of them that the son of a sea captain had hounded them into a process not limited to campuses. Wherever people were in bonds of duties and commitments together, they could take each other on, within these bonds, and pull each other up to optimums. The process was time-consuming, and threatening to all who habitually hid behind roles and offices. But it was also wondrously yeasty. It worked in a bank, it worked in a musical ensemble, it worked in a military base, it worked in a plastics factory, it worked in a Senator's staff. Wherever people would take the time together to declare themselves to one another in the light of their considered goals and world views, bringing their specific daily work and growth under the judgment of such perspectives, and lowering their defenses for full exchange and criticism and appreciation, something remarkable happened. To be sure, the process had to go on under unwavering task-oriented pressure toward excellence. It had to be done in a set to draw forth the best in one another; it had to be seasoned with humor and spiced with time to clown, and allowed to rise in retreats or breaks away from the daily order of things. But when all this was tried, so much followed that some mused that they were touching the process described in the New Testament as "the kingdom of the Coming Reign of God." Others said, however, that they had watched the son of a sea captain make a tight ship.

The politics of love, in such an adventure, may be more potent for permanently altering consciousness than any drug yet known. Wherever the world's work must be done, and institutions operated and improved and operated some more, whether they be whaling ships or marriages or campuses or governments, there the force of such politics may be tested. The set of the politics of love is twofold, toward task achievement, and toward people building at the same time. In the politics of power within love, people carry on institutional traffic and yet bet on each other. They struggle over routines and duties and costs and punishments, yet bet on each other. They may repair to the flexibility and security of encounter groups or love affairs, where the people-field is almost everything, in order to quicken their vision and patience and confidence. But in this kind of power using, they step forward again to join task with personhood in each co-creator, to find each one's hidden greatness amid the day's doings. They invite the upsetting and ennobling Third, the Creative Forces, to the desk, the counter, the tractor, the podium, the assembly line, the racetrack, the bed, the concert hall—wherever they need eyesight and courage to tug and shove each other forward to optimums. The game in each instance is so to set a man before himself that he becomes his own midwife, his own angel and tormentor, while around him others cheer his every labored step to new freedom and productiveness in high play. In the politics of love, power is used to tighten the bonds made by the best commitments a man can offer, within the round of his principles and practices. It is gambled that when any man is asked his own questions long enough, he will produce his own man-sized answers, though the answers may be shatteringly unexpected, to him or to others. More than talk is involved in this process, however, for in this venture the pressures of real duties, real hopes, real roles must be heightened to maximum bearable creativity. This is not therapy, not rescue. This is seeking a flowering which occurs at the top of each one's potency, not in the collapse of it.

The double set of the politics of love piles stress of task upon the stress of growth, keeping in view the unique life form and necessary ego strength of each player. Such a process allows building immense force in the stresses, which can spring the altering mind to towering heights. Because so much is risked in the politics of love—all protecting of face and even at times the protecting of life itself—the stresses must be the right ones, the worthy ones, the authentic ones. When splits develop in the stressed psyche, they must occur along the true cleavage lines of the person, reaching all the way to his inner fire-ringed individuality. To build just such stresses, it is necessary to get people to stand forth in their actual vocations and ideals, in their real covenants, where alone they may be pushed to greatness—as the entranced Cayce pointed out in emphasizing the primacy of ideals for any deep growth. When this is accomplished, then stress may be seen as not simply between opponents, though opponents must keep up their principled and passionate struggles for excellence with each other, but between each man and his next self, as he responds to the unpredictable gifts of the unspeakably creative One.

Accordingly, the thrust of the politics of love must be towards building the best of each person, even in those dark times when he must be run out of office, or exposed as a sloppy workman or an incompetent parent. To so build requires marvelous insight from all players. If psi did not exist, it would require inventing, for the enduring good of a man is harder to find than his evil or weakness. Yet the unique and elusive good may be found, exactly where his low play is fastened, to keep the good from being lost to view. To take up the politics of love, then, is to look for the God-ignited fire of creativity in another, in the stranger and even in the enemy, though that fire be only a spark burning behind much rubbish. For the hard truth of the politics of love is this: a man reinforced in his true strength and identity can bear to face his weaknesses, while a man mocked can only strike back.

But will the man so strengthened come at last to face his weaknesses, his evil? This is the question which haunts many who debate risking the politics of love. But those who are seasoned in this rough and lovely game know that any man's strengths are but the obverse of his weaknesses (in the Cayce view, two sides of the same karma). Leadership is the other side of tyranny. Tenderness is the other side of possessiveness. Skill at beauty and form is the other side of manipulation. Endurance is the other side of stubbornness. To build on any one strength will assure that its accompanying evil will be exposed for decision, as surely as night follows day. For the psyche which must press into heroic service all of its strong resources will use not only its primary skills and defenses, and the problem-solving flow in the unconscious, but its eruptive compensatory flow as well. And when the weaknesses which go with the compensatory material are exposed in the midst of a man's high achievement, before those who have bet on his best promise and choose still to bet on it, then he can bear to slay his demons and dragons—as at last he alone must.

Further, to build on a man's strengths elicits from his psyche not only the half-truths, weaknesses, and demonism exposed in his compensatory material, but the deeper matching opposites needed for his growth to new stature. To be called to practice true justice breeds the love of mercy, under the refining support of those who politick in love. To work for freedom is to be quickened to find worthy destinies for oneself and others, in which freedom may be used. To cherish wisdom is to find how knowledge is ripened into wisdom by that caring for others which fits knowledge to particular persons. Thus, building on strengths sets off radioactive chains of becoming, chains of what Cayce called ideals—the crown and glory of the soul—far within the person trusted and challenged to be his best self. The man whose consciousness has altered once, in the high and dangerous play of the politics of love, knows something about how his own next initiating must proceed. Jonah can make it sitting on a hillside, next time, without running off to sea.

Yet the dangers in using power within love are as great as the potency. In the name of matching justice and growth, work and love, productivity and personhood, Jeremiah is dropped into a well, Calvin burns Servetus, the bishops burn Joan of Arc, New England fathers drown psychics as witches, Christians and Muslims and Jews fight for a holy land, and Gandhi is shot by one of the countrymen he loves. No enemies are more to be feared than one's friends who practice the politics of love as low play.

Fending off such autointoxication requires recognizing the value of the politics of limits, where the set is chiefly and properly to get a job done. Certainly there are times and places where pressure must be applied, power seized or used, with minimal thought of the real and final beings of participants. Crimes in progress must be stopped, discrimination barred, poverty and tyranny redressed. Divorces must be wrought, children rescued from parents, employees fired, invaders halted, diseases quarantined, psychotics committed, and statesmen impeached. The trance-heightened Cayce did not hesitate to counsel such limits, when they seemed to him essential. Yet that society which knows and practices only such emergency politics, the politics of limits, gives up a potent agent for its present and future life: the use of power in person-transforming love, which Cayce identified as "the Christ way." Too often, the society which trusts only the politics of limits fosters crusades in all-engrossing sets towards preannounced goals, goals which it is claimed cannot be revised or jettisoned along the way without confusing the mobilized emotions of participants. Timely and spontaneous shutoff and starting again are not the style of this action. People must, it is claimed, be kept stimulated and polarized, for change comes only in times of crisis and craving. But those who trust human beings only insofar as they are inflamed trust them but little; they have not found the long, steady quickening of the high-play cycle, which must be awakened in a few at a time, but is not easily quenched.

As the first stage begins, in the high play of politicking with love, it often affords a startle or spin effect, which discloses the hidden promise in an opponent or a frozen partner. The startle may afford just a flick of hope, as when marital partners seriously consider divorce, and find that each day afterwards in which they stay married is a day of marriage by choice rather than by habit, and therefore a day of hope for higher loving than they have yet known. With the hope of this stage may also come a concrete suggestion of how to build on the strength of another—what to recognize, what to honor, what to salute, even in hot fray. At the next stage, the lift stage, memory may offer warnings against taking risks, and analogies may teach despair, but the lift says try now, and try again. Such a lift is more than goodwill, for it tugs interest directly toward the area in which the politics must proceed, toward the vows which can be renewed, toward the ideals which can be celebrated even while they are contested. The characteristic lift is cool, though exciting; it is not overpowering like the prospect of besting another, but more like the salute of wrestlers soon to hit the mat. The lift may offer that kind of nonviolence which is determination to stay with the other in vast hope for him, to keep looking him in the eye and calling him by name and saluting his colors, until hell freezes over. So long as there is hope of the other's change, or hope of the hope of change, the sword may be stayed, and the strength of the other built upon in nonviolence which does not fail to make immense demands. In the spirit of this stage the trance-counseling Cayce advised more than one person to "So live that you can look anyone in the eye and tell him where to go," and yet insisted at the same time, "Magnify the agreements; see ever the good in the other person, for as ye treat him, ye treat thy God—they are the same One Force."

The focus stage offers timing and strategies to accumulate resources for the struggle at hand. Each player at this stage must ask, "Is this struggle for me, now?", recognizing that if he postpones the encounter he may seem to others to give up the game, or not to care about his opponent. But the psychological currents at this stage are touching the inner life forms of all players and offering back guiding signals—perhaps not a few by ESP, as Cayce suggested. What the lift stage has promised may be correct, but the time for action may not be now, or the players may not be these players. Jesus does not confront Herod when that ruler slays Jesus' relative, John the Baptizer; instead, Jesus takes his disciples in full retreat to the hills. But at another time, when there are in play Jesus' covenant with Judas, one of his own, and the full meeting with the tradition-steeped leaders of Jesus' people in the central city of Jerusalem, Jesus does not move away, but stands fast without violence, to his death. The point of the game, as he made clear, was not protracted existence but the becoming of all players. Even deeper than timing or expedience, however, the focus stage of the politics of love lays bare what each must endure and gamble. To honor the best in the other requires knowing him, even though one may not like him; it requires learning his language and perhaps some of his trade and associates, though these may bring one ill-repute. To build on the other's strengths requires engaging those strengths, and they may overpower one, ending the game for the present. The force-field which emerges at the focus level warns: Count your resources, for you may never be the same again. This is frightening business, in the cycle of high play levels. Who does not hold in him some dark corner, some ugly streak, some unhappy weakness, which he hopes to compensate by valorous effort, but not to address in the full light of day? Yet there is no way to serve another's coronation without risking one's own exile, in the politics of love.

The "on" stage may be a surprisingly happy one in the risky politics of loving, for it often brings humor in the engagement of an opponent, revealing how readily "a soft answer turneth away wrath," and the spear of satire stuck in one's own behind may be a stronger weapon to disarm the enemy than direct attack. The "on" stage may offer many an original strategy, and part many a Red Sea, when the player's activity is seasoned with inactivity, and his will matched with waiting, especially under the cleansing action of meditation with the Third. For example, it may be discovered at this level that institutions cannot be perfected, but that it is enough to keep them, like impersonal occult powers, with their necks underfoot. At the "on" stage, promptings of when one should speak or not speak are matched by swift awareness of what the other's speech tells, even when he does not say it; insights show how his answers mirror questions which are larger than his heated answers, and how denials mean unspoken affirmations which matter for his greatness.

If the kickover comes in the politics of love, it may be to high adventure indeed. In the sudden surge of this stage may come glimpses of the perspective of the One. There are moments when it seems perfectly fitting that the Buddha died of a bellyache, and that Lao-tse rode into the mountains on a trail marked only by bull droppings. This stage can illuminate how Cayce could have insisted, as he did, that Jesus laughed even on the cross—when Jesus was able without trivializing his effort to grin ruefully at his few remaining associates, from out of his raw and fatal pain, and indicate something like, "This time I've done it, haven't I?" In the light of such kickover times, great evils offer themselves for fresh approaches. It may become apparent that international war will go the way of personal dueling, not only by mighty crusades against it, which have their place, but also by being laughed out of men's sight, ribbons and medals and blood and all. In the kickover can be found those moments when it is right to yell bloody murder and to swing at those one loves, for only such all-risking encounter will show them that someone really loves them, really cares, and is not going away. Jesus' rough handling of the devout Pharisees was surely such kickover love. But right beside such vigorous promptings at this stage may come the quickening to be still, to wait, or even to stand fast while one's head is lopped off, and the opportunity arrives at last to discover whom mediums talk to in their trances. It can lead to far-inward disporting in the midst of a slaughter of whales. It can bring a black man who will one day be assassinated to cry out, "Free at last, free

283

at last!" It can lead a neurotic housewife, in her loving and struggling power moves with the psychologist and nurse who have given her LSD, to report that she has found God.

In the quieting of release and readiness which crowns the high-play cycle of joining power to love, there may come perspective on how true growth among co-creators finally occurs. Northern Buddhism summarized the process in the idealized figure of the Bodhisattva, that saint who had lived through many lives of growth and service until he came to the very door of Nirvana—and refused to enter. For the Bodhisattva was he who would not claim the bliss of Nirvana until he could enter with all of his fellows, and enter with even the blades of smallest grass ennobled to their fullest being. Such a view was not wholly different from that of the trance-speaking Cayce, who reported that from his perspective all souls would continue journeying and growing until each soul not only responded to the Christ spirit, but in some way and day and cosmos had the opportunity to become a Christ—for others. In whatever view or tradition of East or West, the man who renounces his own delights and visions—won with or without the aid of drugs—in order to be a full co-creator with others is surely the one who practices to the end the politics of love.

Ahab, who knows so well the politics of power and command in whaling, is not the only captain of heroic ego and skill in the tale of the white whale. There is also the rugged and venerable captain-turned-pastor, called Father Mapple by the whalemen and their families in his New England seacoast parish. He is the man who climbs into his pulpit in the solemn high play of mounting a ship's ladder that he pulls into his pulpit after him—in an act free of pretentiousness or showmanship, but true to his own life form and those of his congregation. He is a man who enters the politics of love as he preaches, drawing on everything in his seagoing experience to engage his listeners within their true sets and stresses. And in that act so true to the politics of love, he turns the Jonah story of his sermon upon himself, speaking of his own weaknesses and shortcomings, and inviting his hearers to the honest self-wrestling which such searching of soul can prompt. In his closing words he speaks out of his own full ego strength, full identity, full service, in terms which suggest a man as towering as Ahab. And Father Mapple can do at last what Ahab cannot: he can invite others into his own struggle, and thereby open the way for him to enter theirs. He does it despite his pride, by kneeling before the One, though he cannot and properly will not bow to any man, nor to any exigency of land or sea, apart from this Face. He brings to an end his uncontrived outpourings on Jonah by sinking into that silence where great high play with men and the divine has its beginning and middle and end.

Yet, like Ahab, Father Mapple works an incomplete doing. He speaks, but whom does he reach? Ahab is not there, nor are the senators and judges of whom he tells. The seamen before him will fail to struggle with Ahab's vengeance when it threatens to sink them. Father Mapple's pulpit and congregation are a half-venture into human freedom and optimums, as are Ahab's bridge and crew. If Father Mapple steers a course which can bring him delight, highest delight, it is still but a course begun, and incomplete if contained in a chapel. His closing words, as fierce in their own way as Ahab's challenges to Moby Dick, and steeped in joy which Ahab does not know, echo into the unknown which confronts all men who would risk everything for the optimums they see.

"But oh! shipmates! on the starboard hand of every woe, there is a true delight; and higher the top of that delight than the bottom of the woe is deep. Is not the main-truck higher than the kelson is low? Delight is to him—a far, far upward and inward delight—who against the proud gods and commodores of this earth, ever stands forth his own inexorable self. Delight is to him whose strong arms yet support him, when the ship of this base, treacherous world has gone down beneath him. Delight is to him, who gives no quarter in the truth, and kills, burns, and destroys all sin though he pluck it out from the robes of Senators and judges. Delight—top gallant delight is to him, who acknowledges no law or Lord, but the Lord his God, and is only a patriot to heaven. Delight is to him, whom all the waves of the billows of the sea can never shake from this sure Keel of the Ages. And eternal delight and deliciousness will be his, who coming to lay him down, can say with his final breath —O Father!—chiefly known to me by thy rod— mortal or immortal, here I die. I have striven to be Thine, more than to be this world's or mine own. Yet this is nothing; I leave eternity to thee; for what is man that he would live out the lifetime of his God?"

He said no more, but slowly waving a benediction, covered his face with his hands, and so remained kneeling, til all the people had departed, and he was left alone in the place.

The man of reflection, of inward visions and silences, kneels in his rainswept chapel, far from the whale-churned seas of Ahab, the man of action. Whether the two kinds of men can meet at last, in that high play of co-creating with the Creative Forces which completes each man, and opens the way for the politics of love with others, Melville does not say. Perhaps Melville understands, as did the Buddha long before him, that the best psychology tells only what man is not, and leaves the rest for living.

Have you read all of these fascinating books about Edgar Cayce, America's most famous seer?

—**EDGAR CAYCE ON REINCARNATION**
  by Noel Langley (65-752, 95¢)

—**EDGAR CAYCE ON ATLANTIS**
  by Edgar Evans Cayce (65-762, 95¢)

—**STRANGER IN THE EARTH**
  by Thomas Sugrue (65-456, 95¢)

—**DREAMS IN THE LIFE OF PRAYER**
  by Harmon H. Bro, Ph.D. (64-513, 75¢)

—**EDGAR CAYCE ON THE DEAD SEA SCROLLS**
  by Glenn D. Kittler (65-494, 95¢)

—**EDGAR CAYCE ON JESUS AND HIS CHURCH**
  by Anne T. Read (64-422, 75¢)

—**EDGAR CAYCE ON RELIGION AND PSYCHIC EXPERIENCE**
  by Harmon H. Bro, Ph.D. (65-216, 95¢)

—**EDGAR CAYCE ON ESP**
  by Doris Agee (64-122, 75¢)

—**EDGAR CAYCE ON DIET AND HEALTH**
  by Gammon, Read and Ilstrup (64-095, 75¢)

—**THE EDGAR CAYCE READER**
  edited by Hugh Lynn Cayce (64-037, 75¢)

—**THE EDGAR CAYCE READER #2**
  edited by Hugh Lynn Cayce (64-086, 75¢)

—**EDGAR CAYCE ON DREAMS**
  by Harmon H. Bro, Ph.D. (54-776, 75¢)

—**EDGAR CAYCE ON PROPHECY**
  by Mary Ellen Carter (54-699, 75¢)

—**VENTURE INWARD**
  by Hugh Lynn Cayce (54-792, 75¢)